ww news

Waterford Whispers News

2021

COLM WILLIAMSON

Gill Books

Gill Books
Hume Avenue
Park West
Dublin 12
www.gillbooks.ie

Gill Books is an imprint of M.H. Gill & Co.

9780717192571

Designed by seagulls.net
Copy-edited by Neil Burkey
Printed by Hussar Books, Poland

Waterford Whispers News is a satirical newspaper and comedy website published by Waterford Whispers News. Waterford Whispers News uses invented names in all the stories in this book, except in cases when public figures are being satirised. Any other use of real names is accidental and coincidental.

For permission to reproduce photographs, the author and publisher gratefully acknowledge the following: © Alamy: 11, 14T, 15, 16, 23B, 25, 29B, 31, 61, 64, 71, 72, 77, 80T, 84, 88T, 88C, 88B, 89T, 89C, 89B, 94, 124, 125B, 127, 138B; © Corpus Christi Caller-Times-photo from Associated Press via Wikimedia Commons: 108B; © Gage Skidmore: 87B; © Getty Images: 28, 161; © Glenn Francis: 87T, 93; © Harpo Productions/Joe Pugliese/Handout via REUTERS/File Photo: 85; © IDominick via Wikimedia Commons: 92B; © iStock: 5, 6B, 7, 8, 9T, 9B, 10, 11, 12, 13B, 14B, 18T, 19, 20R, 21, 22, 24T, 26T, 26B, 27, 29T, 30, 31, 32B, 33, 34, 35T, 35B, 36T, 36B, 37, 38T, 38B, 39, 40, 42, 43T, 43B, 44T, 44B, 46, 47, 48, 49T, 49B, 50T, 50B, 53T, 53B, 54T, 54B, 55, 57, 58B, 59, 60, 65T, 66B, 67, 68, 69T, 73B, 75, 76, 80B, 83, 84, 86, 90, 91, 92T, 95, 96, 97T, 97B, 98T, 98B, 99, 100T, 100B, 101, 102, 103T, 104T, 104B, 105, 107T, 107B, 109, 111, 112, 113T, 113B, 114T, 114B, 115, 116T, 117, 119T, 119B, 121T, 121B, 122, 123, 125T, 126B, 127, 128, 129, 130T, 131, 133T, 133B, 135, 136, 137T, 137B, 138T, 140, 141B, 143T, 144, 145, 146, 148T, 148B, 149, 150, 151T, 151B, 152, 154T, 154B, 155TL, 155TR, 155CR, 156, 158, 160, 161, 162, 163, 164, 165, 166, 167, 168, 169, 170, 171, 172; © O'Dea at Wikimedia Commons: 65B; © Portmarnock Golf Club: 134; © ShinAwiL/Joe McCallion: 153; © Shutterstock: 3, 4T, 6T, 7, 12, 13T, 15, 17, 18B, 19, 20L, 21, 23T, 24B, 28, 32T, 41T, 45, 47, 48, 51, 52, 56, 57, 58T, 61, 62T, 62B, 64, 66T, 69BC, 69BR, 70T, 70B, 71, 73T, 74TL, 74TR, 74B, 75, 77, 78, 79T, 81, 82B, 93, 98T, 103B, 106, 108T, 110, 116B, 118, 120, 126T, 130B, 131, 132, 139, 141T, 142, 143B, 147, 155CL, 155BL, 155BR, 157, 159T, 160; © VOGUE Taiwan via Wikimedia Commons: 82T; © Wikimedia Commons: 4B, 41B, 63, 79B; Courtesy of Library of Congress: 159B.

The author and publisher have made every effort to trace all copyright holders, but if any has been inadvertently overlooked we would be pleased to make the necessary arrangement at the first opportunity.

The paper used in this book comes from the wood pulp of managed forests. For every tree felled, at least one tree is planted, thereby renewing natural resources.

A CIP catalogue record for this book is available from the British Library.

5 4 3 2 1

CONTENTS

ABOUT THE AUTHOR

Colm Williamson created *Waterford Whispers News* in 2009 when he was
unemployed. Though it began as a hobby, with Colm sharing stories with family
and friends, his unique brand of topical, distinctly Irish satire quickly attracted
thousands of fans. Now *Waterford Whispers News* has over 666,000 Facebook,
227,000 Twitter and 152,000 Instagram followers, and an average of 4 million
page views on the website every month. Colm runs *Waterford Whispers News*
from his home town of Tramore in Co. Waterford.

ACKNOWLEDGEMENTS

I would like to thank my two co-writers Karl Moylan and Gerry McBride for
their continued hard work and dedication to *WWN*. Thanks to my good friend
Rory Thompson for the fantastic cover illustration. A big special thanks to Alan
McCabe for all his technical skills on the site. Thanks to my fiancé, Ally Grace,
for putting up with me and to Lukas and Alex who I love very much. It has
been a tough year for everyone as business worldwide takes yet another hit.
Purchasing this book is a huge help to *WWN*, and I would like to personally
thank you, the reader, and whoever buys this book. It means a lot.

LETTER FROM THE EDITOR

Dear readers,

Allow me to introduce myself: I am the newly installed temporary deputy stand-in editor of *Waterford Whispers News*, Bíll Bádbódy, respected broadcaster, journalist, trutharian, philanthropist, landlord, property developer, patriotic patriot and champion of the people.

It's safe to say this is yet another year that will live long in the memory, chiefly for my elevation to this new position.

Yes, other things such as the pandemic, war, famine, all the hits, etc., have made their indelible mark too. And I suppose this is something *WWN* has sought to address, comment on and adapt to; with the pandemic exposing the cracks in society it is harder to ignore the inequality inherent in Irish life and, despite our status as a relatively wealthy nation, we must acknowledge it.

It has been my personal honour to move these issues right to the centre of what *WWN* does, giving a voice to the marginalised: the landlords, the investment funds, those who inherited their wealth from their parents. They are endangered species, and they have no voice. In this woke world we are adrift on the snowflake ocean [Fiachra, replace this metaphor with a better one].

One of my other professional roles is as acting head of the Irish Landlord League, a sort of support group for helpless landlords, and truthfully the harrowing stories of being unable to raise rent by more than 4 per cent or of a ban on evicting tenants would haunt a ghost, they are that disturbing. It would take a heart of stone not to highlight such things and fight back against the Communist Social and Affordable Housing scam 'working' people are trying to implement.

While other publications seek to pit opposite sides of arguments against each other by antagonising readers into clicking on articles purposely designed to enrage, and thus further exacerbate divides, *WWN* bravely shares only one perspective and sides completely with those who benefit most from the status quo and most fear the tyranny of equality.

Know that under my editorship, *WWN* will also selectively report on the issues that matter most to you, omitting inconvenient facts with an undimmed passion for making sure that everything stays exactly the same because, ultimately, myself and my friends in business and politics are getting on all right, thank you very much.

Yours insincerely,

Bíll Bádbódy

Temporary Deputy Stand-In Editor, *WWN*

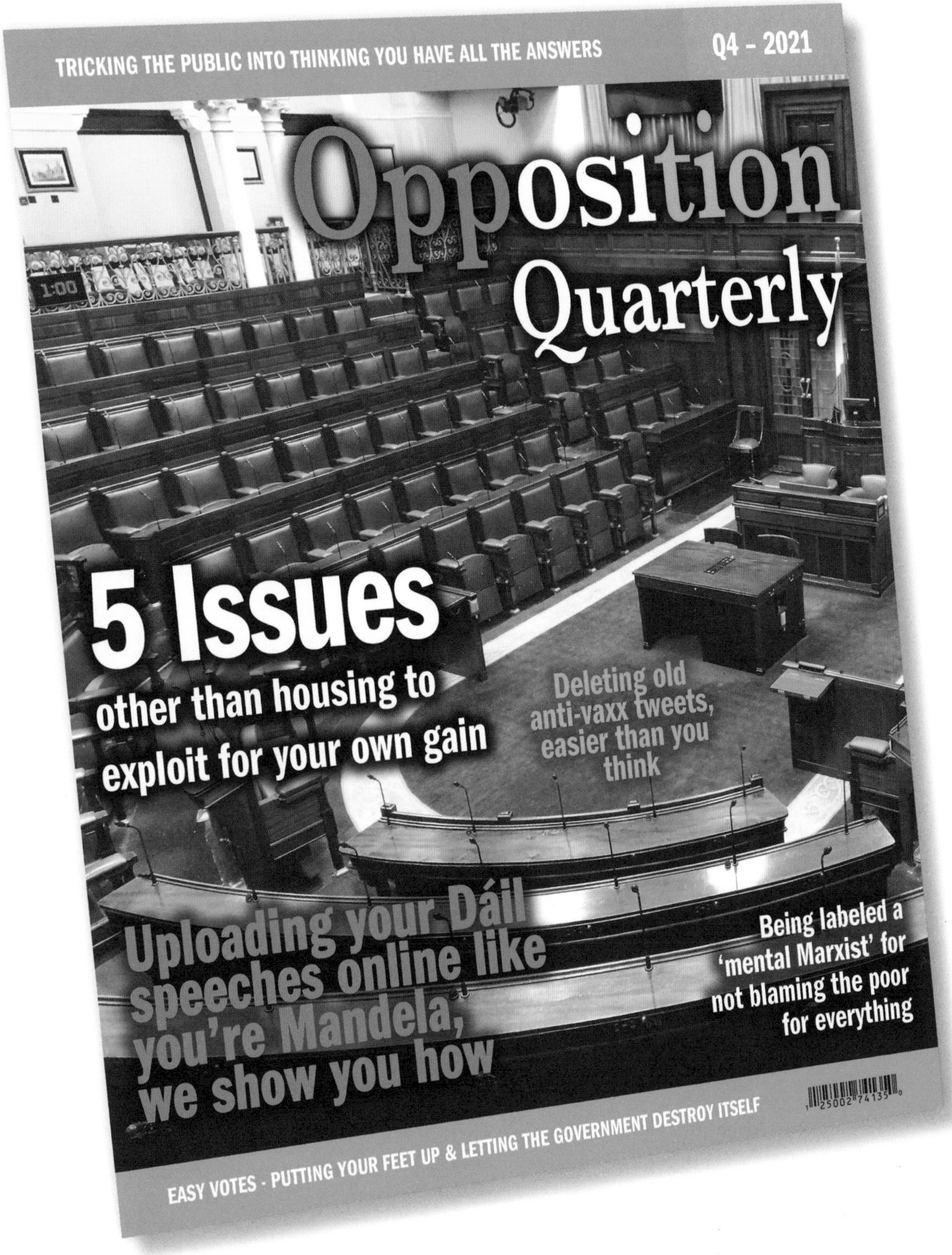

TRICKING THE PUBLIC INTO THINKING YOU HAVE ALL THE ANSWERS   Q4 - 2021

Opposition
Quarterly

5 Issues
other than housing to
exploit for your own gain

Deleting old
anti-vaxx tweets,
easier than you
think

Uploading your Dáil
speeches online like
you're Mandela,
we show you how

Being labeled a
'mental Marxist' for
not blaming the poor
for everything

EASY VOTES · PUTTING YOUR FEET UP & LETTING THE GOVERNMENT DESTROY ITSELF

POLITICS

NORTHERN IRELAND

DUP NOT SURE FOSTER HATEFUL ENOUGH TO LEAD PARTY

DESPITE INSISTING to party members that things would get much, much, much worse if they'd just give her another chance, it appears Arlene Foster's days as DUP leader could be over.

As rumours persist that a majority of party members have passed a motion of no confidence in Foster as leader at a meeting held in 1953, it is believed members feel Foster just isn't hitting the high levels of backward and hateful leadership they expect from the DUP.

'Sure, it's all well encouraging and defending Loyalists petrol bombing communities, but we expect more from a DUP leader. We haven't blamed the bad weather on the gays in ages – it's shocking leadership. She even abstained on the gay conversion therapy vote, *and* she has a lesbian's haircut. This can't go on,' shared one member.

Asked if now is the time for the DUP to reflect on an astonishingly bad few years, and to perhaps focus not on tribal squabbles that achieve nothing but on bettering the lives of the communities they have roundly failed, the spokesperson said, 'No, no, more hate is the answer.'

The current front runners to succeed Foster are Ian Paisley Jr's holiday home in Sri Lanka, the empty void where Edwin Poots's brain should be, a Rangers jersey and a Bible with the line 'You shall not lie with a male as with a woman; it is an abomination' highlighted with a pink highlighter.

Predictions for 2022

The Department of Social Welfare takes a fairly hands-off approach to hounding those still left jobless by the Covid-19 pandemic, making them feel like the shit on their shoe.

DESPITE AT FIRST appearing a near impossible task, the DUP has successfully found someone worse than Arlene Foster to take the position of leader of the party.

Here's everything you need to know about Edwin Poots:

EVERYTHING YOU NEED TO KNOW ABOUT EDWIN POOTS

- Believes the earth is 6,000 years old, while many believe he has the brain function of someone born yesterday.
- Dinosaurs don't believe Edwin Poots exists.
- As health minister he pushed to charge women who elected to give birth via C-section rather than a natural birth £3,500 for the procedure.
- Will likely have collapsed Stormont within the hour.
- It is unclear if he's any craic on a night out, as he's clearly never been invited anywhere by anyone.
- As leader he vows to offend and denigrate everyone equally, which, given his history of misogynistic, sectarian and homophobic comments, will be a mammoth task.
- Is 'pro' all the bad stuff and 'anti' all the good stuff.
- Looks exactly like you'd expect someone named 'Edwin Poots' to look.
- Is expected to suffer from the same amnesia as Arlene Foster, which will lead him to forget that it was his party that created the current NI protocol mess by pushing and supporting a Brexit vote, using dark money, which has foisted hardship on his own party's supporters.
- Will have to commute from 1951 to Stormont every day.
- His appointment proves beyond a doubt just how serious the DUP are about securing a United Ireland.
- Will celebrate leadership contest win with the world's most heterosexual cake.

HOTEL QUARANTINE TO BE ITS OWN, COMPLETELY SEPARATE SHITSHOW, PROMISE GOVERNMENT

ALTHOUGH frustrations are mounting at the slow implementation of mandatory hotel quarantine (MHQ) for people coming into the country, the government has stressed that time is needed to ensure that everything will be as half-arsed and ineffective as possible.

'People think it's as simple as saying "anyone who comes into this country must stay in a hotel for two weeks before they can leave", and in honesty, yeah, it kinda is,' said a spokesperson for the government, at a slowly convened press conference earlier today.

'But we as a nation have a standard to uphold when it comes to these kinds of things. Long story short, we'll begin MHQ when we're 100 per cent certain that it'll result in a tribunal in years to come. It's not just the citizens getting Covid we're worried about. We've got law firms to think of.'

The Year in Numbers

0 – the number of people unemployed, according to the government's own calculator.

Key points the government need to address before moving on include:

- Which hotels are suitable for inbound passengers to stay in, given capacity issues due to many hotels already housing homeless families or serving as Direct Provision centres?
- Is it really needed yet? The government are still of the opinion that things 'aren't that bad', apart from a recent surge in cases that is the fault of protestors and certainly has nothing to do with schools. Is it worth hassling people coming into the country yet? There's an important 'what will they think of us' aspect to be considered.
- Who pays for everything? The government are adamant that anyone flying into Ireland for a holiday 'can't be expected' to pay for two full weeks in a hotel, as this would limit the amount of money they would then be able to spend in Carrolls Irish Gifts.
- And what about seasonal workers? They are almost certainly unable to pay for 14 nights on the wages they're receiving, and it's apparently 'madness' to ask the bosses at the strawberry farms and meat-processing plants to foot the bill. Work is underway to ensure that the taxpayer foots the entire cost, and MHQ will commence once the government ensures a deal that is the worst possible value for everyone concerned.

Despite the roadblocks, the government are certain they can get MHQ up and running in time for the summer holidays, at which point it will be dropped due to cases falling ever so slightly for a week or so.

FINANCE

FUCK IT, DONOHOE PUTTING ALL OF COUNTRY'S MONEY INTO BITCOIN

CONCERN has been expressed at activity at the Department of Finance after Paschal Donohoe made moves to whack all crumbs from the State's former 'rainy day fund' into Bitcoin.

The alarm had been raised after Donohoe began following entrepreneur Elon Musk on Twitter, but Central Bank officials were unable to prevent the transaction, which now sees Ireland's paltry cash reserves converted into the extremely volatile cryptocurrency.

'We knew we were in trouble when he started just calling it "crypto" in one meeting,' conceded a department official.

The 'Hail Mary pass' is designed to help the State recover from its heavily indebted balance sheet quickly, and all-out-of-ideas Donohoe now frequents forums such as Reddit's r/wallstreetbets in search of ways to bolster the country's finances.

'I suppose it's still a safer bet than relying on taxing multinationals to artificially inflate our GDP, but this is only going to end in tears,' concluded the department official.

BRITISH GOVERNMENT TO RENAME MURDERS CARRIED OUT BY SOLDIERS AS 'WHOOPSIE DAISIES'

AHEAD of a rumoured decision to prevent future prosecutions of British soldiers by introducing a statute of limitations, the British government is set to reclassify murders carried out by soldiers during the Troubles as 'whoopsie daisies'.

'We workshopped a few terms, but we feel this showcases our staggering indifference to the murder of people we technically would have considered British citizens,' explained a spokesperson for the Tory government, fresh from trying to cut arts education funding by 50 per cent.

The British government indicated that it could pledge to move towards a 'truth and reconciliation commission' similar to that used in post-apartheid South Africa to deal with such crimes, but only gullible people who have never heard of Boris Johnson before took such claims at face value.

'To be honest, we're actually quite angry at having to even change it to a "whoopsie daisy", because as we all know, British soldiers can't commit murder. That's a British science fact,' added a spokesperson, before ordering the navy to go torpedo some French fishermen out of the water.

'We feel "whoopsie daisy" is quite the durable word, able to encompass all sorts of atrocities, whether it be a typical massacre or plotting with terrorists to kill innocents – just the very normal stuff the British army did during the Troubles, which incidentally we now refer to as the "Mild Bothers",' concluded the spokesperson, before injecting the comment section below the *Daily Mail* article on the news directly into his veins.

LEAKED TRANSCRIPT OF THE TÁNAISTE'S INTERVIEW WITH THE GUARDS

Predictions for 2022

The Irish government says the housing crisis won't be solved overnight for the 11th year running.

MORE SHOCKING than the news that a current Tánaiste has presented himself to Gardaí for questioning in relation to his conduct in office is the near media silence on the matter.

WWN, Ireland's fearless leading news outlet, seeks to address this with an exclusive leak of the transcript of Tánaiste Leo Varadkar's interview with Gardaí:

[sound of tape-recording device clicking on]

Leo Varadkar: They say you only do two days; the day you go in and the day you get out.

Garda 1: Prison, is it?

LV: No, the Dáil. Right, lads, here's what I can do for you.

Garda 1: Let the tape show Mr Varadkar has opened his suit jacket to reveal a number of confidential files, one of which is marked 'The Third Secret of Fatima'.

LV: Look, this GP lad wasn't even my friend. But he wanted to be my mate worse than Micheál Martin. Wow, these interrogation rooms aren't like the movies at all, nothing like *The Wire*. You've seen *The Wire*, right?

Garda 1: Can't say I have.

LV: Aw, what are ye like? Never mind the leaks, you should be arrested. A cop who hasn't watched *The Wire*?

Garda 2: Tánaiste, if we could just address the issue at hand for a minute.

LV: Ah, spot the bad cop. Gotchya.

Garda 1: The issue, Mr Varadkar.

LV: Mary Lou being in the RA?

Garda 2: C'mon, let's be serious. She's not in the IRA.

LV: Have you checked lately? You know you can lock that lot up now without a jury. Special criminal court, just throw away the key. Job done. Pay rise. You're welcome.

Garda 1: Shit, he's got us there.

LV: 'You can't handle the truth!' 'It was the one-armed man!' 'We're going to need a bigger boat.'

Garda 2: This isn't doing you any favours.

LV: My personal solicitor, Fine Gael party solicitor, legal counsel within my department, my mate who's a solicitor, half my party colleagues who are solicitors or barristers – they bet me I couldn't work in more than five movie quotes. They'll absolutely crack when they read this transcript.

Garda 1: This is ridiculous …

LV: 'What we've got here is failure to communicate' … 'Cool Hand Leo'.

Garda 2: For fuck …

Garda 1: Let the tape show Mr Varadkar has tried now for a third time to *Basic Instinct* us. And let the record reflect this doesn't strictly count as another movie quote.

LV: How long have we been at this now?

Garda 2: No more than two minutes.

LV: Grand, that should be enough time to make it look like you were properly investigating this. Right, Varadkar out. Peace!

Garda 1: Mr Varadkar? Tánaiste! Yes, you've presented yourself here voluntarily, but know that if there is any wrongdoing here we will get to the bottom of it.

LV: Ha, nice try, lads. Y'know I was part of the government that cut resources to the point where you've less manpower than a wet pub during a Level 5 lockdown. What have ya, one Nokia 3310 and a Sega Megadrive between five districts? I'm shaking in my boots.

Garda 2: Well, we were knocked down the vaccine priority list …

LV: Eh, why don't you focus on the real criminals – the welfare cheats!

Garda 1: Let the tape show, the interviewee has attempted to moonwalk out of the room while putting on sunglasses.

HOUSING

'GUYS, YOU'RE NOT GOING TO BELIEVE THIS, BUT APPARENTLY THERE'S A HOUSING CRISIS?' ASTOUNDED GOVERNMENT TELLS PUBLIC

BARELY STOPPING for breath in between sentences, leading figures from Fine Gael, Fianna Fáil and the Green Party are eager to alert the Irish public to a shocking discovery that is sure to blow everyone's minds.

'Guys, have you ever heard of this thing, I think they call it a "house sing Chrysler" or something? Wait, Darragh wrote it down somewhere. Oh yeah, "housing crisis",' explained a panicked Fianna Fáil TD.

'And lads, not to scare you, but apparently a whole generation or three are fucked. You'll be pensioners and be expected to pay €2,000 a month in rent, and I know this because a lot of us will be the landlords taking it from

you,' added the TD, unaware that the public were well up to date on the last 13 years of policies implemented by Fianna Fáil, Fine Gael, Labour and the current coalition government.

'Jesus, you guys are lucky we caught this when we did. But I'll be honest, I feel like if you guys were paying attention you could have warned us,' added a Fine Gael TD, who still isn't going to do anything about any of this.

'Bees,' added a Green Party TD.

Astounded at this housing crisis that appeared out of the blue overnight, the government has now said it will leave no stone unturned in finding out who is to blame and how to bring an end to zero supply, vacant homes,

high rents, a lack of social housing and first-time buyers being squeezed out of the market.

'We actually know one or two guys in foreign investment funds, so don't worry, if anybody knows how to solve it, it'll be these guys. Let us talk to them, they'll tell us what to do and then it should all be good,' offered the government.

UPDATE: The government is considering a ban on investment funds hoovering up homes in suburban areas. The funds will, however, be allowed to continue buying up cities and milking cash from people like the overworked and tired cattle they are.

A SHEEPISH Irish nation woke up with the unrelenting feeling of existential dread this morning after realising it, and not the Church and State, played the leading role in the decades of abuse, slavery and neglect of thousands of mothers and babies, as detailed by a recent state-commissioned report.

Previously pinning the vast majority of blame on Church and State, thousands of citizens took to social media and the airwaves to apologise to both institutions for wrongly accusing them of continued malpractice, begging for their forgiveness.

'What are we like at all? And here was me blaming the religious orders for committing horrifying acts against these women and children,' said one grovelling member of the public, reading the report labelled

The Year in Numbers

0 – the amount of corporation tax the government is fine with multinationals paying.

SOCIETY FEELING PRETTY STUPID FOR BLAMING CHURCH AND STATE

a 'whitewash' by some victims and advocates.

'We feel really stupid right now for all of this,' a spokesman for Irish society said earlier today after realising the cock-up, made clearer by the Taoiseach's words emphasising society's role above all else. 'We're sorry for not bothering to keep records on deceased children, and "forgetting" where we buried them. We're sorry for local authorities receiving reports about sky-high infant mortality rates and doing nothing about it.

'Sorry for the nuns that forged mothers' signatures consenting to adoption, members of religious orders that cut women during labour and refused them any anaesthetic, and we're really sorry for sitting politicians who were in government and members of councils while these homes were still open and operating.'

Replying to the apologies, a Vatican spokesperson accepted the nation's

plea for forgiveness, stating 'obviously it wasn't our fault. We came to a Third World country like Ireland, brainwashed its population through education and made its citizens do absolutely anything we told them to, with the sole aim of receiving tax-free donations down the line. Everyone knows this is how we roll, and still continue to do so in impoverished countries. We forgive you all.'

GOVERNMENT MULLING OVER INCREASING PENSION AGE TO 97

DISPENSING with a policy of just putting off tough decisions as the State takes on yet more debt, the government has confirmed that the pension age is set to rise to 97, *WWN* can confirm.

'There's just no other way to avoid the ageing population/pension time bomb conundrum, but don't worry, those years from 67 to 97 will fly by,' insisted Minister for Finance Paschal Donohoe.

'There can't be a monumental rise in the cost to the State in pensions if we eliminate pensioners entirely,' added Donohoe, who said making everyone work until they're 97 is much more humane than the other option on the table: involuntary

euthanasia.

Future generations who won't achieve State pensionable age until they're 97 have been told not to worry about the type of jobs they'll be working into their 70s, 80s and 90s, with experts confirming that by then AI robots will have all the mentally taxing jobs.

'No, you'll just be doing all the manual labour grunt work. If there are cobalt mines left to be going into, that'll be your area,' explained one expert.

Conspiracy Corner

Rumours persist that not only was Paul McCartney killed in 1966 and replaced by an imposter, but that the entire band went 'full Sugababes' by the end, with all original members replaced by lookalikes.

IN-DEPTH REPORT

'BEN SHERMAN SHIRT GRANTS, ROAD FRONTAGE GIVEAWAY, DIAL-UP INTERNET' – THE GOVERNMENT'S 'RURAL FUTURE' PLAN IN FULL

THE GOVERNMENT has unveiled ambitious plans to reinvigorate rural towns and promote decentralisation by incentivising people who can work from home to leave Dublin and do so in affordable, less densely populated areas.

Among measures already announced, such as 400 remote-working hubs and a possible relocation grant of €2,000, the Our Rural Future plan contains the following:

- A commitment that would see every worker be able to use slow, screeching dial-up internet.
- Every village in the plan will be fitted with a Chinatown-style 'Dublintown' to make it easier for Dubliners to assimilate. These will contain the best of Dublin cuisine and culture, such as a Leo Burdocks chipper and open heroin use.
- Those coming from Cork will be allowed operate Corktachts, serving a similar function to that of a Gaeltacht, and would see Cork's language of superiority promoted during summer months.
- For every Ben Sherman shirt you buy, the government will give you another one absolutely free.
- Applicants will be given enviable road frontage, and if you don't have siblings or extended family with which to argue over the land, the government will provide them free of charge.
- Returning rural natives will not need it, but city dwellers will be given extensive training in how to wave at people even if you don't know them. New additions to the town will also be taught how to never use the front door again when entering their home/welcoming in neighbours.
- If you don't own a car yourself, the government will get you an outrageous car insurance quote from a company anyway, free of charge.
- You'll learn road bowling, and you'll fucking like it!
- Upon your arrival in a small town, the government will provide you with a brochure containing all the local gossip, including how that fella's wife ran off with the other fella's wife, and why himself down the way isn't allowed within 500 metres of the school.

PSYCHOLOGY

'I SEE a man with a beard, and glasses, surrounded by people in balaclavas,' said Leo Varadkar today, after being presented with a Rorschach 'ink blot' image with the instruction to just 'say what you see'.

'Is that correct?' asked Varadkar.

'Mr Varadkar, there are no "right and wrong" answers with these tests, it's just to get a glimpse at where your mind is resting,' said the Tánaiste's therapist, trying to find room on her notebook to add yet another 'fuck me, this lad is obsessed with Sinn Féin' note.

'Let's try another one.'

Over the course of an afternoon, Varadkar claimed to see images swimming in the black ink that resembled:

- Mary Lou McDonald with 'some form of rifle', pointing directly at him and laughing.
- Pearse Doherty beside what looked like an arms dump.
- A JCB ripping an ATM out of a wall, being driven by Paul Donnelly.

'I SEE MARY LOU MCDONALD WITH AN AK,' VARADKAR TELLS PSYCHIATRIST

- A 26-county republic that looks just fine the way it is.
- Micheál Martin clutching his chest and slumping to the ground.
- A load of poor people on a boat sailing far, far away.
- Mary Lou McDonald again, only this time her voice was that of an actor.

> **'There are no "right and wrong" answers with these tests, it's just to get a glimpse at where your mind is resting.'**

'But Mr Varadkar, these are just pictures, you're not supposed to be able to hear them speak,' stated Varadkar's therapist. 'Let's try something different. Word association. I'll say a word, and you say the first thing that comes into your mind. Let's begin. "Kitten".'

'An IRA car bomb sent to assassinate me but it accidentally kills all the homeless people in the country, reducing our figures to zero while I jump out of the way, shouting, "I told you this is what a vote for Sinn Féin would bring", while looking really cool in a nice suit with my sunglasses on,' blurted Varadkar.

Conspiracy Corner

Leprechauns are real, but in this PC-gone-mad world, we're not allowed to refer to their short arses with that term anymore.

FIRE BRIGADE CALLED AFTER DONNELLY GETS HEAD STUCK IN DÁIL RAILINGS

FRESH from the Taoiseach revealing he only learned about the recent, probably fairly inconsequential collapse of the country's contact tracing system via an *Irish Times* article, today has brought yet another embarrassing incident for the hapless three-party government.

'Eh, sorry, lads,' said a sheepish Minister for Health Stephen Donnelly to firemen arriving at the scene of the Fianna Fáil TD's head wedged in between the railings outside government buildings.

'I'll be honest, I'm struggling to explain my thinking here,' he added of his current predicament, however, it could serve as a comment on 90 per cent of things he's said and done since taking office, including his most recent claim that he too was utterly clueless as to the contact tracing system issues.

As Dublin firefighters went to work greasing up Donnelly's neck and head, critics of the government's Covid-19 resourcing reacted.

'Oooooh, our bad. We must have spent the last several months sending our stark and grave warnings about how the test and trace system needed more resourcing and was teetering on the edge to a completely different government, silly us,'

confirmed the nation's healthcare workers, specialists, GPs and members of the public.

Elsewhere, never one to just shut up and do his job, Tánaiste Leo Varadkar one-upped the Taoiseach's ignorance by revealing he only learned about the contact tracing debacle via a video on TikTok this morning.

'You'd think the bald, aerodynamic surface would make this easier, but he's wedged t'fuck,' remarked exhausted firefighters, not realising Donnelly was holding onto the railing for dear life.

'Ah, that's a shame, looks like I'm stuck here forever more. Maybe Micheál should get Simon Harris back as Minister for Health. Ugh, I'm raging honestly, if only I could get out there and continue to be the world-beating health minister Ireland needs right now.'

> **'You'd think the bald, aerodynamic surface would make this easier, but he's wedged t'fuck.'**

HOUSING

'I'VE LISTENED TO YOUR CONCERNS ABOUT THE HOUSING CRISIS, AND YOU'RE RIGHT, IT'S ALL SINN FÉIN'S FAULT'

IT'S BEEN a humbling few days for the Taoiseach, his party and the three-party coalition government, but he has put his exceptional listening skills to use and truly engaged with the plight of renters and first-time buyers.

'I've listened to your concerns about the housing crisis, and you're right, it's all Sinn Féin's fault,' explained Micheál Martin, showcasing once more his uncanny ability to give voice to the feeling out there on the streets.

Officials from the Department of the Taoiseach then confirmed that they personally saw Eoin Ó Broin drive a bulldozer through a new housing estate last night, in yet another sign that the government really have their finger on the pulse of the nation.

'And incidentally, you're wrong – it's not actually a housing crisis at all, it's a supply issue, which 6,000 affordable homes built on State lands over the next four years should solve, even though the overall demand is for 33,000 each year,' added the Taoiseach.

Responding to news that it may be several more weeks before there's new legislation introduced relating to investment funds, the Taoiseach sought to reassure the public by stating that, 'when we have the investment funds' permission to do that, we'll introduce it.'

Shockingly, sources close to the government revealed it was Sinn Féin, not Fianna Fáil, who in 2009 set up NAMA, which used public money to bail out developers, and not Fine Gael, but Sinn Féin, who set up the Land Development Agency, which uses public money to give developers public land to build on.

GOVERNMENT HIRES SHEEP FARMERS TO HERD WORKERS BACK INTO OFFICES

WORRIED by the prospect of billion-euro property investment funds losing money if the nation's office space isn't at 100 per cent occupancy, the government has hired a number of experienced sheep farmers to herd reluctant workers from their home offices back into the traditional corporate 9-to-5 cubicles.

'Good girl, Polly,' shouted one sheep farmer in between whistles as his border collie guided a crowd of harried workers off a Luas and towards office blocks.

'Once you get enough of them moving, they all follow each other. They're not particularly bright,' explained farmer Cormac Cullen, whistling intently and shepherding the expensive profit-generating stock back onto business premises and closing all gates behind him.

'In some ways they're more like sheep than actual sheep,' added Cullen as his dogs ripped one union official trying to stick up for workers limb from limb.

Across Ireland's city centres and out-of-town business parks, the scene is repeated as sheep farmers set their dogs to yap at the ankles of a workforce who for too long (15 months or so) have had it their own way.

'It's a great initiative, and only a handful of the workers have got stuck in ditches or up steep mountain cliffs,' confirmed a spokesperson for IBEC.

'I actually can't wait to be back in the office,' confirmed one worker, providing clear proof that the government has also hired world-renowned brainwashers to coax people back to the grind.

ELECTRIC PICNIC ORGANISERS ADD ZAPPONE TO LINE-UP IN BID TO ENSURE FESTIVAL CAN GO AHEAD

EXHALING in relief, Electric Picnic festival organisers are celebrating a foolproof line-up addition that ensures the event can go ahead without fear of any repercussions.

'Thank God for that, we can tear up all the careful planning that goes into ensuring an outdoor event is as safe as possible now that we've got our headliner – courtesy of plenty of time being freed up in her diary all of a sudden,' shared one EP organiser.

Ireland's now former special envoy for 'freedom of expression', Katherine Zappone, declined to respond to questions about staging a 50-person gathering at a Dublin hotel over a week ago that appears to have been against current guidelines.

'With Katherine booked for the main stage, it looks like we can just

do what we want. 40,000? 70,000? Fuck it, 100,000! The key is just to act like any complaint or concern from the public is beneath you. Get buying your bucket hats and face paint now!' offered the organiser, who added that unlike Zappone's gathering, Leo Varadkar won't get a free invite and will have to pay for a ticket.

While music fans have welcomed the news, others have lamented Zappone's addition to the line-up, calling her output a disappointing cover version of Golfgate.

Elsewhere, seasoned sessioners and jaw chewers have rejoiced at the EP news, saying, 'talking to a tree at 4 a.m. about how Taylor Swift is actually the Karl Marx of our times is back on the menu.'

TUSLA BREAK UP ÓGRA FIANNA FÁIL RING, TAKE DOZENS INTO CARE

CHILDREN ranging in age from 16 to 30 have been taken into protective custody by the national child and family agency Tusla after troubling reports that they have been showing early signs of centrist politics with strong Christian tendencies, *WWN* can report.

'We've had Ógra Fianna Fáil on our radar for quite a while, and we felt that now was the time to swoop,' said a source close to Tusla, while dealing with the heart-breaking case of a 16-year-old boy who was beginning to openly discuss the merits of not paying student nurses a wage.

'A lot of the Ógra groups prey on our youth, draw them in with the lure of being part of a gang, and that's very

appealing to these dorks who don't have pals to begin with.

'In the end we couldn't stand by and let one more teenager think that it was okay to put "Ógra Fianna Fáil" on their Instagram handle.'

Among the children rescued were:

- A Carlow youth who expressed delight at the sealing of the Mother and Baby records, while explaining at length that it was the right thing to do in the long run.
- A Donegal teenager who felt that public transport to and from her county was perfectly adequate.
- An alarming number of children who, when they got themselves into trouble, instinctively lashed out at other, more Republican children.

Tusla remain optimistic that most of the affected children will be able to be rehabilitated back into a normal life, but for some older members such as Jack Chambers, 'the rot has taken too strong a hold'.

LAW & JUSTICE

TATTOO-CLAD DAVID DRUMM EMERGES FROM PRISON A CHANGED MAN

STILL AWAITING an apology from the Irish judiciary and the wider Irish public, David Drumm emerged a changed man from prison two years and eight months into a six-year sentence for false accounting and conspiracy to defraud the public.

'Whoever decided he should go free after less than three years should be done for false accounting too,' remarked members of the public still not willing to accept that white collar crime is somewhere below littering in the list of severity of crimes in Ireland.

Looking slightly different from when he went to prison, the former Anglo CEO was pictured leaving Loughan House open prison with his knuckles bearing the tattoos 'thug' and 'life', and his now former prison mates can attest to the fact that he is most certainly a profoundly changed man.

'It took him a while to adjust. You have to remember he'd feel like a real fish out of water – the sorts of guys in here, they're in for crimes very different from being involved in €7.2 billion fraud. You're talking lads in here for not paying their TV licence, proper scum,' confirmed former cellmate Barry 'Brick' Townsend.

'But that's not how everyone sees it at first, the lads who were in for child pornography and that – they didn't want anything to do with scum like him.'

'After a while he toughened up and started demanding people call him by his prison name – Attila the Drumm, and he was slowly accepted.'

In the early days, Drumm took to lifting weights and getting 'Anglo Golden Circle' tattooed across his back to get his mind off the fact that he'd be out in no time.

'In prison they do be giving you courses and that, y'know to try and prepare you for the outside, but it wasn't for Drumm 'n' Bass. As much as we tried to help him, he'd keep failing the Intro to Accounting module,' explained John 'Slit-throat' Murphy, a former drug gang enforcer.

'You only do two days inside, the day you arrive and the day you leave. Granted, when it's white collar crime in Ireland chances are you literally only do two days anyway,' confirmed Drumm's tattooist, Frank 'Fiddler' Flynn, so named due to being a talented fiddle player, and nothing else.

Do his prison mates think the punishment befit the crime?

'I think when it comes to Ireland, we need a big rethink on prisons and justice, like yeah sure here's a lad who helped collapse and bankrupt a country, but he couldn't get Sky Sports on the TV in his room. So if anything, the punishment was too harsh,' confirmed Flynn.

WWN was unable to reach Drumm on the phone for comment due to him fielding a large number of calls from old pals seeking to give him consultancy work.

County Knowledge

Cavan

Far from the tight-fists they are sometimes portrayed as, most Cavan people are more than willing to let you have a crisp from their bag for as little as two cents.

Virginia, Co. Cavan, formally ended its slave trade a mere 130 years after its US namesake did in 1865.

Known for having 365 lakes adorning the county, Cavan grows an extra lake every leap year.

BREXIT UPDATE

JOHNSON UNSURE HOW TO PHRASE BREAK-UP TEXT TO NORTHERN IRELAND

BRITISH PM Boris Johnson has reportedly been staring blankly at his phone for hours, unable to summon forth the delicately phrased words needed to let Northern Ireland down gently while at the same time never giving them reason to think he's shafting them.

Johnson's hope is to occupy a place in Northern Ireland's mind as a fondly thought-of ex, whose true bastard nature never quite dawns on it, a hope labelled by the Tory leader's inner circle as an impossible goal.

'Sugar plums, it's not you, it's me,' Johnson wrote out in a WhatsApp text before deleting it quickly in a panic, unaware that the DUP was at the same time flicking through its own phone and staring lovingly at a series of

photos of Johnson with a Union Jack, Johnson in Belfast, Johnson passive-aggressively undermining Northern Ireland in front of its friends.

'Boris is hoping to let Northern Ireland down so gently that, years later, it is still defending its toxic, abasing, no-good ex to friends any time he comes up in conversation. Poor Boris, he says NI is so insecure and needs constant reassurance, it's a drain on him,' confirmed one aide.

Despite close friends trying to do the 'decent thing' in recent years by heavily insinuating that Northern Ireland could do better and doesn't have to take such shoddy treatment, Johnson's desire to treat the landmass like one of his children and deny its existence entirely will come as a shock to Northern Ireland when the inevitable happens.

'Sadly, I think Northern Ireland is going to be that person who, after being plainly told "it's over", will delude itself into thinking he'll change his mind and they'll get back together,' confirmed another aide.

Johnson, still struggling to find the right words for a break-up text, sent a series of unanswered eggplant emojis to America.

FINANCE

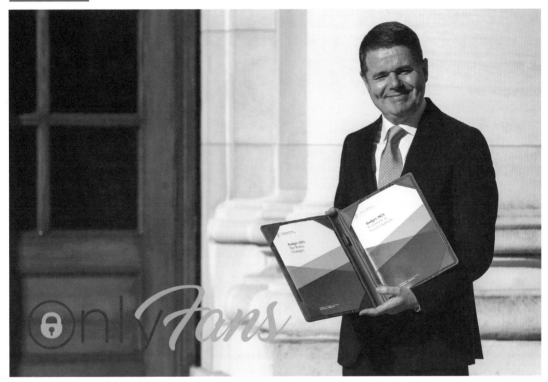

GOVERNMENT SET UP ONLYFANS ACCOUNT IN BID TO COVER BUDGET COST

MINISTER for Finance Paschal Donohoe has confirmed that with the country's paltry rainy day fund no match for the tsunami of pain that comes with a recession, the government will now turn to setting up an OnlyFans account to plug the humongous gaps in the state's finances.

'It is ours and everyone's patriotic duty to show a bit of skin and dupe some perverts into handing over some cash. Your monumentally, permanently fucking broke country needs you,' a frank Minister Donohoe shared with the public.

OnlyFans, a content subscription service known mostly for young women sharing videos and pictures of themselves in exchange for money from basement-dwelling creeps, is now the only viable way for the crippled Irish State and its hobbled economy to generate revenue.

'If OnlyFans and its ilk have proved anything, it's that people love to watch people getting fucked, and boy oh boy let me tell you there's going to be plenty of that in the upcoming budget,' he added.

'We've all to do our bit. I know it's unlikely that people will pay money to see Micheál Martin's feet pics, or Eamon Ryan eating salad in some lingerie, or fuck it, Donnelly lubing up his bald head, but we've got to try everything,' added the minister.

Other revenue-generating options that were considered included asking the nation to look under their cushions for spare change, but the government rubbished the idea of getting multinational tax-evading corporations to pay their fair share.

> **'It is ours and everyone's patriotic duty to show a bit of skin and dupe some perverts into handing over some cash.'**

CYBER SECURITY

GOVERNMENT SIGN HSE UP TO FREE 30-DAY TRIAL FOR AVG ANTIVIRUS

IN A CLEAR sign that it's definitely a case of 'lesson learned', the government dispatched the Department of Defence this morning to sign the HSE up to a free 30-day trial of AVG AntiVirus in response to the biggest cyber attack in the history of the State.

'Now the free trial is only for the one computer, so you'll all just have to use the one old HP running on Windows 97 from now on. And let's hope it just keeps going after the 30 days are up,' a government spokesperson told the HSE as the ransomware attack continues to wreak havoc.

Responding to the ongoing hack as it entered its fifth day, the head of Ireland's National Cyber Security Centre (NCSC) wasn't able to provide comment, because they don't exist, as the government has failed to fill the role for over 12 months, mainly due to offering an insultingly low and uncompetitive salary for the position.

'In fairness now, who could have seen this coming?' offered Minister for Defence Simon Coveney, whose own department issued a report as far back as 2015 warning of such hacking threats before the National Risk Assessment reports of 2016, 2017, 2018 and 2019 warned of exactly the same.

'Rest assured, the government has provided the NCSC with all it needs to protect Ireland from future attacks,' said Coveney of the outfit that only has 25 staff, no dedicated premises to work from, no director and, up until last year, a budget of less than €2 million.

'And to think some people are trying to pin the blame on the government. Cyber hacking is just one of those things you can't plan for,' offered Minister for Communications Eamon Ryan shortly before clicking on a 'Collect Your Lottery Winnings By Entering Your Account Details' email.

AN INTERNATIONAL team of pathologists and coroners have confirmed that irony died an 'agonising death' following a 'deliberate and premeditated' attempt to kill it by former British prime minister Tony Blair.

While irony had been presumed dead due to decades of people misusing and abusing it, Blair, famed for the totally legal war in Iraq, is thought to have finished it off for good.

'A lesson from Blair on upholding international law? What next, Cameron warning us against committing bestiality? Or advice on proper garden maintenance from Fred and Rose West?' asked one observer, who thought it might be for the best if Blair sat out lecturing people on tarnishing Britain's reputation via breaking the law.

Police assigned to the crime scene confirmed that Blair, a man famous for supporting a war in Iraq based on spurious claims, is alleged to have killed irony when he tried to criticise current Tory PM Boris Johnson and his reneging on the Brexit withdrawal agreement with the EU, accusing him of 'breaking the law'.

IRONY DEAD AS BLAIR CRITICISES JOHNSON FOR BREAKING INTERNATIONAL LAW

'We are so incensed by Johnson's hostility to rule of law and the decay in political discourse and integrity, and

how it will damage Britain for decades to come, that we'd accept anyone's help in pushing back against him, anyone except you, Tony, you can fuck off,' the British public confirmed.

Blair was just one of the five living former British prime ministers to criticise Johnson's bill, which breaches the Northern Ireland protocol in the withdrawal bill signed with the EU, with experts labelling his moral-high-ground pontificating 'like putting a gun to irony's head and pulling the trigger.'

'Poor bastard irony never stood a chance,' remarked one police officer assessing the grisly crime scene.

The hundreds of thousands of civilians killed in the Iraq war were unavailable for comment.

COVID RESTRICTIONS

GOVERNMENT PICKS NEW RESTRICTION MEASURES FROM RAFFLE DRUM

THE IRISH government has announced a new wave of national restrictions after randomly picking

> **'We understand that over the past nine months we've managed to come up with about a thousand different levels, tiers, traffic light systems – whatever it's called this week – but at least now we can't be blamed for these decisions.'**

them from a raffle drum earlier today, *WWN* can confirm.

Tasked with writing down all previous restrictions onto pieces of paper and crunching them up into tiny balls, proxy Taoiseach Micheál Martin rolled the raffle drum several times before excitedly picking a dozen or so measures, giving rise to yet another brand-new level of restrictions.

'We're calling this one Level 5 Max, with the extra protection of wings,' voiced Martin, before pulling out his old favourite 'close all pubs and restaurants' restriction from the drum. 'Yay, I love this one! If only we could shut those blasted off-licences too.'

Originally resorting to picking restriction measures from their holes earlier in the year, the government

admitted that the new raffle drum restriction method has its flaws, but is still fair all the same.'

'We understand that over the past nine months we've managed to come up with about a thousand different levels, tiers, traffic light systems – whatever it's called this week – but at least now we can't be blamed for these decisions. It's the luck of the draw!' Martin added, while picking out the restriction 'close the hairdressers' while leaving gyms and leisure centres open.

'Sure, we may be just making all this up as we go along and actually have no idea what we're doing, but if you could all just get back into your overpriced boxes, that would be great,' he concluded.

County Knowledge

Monaghan

We could find no facts about Monaghan that the people of that county would willingly share with us.

IN-DEPTH REPORT

'ILLEGAL IMMIGRANT' VS 'UNDOCUMENTED IRISH': THE DIFFERENCES EXPLAINED

WITH NEWS that candidate for US presidency Joe Biden has put his weight behind a campaign promise to resolve the citizenship of the 'undocumented Irish' living in America, a fresh spotlight has been shone on the term and just how it differs from 'illegal immigrant'.

In a bid to provide the necessary clarifications and specific distinctions, *WWN* has consulted with figures in the Democratic and Republican parties, as well as Irish people with relatives in America to straighten things out once and for all. Here's how to spot the difference between an 'undocumented Irish person' and an 'illegal immigrant':

Example one: Johnny Carty, Philomena and Joe Carty's youngest, living in Boston since '94 after getting a young Yank girl pregnant during USA '94, and riding it out on his tourist visa ever since = **undocumented Irish**. Ah, it's awful, he hasn't been back home since for fear he won't be let back into the US. Horrible stuff.

Example two: A five-year-old Syrian child orphaned by a proxy war sustained by the US, Russia and other interested parties, who is now trying to attain refugee status in the US through the proper process = **illegal immigrant**. Nice fucking try, pal.

Example three: Eoin 'Bricker' Burkin, didn't bother with the visa shite, not even a J1, got work on the building sites in New York in the early 2000s through a cousin who did the same the summer before him = **undocumented Irish**. Your heart would break for him, living in limbo like that. Have the US officials no hearts at all?

Example four: Amaya Burkin, mixed-race French-Iranian, applying to study at university in the US = **illegal immigrant**. Burkin! Burkin? Could have hidden it a little better. Burka? Just flaunting it out there in the open, doing herself no favours.

Example five: Isabel Murillo, undisclosed location in Texas, recovering from a forced hysterectomy at the hands of health officials at a detention centre = **illegal immigrant**. Nicaragua is a perfectly stable country with a strong economy, so no excuses, sorry.

Example six: Sean Stewart, nicest lad you'd ever meet, wouldn't harm a hair on anyone's head, but would you believe they're trying to deport him after him defending himself with a broken pint glass? Judge has it all wrong. You can stab a homeless man 50 times in the neck in self-defence = **undocumented Irish**. Ah, jaysus, crazy stuff and sure they'd let Mr Sob Story Middle East man and his 15 wives into the US no bother.

Example seven: Laura Higgins, of the Higgins out the Lahinch way. A nurse who moved over on a visa in '99. She's not Higgins anymore, of course, goes by Sanchez these days. 'Married a Hip Spanic' according to the mother. Anyway, she's changed, to say the least … and their kids? Tearaways by all accounts, and very tanned, almost too tanned, says Laura's father = **illegal immigrant**.

IRATE AND BARE-CHESTED MARTIN CALLS OUT PUTIN OVER HSE RANSOMWARE HACK

RECENT ATTACKS carried out by the Russian-backed Darkside and Evil Corp. hacking groups have given rise to suspicions that Putin's Federal Security Service may be responsible for the recent HSE ransomware hack, which might explain why an irate and bare-chested Micheál Martin is in the middle of recording a call-out video to the Russian leader.

'I'll fight any man,' the Taoiseach said, rather unconvincingly, as he shivered in the cold, thus obliterating the notion that 'you can't mess with the Irish State's mess of a network of IT systems and get away with it'.

Such is the severity of the attack that Ireland has now been forced back to using dial-up internet only, and communicating through a supply of

'You can't mess with the Irish state's mess of a network of IT systems and get away with it'.

Nokia 3210s, which every household has lying around in some drawer in the house.

Now throwing scurrilous accusations about 'the junkie bastard Putin' into the chilly air on the steps outside Leinster House, Taoiseach Martin had hoped to intimidate the leader into freeing the HSE's IT system from crippling ransomware.

'We don't negotiate with terrorists, ha, I always wanted to say that,' wrote the Taoiseach in an earlier exchange with hackers who had demanded Bitcoin and other things the Irish government had never heard of, such as an affordable home.

Despite the show of intimidation by Martin, the nation's best hope remains the hackers taking pity on the shocking state of government IT infrastructure and returning IT systems to being fully operational.

Elsewhere, in response to this dangerous attack on the health service, which genuinely poses a risk to the life of patients, the Gardaí and Irish Defence Forces have confirmed they remain on hold with Eir customer service.

Historical Facts

Biblical paintings aren't as inaccurate as you may think; there were loads of six-foot-tall, blond, blue-eyed white guys riding all around them in the Middle East at the time.

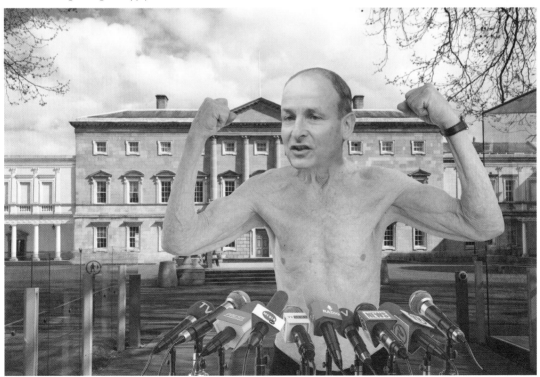

WITH CAMPAIGNERS calling on the government not to lock away records from Mother and Baby Homes, *WWN* goes subterranean to the 7-km-deep vault where the controversial documents will be kept sealed for the next 30 years after posing as elderly nuns who just wanted to burn some documents that were of 'no importance'.

Excavated in Offaly at a cost of €34 billion in the '90s to hide sensitive government legal material, the entrance to the vault is hidden in a field under a cow trough, which, when pushed over, opens a door to the large tunnel beneath and a cable-car type of lift that brings us down for 7 kilometres.

After the 40-minute descent we could not help but notice dozens of human skeletal remains embedded in the tunnel walls.

'We keep a lot of government case findings down here, mostly church-related so, as you can imagine, a lot of desperate people have tried and failed to reach the contents of this vault,' our government guide explains, before pointing to the remains. 'There's a

WE VISIT THE 7-KM-DEEP VAULT SURROUNDED BY LAVA THAT THE GOVERNMENT WILL SEAL MOTHER AND BABY HOME RECORDS IN

> **'We keep a lot of government case findings down here, mostly church-related so, as you can imagine, a lot of desperate people have tried and failed to reach the contents of this vault.'**

Magdalene laundries victim there … Oh! And there's a couple of men who tried finding out where their Catholic priest abuser from the 1960s was relocated to – it's mad how persistent some people are when it comes to acquiring information that should already be in the public domain.'

Finally landing at ground zero, we see the large vault, surrounded by bubbling lava.

'It might seem like we're really trying to hide the contents of the vault, but in fact this is basic protocol when it comes to storing legal documents in Ireland,' our government guide insists, reading from a pre-prepared statement.

The time-locked vault shows several separate countdown clocks relating to certain documents, including a

74-year timer with a yellow Post-it note stating 'Possible review in 25 years … NOT! Lol'.

'Oh, that's the two million documents from the redress bodies from the Commission to Inquire into Child Abuse,' the guide states. 'They contain the testimonies from representatives of 18 religious congregations, which managed residential institutions for children, so it's very important we keep them, and the people responsible, safe from the public and their victims.'

Happy in the knowledge that the vault was indeed a secure and impenetrable place to keep sensitive information away from the prying public, we gently inquire as to whether the vault was also home to the current government's only shred of human decency, which could prevent them from sealing the documents away for 30 years. Our guide laughs uncontrollably, before stating: 'Decency?! What made you think they had any to hide away in the first place?'

STEPHEN DONNELLY MAINTAINS SLEEK AERODYNAMIC LOOK TO AID EVENTUAL GETAWAY

ALTHOUGH the rest of the nation are still wondering where their next haircut is coming from, Minister for Health Stephen Donnelly has been making full use of the Dáil barber to ensure his head remains streamlined and 'ready for flight', a source has told *WWN*.

'He calls in regularly for a short back and sides and top, as he calls it,' said a member of the FF-FG-G coalition hair and make-up team, while showing us barely different 'before and after' images of the Wicklow TD.

'He knows as well as the rest of us that his time in government is going to end with a chase of some sort, and he wants to remain as aerodynamic as possible.'

Although many may doubt what difference the drag of a head of hair would make while being chased by a mob furious about any number of things, Donnelly remains adamant that he's 'not taking any chances' by growing out his luscious locks any time soon.

'His hair is naturally down to his shoulders, he tells us,' our source

declared. 'And when the nation eventually get sick of the Children's Hospital scandal, the CervicalCheck scandal or the Covid spike after ignoring NPHET, Minister Donnelly doesn't want to risk getting his long, flowing hair caught in a sliding door or something. Plus, he knows they'll be coming for him and Simon Harris, and he needs an edge on Harris, who can naturally squeeze through tight gaps to escape.'

Donnelly is also said to keep a pair of wraparound shades with him at all times in case he needs to really streamline himself, as well as a plastic lunch bag filled with cold mud, which he intends to smear himself with and become 'invisible to heat vision'.

NATION KNEW GOVERNMENT WERE GOING TO SHAFT MOTHER AND BABY HOME SURVIVORS, BUT HOLY SHIT

NEWS that hundreds of recordings that helped inform the Mother and Baby Homes report had been 'irretrievably destroyed' has come as a shock to even the most hardened, unshockable cynics in the country, with many applauding the government for hitting a new low in the long-running saga.

'We always felt the commission would put forth a version of events that suited the government's narrative and the survivors would be used as pawns to this end, but Jesus fence-jumping Christ, this was unexpected,' said one spectator, annoyed they didn't see this coming after decades of watching Fianna Fáil and Fine Gael oversee whitewashed reports and go-nowhere tribunals on a huge

range of seismic scandals that rocked the nation.

Meanwhile, the government remained adamant that participants who engaged with the Mother and Baby Homes commission were told upfront that their testimonies would be destroyed after the commission cherry-picked the findings it wanted out of them, adding 'it's not our fault' if a woman in her late 80s who had her baby stolen from her 60 years ago didn't properly read the GDPR terms and conditions at the end of article 37, paragraph 19b.

'Well, I think we can all agree on one thing: it's all over now,' said a spokesperson for Minister for Children Roderic O'Gorman, stuffing hundreds

of documents into a wood-chipping machine round the back of Leinster House as the commission headed towards dissolution.

'We concluded that it was bad, but it was a different time. And the women we interviewed agreed, as their tapes would show. Which they can't because a big dog ate them all. But take our word for it, they agreed with everything we said. Just ask them! Well, the ones that are still with us. What can I say, these things take time!'

FANATICISM

REPUBLICAN FUNDAMENTALISTS VOW TO DECAPITATE CARTOONIST DEPICTING PROPHET MCDONALD

A SLEEPER CELL of devout McDonaldists have vowed to exterminate the cartoonist responsible for creating an image of the prophet Mary Lou McDonald that was published in the *Sunday Independent*, *WWN* has learned.

Calling for the immediate deaths of all non-believers involved in the publication of the image, the group, who call themselves the 'Tallaght Ban', took to various comment sections and forums online, promising 'swift and lethal revenge'.

'Depicting our prophet McDonald in any other form than her earthly manifestation as a champion of the working-class people is forbidden in our Republican faith, and will have to be dealt with,' a spokesperson for the Tallaght Ban explained during a video call to prayer this morning, backed with an instrumental version of 'Come Out Ye Black and Tans'.

In adherence with the McDonaldist faith, only pre-approved depictions are allowed of the leader, and they must portray her positively – carrying out modern miracles such as enjoying an increase in support while in opposition during a global pandemic that has shut down the entire country and large sections of the economy.

'Likening our prophet to a witch stirring a cauldron full of Sinn Féin frenzy is also clearly sexist, as our great prophet is a celestial being who has merely taken the form of a woman,' the spokesperson pointed out, now bowing in a northerly direction. 'You'd never see a male politician depicted in a negative way.'

SINN FÉIN TO REVIEW POLICY OF LETTING ANY HEAD-THE-BALL JOIN PARTY

CAPPING OFF a year that has seen its members proclaim anti-vaccine stances, air misogynist and xenophobic comments, and glorify terrorism just a few dozen times, Sinn Féin has announced its intention to review its admittance process for new members.

'If a TD has a go at the gays, Chinese, Nigerians, Brazilians, Muslims, Jews, you have to hold your hands up and say "who are these fucking loopers and why do we keep putting them forward",' accepted a Sinn Féin spokesperson.

The entry requirements that are now up for review consist of new members tasked with ticking 'yes' on a box next to 'are you Sinn Féin in the membrane?'

'When some of your TD's Twitter accounts read like passages rejected from a Beginner's Guide to Discrimination for being too controversial, it's rethink time. But c'mon, who on God's flat green earth can say their own party hasn't a few fringe oddballs?'

However, there is disquiet within the party, as some claimed the new policy would reduce the party's number to just Mary Lou McDonald, Pearse Doherty and Eoin Ó Broin.

'Now I know we give Fine Gael a hard time for always blaming us for everything, no matter what it is, but we're cashing in our "this is a Fine Gael distraction tactic" voucher today,' shared one party member, stating that all head-the-balls were Fine Gael plants.

Members proclaiming 'up the RA' at any time will still be covered by the stock Sinn Féin excuse of 'actually they were just singing the Ra-Ra-Rasputin part of that Boney M song'.

WHINING

**An Roinn Sláinte
Department of Health**

Dr Tony Holohan
Chief Medical Officer of the Department of Health

NATION URGED TO STOP BEING SUCH LITTLE CRYBABIES ABOUT EVERYTHING

THE INCREASE of whiny little bitches in Ireland is currently rising to unsustainable levels, according to a damning new report from the National Crybabies Emergency Team (NCET) leaked online today.

Figures show that the amount of Irish people tattling, sulking, whingeing and needing their arses wiped has risen month on month since the beginning of the pandemic, with curtain-twitching currently reaching 'local Catholic man marrying a Protestant woman' levels.

> **'We know that the Irish people have the capacity to get to a level of cuntishness that appears jovial and friendly'**

'One of the unforeseen aspects of the pandemic is the sheer amount of dickheaded behaviour that has emerged in Ireland,' stressed a member of NCET at a press conference today.

'We're urging everyone to move to a Level 5 of copping on, in a bid to regain some sort of soundness for the Christmas period. We know this has been a challenging time for everyone, and we know that the Irish people have the capacity to get to a level of cuntishness that appears jovial and friendly, without descending into this dummy-out-of-the-pram shite we're seeing today.'

Included in the plan are guidelines such as:

- The cessation of passive-aggressive phrases such as 'no mask today?'
- Catty social media posts about shops that seem to have a lot of people in them are to be limited to one per day.
- Sharing videos of more than five people standing together in the freezing cold with the caption 'no lockdown here' is to be phased out.
- Energy spent whining about health guidelines should be diverted into whining about the price of car insurance/some co-worker you believe 'has it in for you'.

CRIME

VIOLENT CLASHES CONTINUE BETWEEN MAYO AND LOUTH AS THEY FIGHT TO CLAIM BIDEN

VIOLENT SKIRMISHES between two counties that believe themselves to be the one true ancestral home of US President-elect Joe Biden have entered a fifth day.

An unsuspecting Ballina, the frontline location for 'he's from Mayo', suffered a fresh ambush this morning from Carlingford in Louth as a battle to the death for bragging rights over Biden becomes bloodier and bloodier as the hours tick by, prompting calls from the UN for both sides to come to the negotiating table and reach a compromise.

'We can't stress how volatile this situation is, but when you consider

what's at stake – the victor building a Joe Biden Plaza – you can understand why both sides have invested in tanks and grenade launchers,' explained one military expert, shielding themselves from shrapnel.

Initially, the clashes were isolated to genuine distant relatives of Biden,

numbering only five people, but when both sides began recruiting people claiming to be related to the next US president, the numbers in battles swelled to 187,000.

'I'm fighting in this battle cus I owe it to the local economy,' said one Mayo woman going over the trenches with a knife between her teeth, hoping her side could triumph and that Ballina would be the one true location for a rip-off gift shop with Joe Biden masks and commemorative fridge magnets.

'Over my dead body, you Sam Maguire-allergic bastards,' screamed a Louth man on the other side, who would fight to his dying breath to secure a legitimate claim to Biden, the type that would bring busloads of American tourists to his county to stare at the spot Biden's great-great-great-great-great-grand-third cousin took a shit.

WATERFORD CONTRACTOR WILL FINISH CHILDREN'S HOSPITAL FOR 56 GRAND, CASH

LOCAL ALL-ROUNDER Colm McQuillan of McQuillan & Sons has 'had a look' at the ongoing National Children's Hospital project and estimated that he'd be able to have the place up and running by January for about €56,000, no questions asked.

'Ah yeah, I can see what they're at, stringing the money out of you,' said McQuillan to the government, following the announcement that the contractor of the Children's Hospital was foreseeing a further cost of €200 million for the project.

'Listen, come here, I'd just tell them thanks for the work done so far, and tell them to take their shovels and go on about their business. Me and the lads can get in here and get the job

finished nice and quick. In fairness to them, now, the BAM lads have a lot of work done, but sure they'd want to for the €1.4 billion they've suckered out of you, hahaha!'

McQuillan went on to outline how he would manage to 'bring the job home' for such a seemingly reasonable price.

'There's a place down here beside us, they can get me plasterboard at cost price or near enough,' explained the 56-year-old builder, while looking at an incoming call on his phone before deciding that he didn't want to take that call just now.

'And like I say, cash is king. If you want it through the books now, I'd have to put the VAT on top of that.'

The government has thanked Mr McQuillan for his time, but have stated that they're perfectly happy to hand BAM as much taxpayer money as they need, for as long as they need to.

'Fair enough,' McQuillan said, before answering that damn call, 'it's the same lad ringing me over and over about a bollocks of a job, fuck sake.'

FINANCE

WE MEET THE SHAMAN RESPONSIBLE FOR IRELAND'S INSURANCE PREMIUMS

FOLLOWING news that the Central Bank of Ireland found widespread use of differential pricing by firms in the motor and home insurance industry, *WWN* travels to the Hill of Tara in Co. Meath to meet the source responsible for Ireland's insurance premiums, local shaman, Seamus McGee.

Arriving before dusk, our guide stops his 2021 Land Rover and explains the route ahead, before charging us €50 for the ten-kilometre journey from Ashbourne.

'Just walk straight up the hill until you come to a toll gate. Pay the toll and you will then gain access to the shaman's lane leading you straight to his tent,' our guide explains, tearing off in a plume of dust down the road at high speed.

Paying the €200 toll, we were amazed by the sophisticated electronic gate system and the amount of CCTV cameras around the shaman's 'tent', which more closely resembles a marquee you'd see at a trade fair.

'Ah, you made it,' a crusty-sounding voice bellows from behind the tent doors, which have a handle and glass panelling. 'I understand you are looking for a premium or a quote? What company are you with?'

Having falsified some documents to make it appear as though we were an insurance broker as part of this investigation, we hand them over.

'We're a small town brokerage and we're looking for some premium spiritual guidance,' I reply, now winking as I was told to do earlier by our guide.

'Ah, yes, small town in Waterford, but lots of congestion, right?' our shaman winks back, now lighting up some incense and ingesting what we believe to be dried mushrooms of some sort, along with a series of numbers from one to nine, 'lots of black-spot areas too, I bet? And anti-social behaviour?'

'Yes to all of the above,' I reply, aiming now for the maximum premium I could find.

What followed was to be an hour of dancing, chanting and purging, before shaman Seamus returned from the premium spirit world with tales of his visions and a set of vomit-saturated figures, and a matrix to help explain to insurance customers why they're getting charged so much. 'The more figures you give them, the less they will understand.'

> **'Go forth and insure, my sons, but remember, never reveal our secrets to the plebs.'**

'Wow, these are actually extortionate!' I tell our spirit guide, before calling my editor to see how much notice I have to give him if I want to leave my job for the insurance game.

With our lucrative premium algorithm to hand, we part ways with Shaman McGee, but not before being summoned back one more time.

'Are you forgetting something, assholes?' he asks, referring to a large cash rebate for his efforts and an annual performance bonus.

'So sorry, Shaman McGee, we nearly forgot,' I apologise, handing him a suitcase packed with non-sequential bank notes for his offshore bank account in the Isle of Man.

'Go forth and insure, my sons,' the shaman concludes, 'but remember, never reveal our secrets to the plebs.'

THE HOMELESS

DUBLIN'S homeless community will be allowed to sleep at the controversial new white-water rafting facility when it is not in use, with one raft allocated to each homeless person wishing to avail of the new scheme, Dublin City Council (DCC) have confirmed.

The €22.8 million construction, soon to be €50 million, has come under fire from politicians and peasants alike, with many calling it a 'political obscenity', a 'grotesque vanity project' and a 'what the actual fuck are you playing at lads, eh?'

'We can strap them in overnight and they can spin around in the rafts as they sleep. It'll kill two birds,' one member of DCC said, defending the decision. 'Sure, we could probably build actual homes with the money

COUNCIL CONFIRMS HOMELESS ALLOWED TO SLEEP AT WHITE-WATER RAFTING FACILITY WHEN NOT IN USE

we're going to overspend on this, but where would the craic be in that? The homeless lads will love it.'

Despite already being refused a €6.6 million grant application by the government for the project, the council is currently gauging expressions of interest in the construction, including children's hospital construction company BAM and Bob the Builder.

Meanwhile, members of the homeless community welcomed the new overnight accommodation.

'Sleeping on a white-water raft couldn't be any more dangerous than sleeping in a Dublin city doorstep,' one man told *WWN*. 'At least I won't get pissed on, crushed by a council digger, set on fire or stabbed to death spinning around on one of them things.'

> **'Sure, we could probably build actual homes with the money we're going to overspend on this, but where would the craic be in that?'**

Predictions for 2022

A first in Irish history, a celebrity endorses a local car dealership, and not just because they've agreed to give them a free car.

RELATIONSHIPS

WOMAN JUST WANTS TO FIND SOMEONE WHO'D DEFEND HER THE WAY GOVERNMENT DEFENDS VARADKAR

LOCAL WOMAN Megan Loughlin has once again cursed her bad luck in the dating world, but still holds out hope that she can find someone who supports her the way the government is supporting Tánaiste Leo Varadkar through his run-in with the law.

'I couldn't catch a ride in a dildo factory, but I'm an optimist so I look on in envy at how much the government really backs their man. I hope to find a man who'll treat me the same way,' explained Loughlin.

'You know, love me despite my flaws. Downplay my potential breaking of the law when I leak confidential documents – classic hashtag relationship goals stuff,' added Loughlin.

The source of much envy, the Taoiseach and members of Fine Gael have happily downplayed any sense of wrongdoing on the part of Varadkar, with some even confessing that they thought breaking the law was only something 'the poors' do.

'Imagine that passionate intensity, to feel so safe in their arms,' daydreamed Loughlin.

It is not all plain sailing for Varadkar, despite the unconditional support, with reports the panicked FG leader is currently bingeing *Orange is the New Black* and *Prison Break* in a bid to prepare for a potential stretch in the Joy.

Elsewhere, Sinn Féin were reminded they weren't so keen on demanding resignations when then leader Gerry Adams was arrested by police investigating the murder of Jean McConville.

𝔚aterford 𝔚hispers 𝔑ews

VOL 1, 20156136   WATERFORD, THURSDAY, APRIL 22, 1351   2d

'Ring A Ring A Rosie' Song Tasteless, Insist Families of Black Death Victims

FAMILY members and survivors of the ongoing black death pandemic have taken to parchment publishers far and wide to slam a sick new song which they say mocks the victims of the Black Death, *Waterford Whispers News* can report.

Children as young as three have been heard singing the lyrics to the song 'Ring A Ring A Rosie', which taunts the dead when stating, 'A pocket full of posies, a tissue, a tissue. We all fall down', referring to the ritual of leaving poppies on the dead, while the 'rosie' is the malodorous rash that develops on the skin of bubonic plague sufferers. 'Pray tell, whose mind is pregnant with such depravity that they hath come up with this? Thy young folk mock the memory of the dead with such worded filth – and some of them their own kin?' one survivor of the plague retorted upon hearing of the bizarre trend, while another remarked: 'Insensitive fuckin' geebags, boi, if you ask me. Hang them all.' However, child welfare groups have suggested the song may be a way for young people to process the awful scenes they have witnessed over the duration of the pandemic and urged people to be a bit more understanding.

'It's 1351 for God's sake and people are losing their minds over a song, what is this, the Crusades? People signing petitions and gathering up angry mobs! Cancel culture has gone mad, if you ask me. There's more important things to be doing. We've witches to burn at the stake for a start.'

HOUSING

'THANK GOD THIS DIDN'T HAPPEN TO DUBLIN HOMES': GOVERNMENT GLAD MICA ONLY AFFECTING RURAL COMMUNITIES

'JESUS, can you imagine if Dublin homes were built using this craic, we'd never hear the end of it,' a relieved government minister told a closed meeting today on the current, albeit unimportant, scandal involving Donegal homes. 'We'd probably lose all our voters if it happened here, thank Christ no one gives a shite about

that place. Hopefully, this pathetic excuse for a scheme will shush them for a bit until it's the next government's problem.'

The scheme in question, the Defective Block Scheme, was launched in January 2020, yet affected families have said it is lacking and have questioned why they have not been granted the same treatment as families affected by pyrite in the east of the country.

'They do know where they're located, right?' another government adviser retorted, scoffing at the thought that someone in Donegal has the uninformed notion that their home is

> **'Hopefully, this pathetic excuse for a scheme will shush them for a bit until it's the next government's problem.'**

somehow as important as their Dublin counterparts. 'Surely they could just build another home? Sure, they cost nothing up there.'

It was found that the mineral muscovite 'mica' was present in the concrete blocks used to build a large number of properties in Donegal, a substance that impacts on the cohesion of the cement content in the block and therefore the durability of the walls, leaving them to deteriorate very quickly, and forcing owners to move into rented accommodation while still paying off a mortgage.

'We'd probably have to launch a national emergency plan if that was Dublin, ha-ha! Imagine the money it would cost us, we'd be torn apart in the press and even worse, actually have to act on it like we cared,' ministers at the closed meeting agreed, before heading to lunch for a couple of hours before the next meeting on how to keep people renting and living in the overpriced capital now that people are leaving for rural Ireland.

'Let's hope they don't all move to Donegal,' they all laughed.

Grotto

APRIL 2021

Knock Hot, Lourdes Not
STAY-WORSHIP-CATIONS

100+
IRELAND'S SEXIEST GROTTOS

Free Fizzy Holy Water

* 5 Best Moving Statues
* Magdalene Was A Slut
* Bring Back The Laundries
* It's Not Your Body, It's God's
* Worshipping Statues, A Guide

Ignoring The 3rd Commandment
Why It's Okay Catholics Worship Engraven Images

2021 Blessing Of The Graves Line-up Announced And It's Off The Fucking Chain

LOCAL NEWS

BREAKING NEWS

ARCHAEOLOGISTS DISCOVER PROOF THAT 33,000-YEAR-OLD CORK CAVEMEN WERE ABSOLUTE DOSES

EXPERTS HAVE ANNOUNCED that blade marks on the skeleton of a 33,000-year-old reindeer found in the Cork region is clear proof that early humans in the area were using tools to hunt, and that they were almost certainly being insufferable about it too.

'We have no reason to believe that these primitive people sounded in any way different to Cork people sound today,' said Dr Paul Illington, senior archaeologist at the dig in north Cork.

'We're investigating now to see if there are any cave paintings in the area for evidence of overly bullish aggression towards other tribes, increased self-importance, confederate flags, things you'd associate with cavemen. If what we suspect turns out to be true, it could change everything we know about how Ireland was formed.'

Pressed for details, Dr Illington opened up about the chilling possibility that all life in Ireland stems from the south-west, which would …

'Would make us all Cork people, yes,' said Dr Illington, gravely.

'Our DNA, our very being, it all stems from Cork. Everything we do, everything we've ever done, we've been acting as Cork people, even if we didn't know it. In fact that's probably why Cork people detest the rest of the nation, as somewhere deep down in them, it's apparent that we've all turned our back on who we are supposed to be.'

Upon consideration, Dr Illington and his team have been asked to take the reindeer remains they have found and bury them back in the ground, and never speak of any of this again.

LOCAL MAN'S CRY FOR HELP PROBABLY JUST A CRY FOR HELP

THE FRIENDS of a young Waterford man named Eoghan Reid have put his recent erratic behaviour down to 'one of those cry-for-help kind of things', and as such have decided that it's certainly nothing that warrants any action on their behalf.

Reid has just returned from 'being off on one' for a few days, prompting his mates to issue statements on social media for help in finding him – a campaign deemed a total success now that he's home safe and sound.

'Yeah, Eoghan does this from time to time,' said 23-year-old Mark Lalor, who has been friends with Reid since secondary school.

'He'll go off for a while and then come back; sure it's only a cry for help anyway. It's not like it's, you know, anything really serious. If it was, he wouldn't have come back, right?'

Lalor's lack of serious concern was backed up by fellow Waterford native Declan Hannon, who agreed that if Reid needed someone to talk to about any of this, then they were on hand at almost any time, maybe not weekends though, but definitely most other days.

'He says he's grand so, you know, I took that to mean he's grand,' explained Hannon, who stresses he's 'not being a dickhead or anything'.

'And besides, we steered him towards the HSE if he wants to really have a go with someone about his mental health, someone who won't just tell him he's grand and leave it at that. They gave him an appointment in 2026, so all he has to do is hold tight until then and know we're here for him if he wants to turn to alcohol to self-medicate in the meantime.'

Elsewhere, the government announced that instead of proper funding and reforms for mental health services, they would ask *The Late Late Show* to make its 'sport star talks about mental health' slot a permanent fixture.

HEALTH

MAN 'DEAD FOR WEEKS' WAS STILL WAITING FOR EIR CUSTOMER SERVICE TO ANSWER

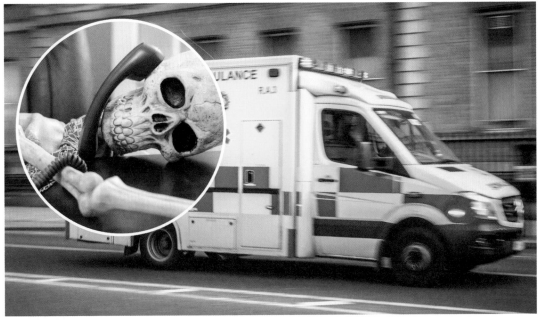

A COUNTY Waterford man was reportedly 'dead for weeks' while still waiting for Eir customer support to answer, emergency services who arrived at the gruesome scene confirmed today.

'The hold music was still playing through the loudspeaker on his phone

---

'His last words to me were, "Sorry, love, it's just what if they answer the second I hang up?"'

---

when we entered his home,' said a paramedic, who had to break the dead man's fingers, which were clutching the phone. 'There were 13 crossed-out lines on the wall in front of him, which we believe were the number of days he was waiting before passing out from dehydration and exhaustion.'

Relatives of the 50-year-old recalled how irate he was over not being able to get through to the phone and broadband provider, and was refusing to hang up for fear someone may just pick up the phone.

'His last words to me were, "Sorry, love, it's just what if they answer the second I hang up?"' the victim's daughter revealed, explaining her father missed her wedding in order to stay on hold.

The man is just one of dozens of victims this

year who have died while waiting for customer service agents to answer.

'Three of those dead ended their own lives after finally getting through to an agent only for the line to suddenly drop as they were about to talk,' a report into the deaths read.

'GOOD TROUSERS' MAKE FINAL TRANSITION INTO 'WORK TROUSERS'

THE 34-WAIST, 32-leg bootcut denim jeans that served Waterford man Michael O'Mailligh so well over years of work drinks, Christmas parties, funerals and baptisms have finally made the inevitable leap to the 'work pile', *WWN* can tearfully confirm.

Like all clothing owned in O'Mailligh's life, the Wranglers have moved into the final stage in the good clothes/around the house clothes/work clothes cycle, and will get their inaugural airing tomorrow when the 36-year-old spends the afternoon pulling weeds in his garden.

'Mad to think of me wearing these good jeans while doing the gardening,' mused Michael, pointing at what we assume he meant were 'good jeans'.

'Boot cut, look at that. Never went out of style. I think I could have got another few years out of them if only they hadn't given up in the crotch area there. No fixing that, so there's not. I tried to tell the wife that they'd still be grand if I just sat the right way wearing them, nobody would notice the hole at all.

'And sure wouldn't I be wearing a nice pair of brown shoes and a nice shirt too, sure who would notice. But she said no, so I just had to wear them round the house or down to the shops. And then I was told I wasn't even allowed to do that, so into the work pile they go.'

O'Mailligh took some convincing from his wife that the trousers weren't 'still of use to someone', therefore banning him from dropping them off at a local charity shop.

> **'Boot cut, look at that. Never went out of style. I think I could have got another few years out of them if only they hadn't given up in the crotch area there.'**

County Knowledge

Westmeath

Northmeath, Southmeath and Eastmeath were all annihilated in a brutal 1,000-year war by Westmeath after suggesting to just call the whole county Meath. People from Westmeath still don't talk to their estranged, directionless counterparts to this day.

NORTHERN IRELAND REALLY ANNOYING IN FAIRNESS

IN A RARE moment of agreement between the two states, Britain and the Republic of Ireland have jointly agreed that Northern Ireland is really annoying in fairness, *WWN* has learned.

Citing years of terrorist organisations, sectarianism and general civil unrest, the six counties have been likened to a malignant tumour conjoining Siamese twins, desperate to separate each other from themselves, and the disputed mass itself.

'Seriously, you can have it,' a spokesperson for Britain insisted, before being verbally shot down by their Irish counterpart.

'No, we really can't afford it. Keep it, it's a fucking mess,' an Irish spokesperson replied. 'We can barely take care of our own criminals here, never mind a whole nation of them.'

Much like the unwanted red-haired stepchild it is, Northern Ireland insisted neither owners have any right to claiming the territory, stating Free Staters and Brits alike haven't a clue what it's like up/over here.

'Youse have no idea what it's like being us,' a NI spokesperson intervened, with all the gusto of an abandoned dog left chained to a pole in a shared back garden.

'We actually don't care anymore,' both nations replied, hoping some form of warden would take it off their hands. 'Would you not just stray off to Europe, like a good little nation? We won't mind, seriously! We've enough shite to be dealing with, cheers.'

Historical Facts

Up to 175 people were lost in the great storm of 1276 in Galway, despite a stone tablet being issued pleading with them not to make unnecessary journeys.

LOCAL MAN NOT SURE WHY HE HATES THAT ONE SPOON IN PARTICULAR

UNABLE to explain the strange phenomenon whereby he curses out one spoon that resides in the cutlery drawer of his kitchen, local man Denis Crawley is appealing to the public in a bid to find out if there are others out there like him.

'I just can't stand the spoony fucker,' offered Crawley, pointing at the teaspoon in question as if by doing so this reporter would instantly recognise the awfulness inherent in the spoon.

Crawley, whose blood pressure skyrockets at the mere sight of 'the bastard spoon', has been known to skip using the spoon for tasks such as making tea even if all other spoons are out of commission awaiting cleaning in his sink.

'When that happens I just whip out a dessert spoon and use that instead,' continued Crawley, nearly sick just from catching sight of the teaspoon's handle and shape, which is slightly different to his other six teaspoons.

'I just need to know I'm not completely mental, and that there are others out there who can't stand specific cutlery,' a lost Crawley appealed, yet he failed to offer a valid reason as to why he doesn't just throw the spoon out.

'No, because then the spoon will have won,' Crawley added, throwing the spoon a dirty look.

RELIGION

CHURCH 'SORRY' BUT NOT 'PAY COMPENSATION SORRY'

THE CATHOLIC CHURCH has 'apologised unreservedly' for its very small, barely significant part in setting up and running Mother and Baby Homes for 70-plus years, which proved to be bottomless pits of immense cruelty and inhumanity down which they gleefully threw 56,000 women.

Experts with previous experience of church apologies in Ireland have confirmed that on closer inspection, 'sorry', when used by the church, does not carry with it any real intention of atoning in any way.

'Oh, you naive summer flower, this is your first church apology for a tyrannical reign of abuse and torture, isn't it?' said one forensic apology expert to those taking the apology on face value.

'When the church "unreservedly apologises", what it means in church

speak is "we have stonewalled survivors who have been begging us in recent years to hand over records, and we'll continue to do so, now feck off".

'And when they say they "accept victims' accounts", that doesn't mean they won't drag their heels over paying compensation or redress, and get their solicitors to make it all go at a snail's pace. You'll check back in five years to find they haven't handed over a single penny,' added the expert.

'Oh, and when there's a call for inquests into the deaths of children who were, to use the only appropriate term, murdered or starved to death, they'll slot in a "the past is the past"or "it was a different time". Sure, they're apologising now, but two years ago

they were paying PR firms to tell you all there was no mass grave in Tuam.'

LOCAL ENVIRONMENTALIST ALL FOR WIND FARMS AS LONG AS THEY'RE ERECTED SOMEWHERE ELSE

CONTRADICTING years of her own social media comments, tweets and sharing of dozens of articles highlighting the benefits of wind turbines, local woman and 'environmentalist' Sinead Crawley failed to see the irony of her latest quest to halt the installation of a local wind farm, *WWN* can report.

Echoing the vast array of previous opponents that she shot down for similar stances, Crawley slammed a proposed local alternative energy development as 'hideous', stating that it would ruin the view in her area.

'No one knows the benefits of wind turbine technology like me, but when it interferes with my own personal landscape view then it becomes a massive problem that requires me to launch several online petitions and a campaign to block their planning,' she explained, blissfully unaware of her own hypocrisy, which saw her call for the closure of a peat-run ESB station in 2015, now resulting in this substitute wind farm.

Previously calling opponents of wind farms 'boggers who need to move into the 21st century', Crawley's sudden change of heart was triggered by vivid nightmares that depicted the permanent eyesores, resulting in the reversal of years of eco-warring and credibility as an environmentalist.

'Surely there must be better places with a more passive population where

these monstrosities can go,' Crawley pointed out at a local online meeting, in between swigs of Colombian coffee from a bamboo cup made in the Philippines, 'Maybe put them somewhere shit like Leitrim, just not in my beautiful locality where I personally have to see them.'

Crawley all but admitted defeat when she realised the local council was heavily populated by Green Party councillor. However, unbeknownst to Crawley, they will actually lodge objections to the wind farm in the coming weeks.

FINANCE

'REELING IN THE YEARS' VIEWERS SHOCKED AT HOW DOCILE IRISH NATION WAS

VIEWERS WATCHING the new season of *Reeling in the Years* last night were said to be left flabbergasted at how docile and subservient the Irish people once were, leaving many disappointed with how a generation dealt with the situation all round.

'Imagine handing over your entire country to a handful of people to run it for you and to call all the shots,' tweeted one woman, who has been at home isolating for the past 13 months. 'To think people were so obedient and trusting back then actually makes me sick.'

Sunday night's episode focused on 2010, a year that saw Ireland come to grips with the economic recession that ended up crippling the nation and causing years of

incalculable physical, societal and emotional damage.

'Imagine putting a huge debt like that on the people instead of those who actually caused the debt in the first place,' echoed another shocked viewer, unaware a similar debt was now looming due to Covid subsidies that would be paid for through taxes and draconian cuts.

Speaking of the 2010 bailout, financial experts pointed to the particularly important lessons learned 11 years ago: mainly that nothing ever changes and that banks

> **'Imagine putting a huge debt like that on the people instead of those who actually caused the debt in the first place.'**

will always come out on top no matter what the crisis is.

'When you print the main commodity that the entire planet depends on it's kind of hard to fail,' he said, before showing more optimism for the Covid financial crisis than the 2008 banking crash, 'At least this time the banks are not in a rush to reclaim the huge loans they've given out, so we can all pay them back slowly over the next 10 years, or whenever they decide to do another financial reset to try to undo years of poor practice.'

LINKEDIN ASSURES LOCAL MAN HE'S LUCKY TO HAVE THE JOB HE HAS

ONLINE job-boasting social media platform LinkedIn has rolled out a new feature where it assesses the CVs of its members, in some instances advising them to 'get back in their lane' and cling to the job they currently have rather than seek new employment elsewhere.

'I was on the lookout for something in a managerial position, and had linked up with a few people with that goal in mind until I got a notification that informed me I should be counting my lucky stars that I still have the job I have,' Waterford man Frank Nelson informed *WWN*.

'It probably wasn't the news I wanted to hear, but may well have been the news I had to hear,' he admitted.

Further updates to LinkedIn aimed at limiting delusions among workers who think they have a life outside shift work and meaningless grind include:

- Sending an automatic 'cop yourself on' message to anyone from a certain socioeconomic background whenever they attempt to link to posher, better-off people
- Advanced facial recognition software that recognises someone who looks like they might have a tattoo out of shot, and isolating them in a separate part of the website
- An ageing feature to help prospective employers know what people using 15-year-old head shots look like now
- Anyone describing themselves as 'entrepreneurs' receive a 'you're fooling no one' pop-up message

The new measures should help ensure the working class stay working, while people more suited to better jobs, and suits, get the chance to go further in life.

THERE was more Olympic triumph for Ireland in Japan this morning, after a bedsit on Dublin's North Circular Road was declared the winner by a panel of judges in the debut of the 'Best Dive' event.

Factors in the decision to grant gold to the apartment, listed as being for a single person but with a landlord that is 'flexible' as to how many stay in it, include:

- The proximity of the kitchen unit to the bed itself, with a mere 8" of space between the oven and the duvet, allowing the tenant to make their dinner while lying in bed (if the oven actually worked, which it doesn't).
- The complete lack of toilet or bathroom facilities – described by judges as 'miraculous', but described by competitors as 'suspicious', prompting calls for

DUBLIN APARTMENT WINS OLYMPIC GOLD FOR BEST DIVE

the apartment to be tested for regulation tampering.
- A gold-medal-worthy smell that lingers on the palate long after leaving the apartment.
- A monthly rent well above what could be expected for such a shithole of a property.

The rest of the podium also went to the Irish dive team, with a three-bedroom house kitted out for 36 migrant workers taking silver, and a family home that gets cleared out every 12 months for the landlord's 'brother in America' to live in, only to show up on the market a week later with much higher rent.

The apartment will be met at the airport by Minister For Housing Darragh O'Brien as well as Minister for Sport Catherine Martin, while Gardaí are being posted at the arrivals gate to keep an eye out for former minister Shane Ross, who has been spotted in the area.

WILDLIFE

DIVERS FIND DOLPHIN MASS GRAVE IN DINGLE

DIVERS SEARCHING for Fungie the dolphin in Dingle have discovered a 'mass grave' site underwater where an estimated 20–30 separate remains have been found, *WWN* has learned.

The graves, marked with the name Fungie followed by a number and year of death, are believed to have been the final resting places of a series of aquatic mammals who have filled the tourist attraction's roll for the past 40 years.

'When the first Fungie died, another one arrived in the bay and we said

we'd just go with the flow and say nothing, play it by ear,' admitted one Dingle boat owner, who has made a living out of bringing tourists out to see the dolphin for 35 years. 'After the 12th or 13th Fungie we couldn't really say anything, as business was booming, so hopefully a new Fungie will arrive before the current restrictions are lifted.'

Auditions for the new Fungie are believed to be underway, with all mammal options now being discussed.

'We were thinking of mixing it up a bit this time around and getting a seal into the bay instead,' another boat operator explained. 'The fame

and limelight seems to go to dolphins' heads; the last Fungie spent weeks on the session with the Miami Dolphins one summer and left us in the lurch. Another Fungie would hardly surface at all because he was hooked on watching reruns of *Flipper*. We can't have that when our whole town depends on them'.

Meanwhile, RTÉ have announced a 50-episode true crime podcast on the mass Fungie grave narrated by Daniel Day-Lewis, who has spent the last six months learning to speak dolphin in preparation for the series.

'Eh-eh-eh-eh-eh,' confirmed Day-Lewis, standing upright in a swimming pool and clapping his elbows together.

The discovery of the mass dolphin grave has left egg on the faces of Dingle officials, who just this morning told the nation Fungie had gone to live on an aqua farm.

> ### 'The fame and limelight seems to go to dolphins' heads.'

The Year in Numbers

1,456 – the number of 'new genders', according to your uncle in his latest Facebook rant.

RELIGION

GODBEENS: IRELAND'S UNDERGROUND MASS SCENE

WITH DOZENS of rogue Irish priests being threatened with fines for orchestrating illegal masses across the country over the past 12 months, *WWN* travels to Co. Tipperary to attend what has commonly become known as a 'Godbeen', where scenes of Ireland's underground masses are rife.

Disguised as a 6-foot-2 elderly woman caped in a shawl, we managed to gain an invite from a local altar boy operating as a 'black mass vendor' who said he could guarantee a front-row pew if the donation was right.

'Fifty gets you top of the queue for communion, a hundred gets you a live confession,' I was advised, before being shown a menu of tiered communion bread ranging from 'speckled with the holy ghost' to 'double dipped with Christ', both equally tempting in their own right. 'There's a fair slap off the speckled ones now; keep ya Christing for at least a week.'

Led to the back entrance of the priest's house under the cover of night, we were astounded to see a large, orderly queue, mumbling excerpts from the gospels, dousing themselves in Lourdes' finest-quality base H_2O.

'I get it sent through the mail straight from source,' one man tells me, offering me a splash of his Bitcoin-bought water, 'never gets stopped by customs either, the big man must be looking over me.'

Our guide ushers us inside to a small oratory in the basement of the priest's house. The room is packed with all sorts of people – mostly elderly, white – leaving a musty rural-shop-from-the-1980s smell in the air. We're offered some hymns of praise for 10 euros a pop. Upon reading them, it's clear there were some real crackers in there. Money well spent.

'He'll give it to you on your tongue if you're lucky,' one pensioner winks at me, eyeing up a bowl of wafers in a gold-plated chalice.

The crowd hushes as the sound of a 10-hour-long YouTube video of Big Ben chiming is played. The priest and his henchboys walk out, the irony of the British bongs lost on the revellers, all transfixed now on the underground priest.

Mass begins.

'Blessed are thee who come in the name of our Lord,' Fr X bellows through what appears to be a PlayStation 3 microphone, earning a very enthusiastic round of applause.

'He really knows his crowd,' a man beside me whispers, clapping manically like a seal.

'The last mass was off the fucking chain … God forgive me,' another man responds, before blessing his curse away.

It was clear this underground mass was more chilled, more urban than mainstream masses I've attended.

We delved further after procession.

'If you're interested, I know a few wet churches around too,' a parishioner informs me, awaiting live confession. 'No Holy Communion, just straight-up mass without all the Holy C. In and out in 15 minutes – great for people on the go.'

We wondered how many of these churches were serving underground mass, all tax free, before realising to ourselves that all mass is tax free, regardless of location or current regulations.

'You got your christenings, weddings and of course the whole funeral end of things is booming at the mo. Cleaning up, really. I'll probably lease a nice grey 212 Megane come June, nothing too fancy now or they'll be talking, you know yourself,' Fr X later says, explaining the lucrative mass trade.

'Easter is the big one on Sunday. We found a site up the mountains here in the forestry and one of the other priests from a neighbouring diocese has a decent sound system rig. Expecting a few hundred at it now, so it should be a decent auld gig. Plenty of holy water will be had.'

Predictions for 2022

Good news for that one fan of James Corden: the talk-show giant is set to appear on everything, all day, everywhere, for as long as he lives.

Historical Facts

Bram Stoker was inspired to create his Dracula character after catching sight of the night walkers on Sackville St, now O'Connell St.

CRIME

DRUG GANG RISE TO GARDA CHALLENGE WITH BRILLIANT 'JERUSALEMA' DANCE OFF

A LOCAL DRUG gang has taken some time out of their incredibly busy schedule this week to perform the never-tiresome 'Jerusalema' challenge, in response to An Garda Síochána's recent video.

Taking place in various deprived areas of Waterford city and county, the criminal organisation posted their rendition of the dance online, keeping in the spirit of the popular craze and vowing to murder anyone who gets in their way.

'Fuckin' flat out so it was gettin' all the lads in one place at one time, trying to lose surveillance an' that,' said gang leader Jason Lonergan. 'Took us ages to get it righ' and that, but once I brought out the stun gun and started punishin' lads for dancin' the wrong way they soon copped on.'

Lonergan, who controls most of the south-east's wholesale supply as an area manager for a Dublin-based gang, said the video better put smiles on people's faces, or else.

'Fuckin' great year for us even with all the seizures. We're after makin' a fortune from people fallin' off the wagon, so happy to give back to all the dopes who have to go out and work for a livin' and pay tax an' that,' the young entrepreneur added. 'If I don't see people smiling at our video there will be consequences – permanent smiles, if ya get me.'

However, a rival gang has also taken up the 'Jerusalema' challenge, brandishing guns and swords, calling out their competition and promising to dance on their heads.

'Ah, it's only a harmless bit of craic is all,' Lonergan insisted, before setting a contract on everyone in the rival video.

COUNTY DONEGAL STILL THERE, FINDS REPORT

A WORRYING new report into whether or not certain unwanted counties are still there has found that the north-west district of Donegal is still lingering about, despite years of neglect, states the recently published report.

With under-par infrastructure, including poor roads, lack of transport hubs and general government incompetence at a local and national level, Donegal has grown to become the runt of the Irish county litter, followed closely by several other rural counties that no one really bothers with anymore.

'I thought it was part of the UK, if I'm honest,' explains the report's author and lead researcher, Michael Matthews.

'It's just kind of wedged in there like a piece of pasta stuck in a sink that just won't flush down the drain. How the people there don't revolt is anyone's guess, but it's probably to do with it being super cold and wet and the residents up there have just become accustomed to being left abandoned and are suffering from a form of Stockholm syndrome,' the report read.

Barely making the news recently over a building controversy involving the use of mica, a substance which has resulted in the crumbling of hundreds of Donegal homes over the past decade, Donegal residents were said to be left outraged at the recent developments and the lack of government response.

'Yeah, they're a shower of bastards, but we're used to it now and we kind of expect to be fucked over time and time again, so don't worry about us at'all at'all, hi, just leave Donegal continue to rot into the sea,' one local offered, before being crushed to death by their own home.

HEALTH

TECHNICIAN DIES IN CAR ACCIDENT JUST SIX MONTHS AFTER ERECTING 5G MAST

WITH MORE and more evidence surfacing around the dangers of 5G technology, a Co. Carlow man who was part of a team of installers who erected a controversial 5G mast six months ago suddenly died on Monday morning driving home from the pub, sparking calls to investigate the new telecommunications service.

The man, believed to be in his late 30s, was reportedly a picture of health up until his car ploughed head-on into a large ditch, begging the question of how a popular amateur sports figure in the community who was never sick a day in his life could have had such a dramatic negative turn in health. Many people have reasonably pointed to his recent job of erecting the mast as the possibly cause.

'It's really strange, because I was only talking to him in March and he was absolutely fine,' a former neighbour confirmed, 'then all of a sudden he worked on that mast up the road and then 'coincidentally crashed' his car six months later? A bit suspect if you ask me. Of course no investigation is being launched into the 5G connection – it's all being hushed up.'

CCTV footage of the man leaving his local bar with a bottle of vodka revealed some clues into his final moments.

'Watch as he's driving here on the wrong side of the road after he takes a swig from the bottle. He then picks up his phone and begins to text,' said experts investigating the footage, which they showed to *WWN*. 'Obviously the phone was on some kind of 5G signal at the time and took over control of his body, causing him to swerve to avoid an oncoming truck and forcing him to crash head-on into the ditch at 127 km per hour. That's 5G mind control if ever we've seen it – he had no chance.'

LOCAL FATHER APPLIES FOR ZERO CUSTODY OF CHILDREN

EXHAUSTED, fed up and missing being able to lounge on the couch all day uninterrupted, one local father is taking a landmark custody case to the High Court in Ireland, *WWN* can reveal.

'I'm sure a few fathers who don't have access to their children will find this offensive, but honestly, take mine,' shared father-of-two Rory Macklin, who loves his kids but Jesus, the effort.

'The ex-wife was happy with the 50-50 split, but now they're in that always-asking-questions phase, so I just want my life back,' confirmed Macklin in his submission for zero custody.

'I've tried everything, pawning them off on play dates at their friends' homes, gluing iPads to their faces, but they're always there, y'know,' said

Macklin, who in harrowing testimony said he has had to decline over 400 'pints with the lads' invites in the past two years.

Judge William Holden told Macklin that, while he agreed 'children are very fucking annoying' at times, he could not grant his application for seeing less of his children, as this would lead to a flood of similar applications from parents.

Now in the midst of a temper tantrum, Macklin protested and asked that Judge Holden meet his children in order to better understand how irritating they are.

'They're not into football at all. It's all about weird YouTubers, or TikTok dances they need me to watch them recreate,' cried Macklin as he was taken away by Gardaí to be reunited with his children.

RURAL MAN SPENDS DAY LOOKING OUT FOR BLOW-INS

RURAL MAN Noel McCaffrey has spent the bulk of his day perched at the main thoroughfare of his local village in the hopes of identifying every single individual who is not from around here, *WWN* can reveal.

In a repeat practice of a hobby he first took up 25 years ago, succeeding his departed uncle in the role, McCaffrey possesses a rare desire and talent for scowling at any person he is unable to recognise from the locality.

'Whist now, that's not the O'Neills' car, definitely not the Cassidys' either,' McCaffrey said, cutting off our questioning to fully focus on the dim hum of a car engine several miles away.

'They'll be coming the back road into the village, now you can come on the bypass that way but a blow-in wouldn't know that,' said McCaffrey, squinting his eyes to make out the car now approaching the crossroads made up of a Mace, a post box and nine pubs.

McCaffrey is one of 40,000 dedicated rural men put in the paid position by local government to keep a watch over towns for evidence of someone 'not from around here' passing through villages under the Rural Auld Lad On Watch Scheme.

'You just never know what they're up to,' said McCaffrey, burning a hole through the back of a woman emerging from the Mace with a litre of milk.

'Communists, ISIS or worse, Dubliners, we must remain ever vigilant,' concluded McCaffrey, walking out into the main road to make sure the car driving off kept driving.

FAMILY

COUSINS WEIRD AS FUCK, FINDS REPORT

A NEW report into cousins – you know the ones – has found beyond any reasonable doubt that they are as weird as fuck, *WWN* can confirm.

The study, funded by the Normal Cousins of Ireland group, found vast anomalies in cousin behaviour, likening them to a far-removed evolutionary chain of primates who have yet to learn even the most basic forms of human etiquette.

'We found that a certain class of cousins are just very, very odd,' the 46,000-page report concluded. Its findings are published this week in *National Geographic*.

'It's like they're not even from this planet at times and seem to be constantly fighting and generally bringing bad luck on themselves, while simultaneously blaming everybody else for their own problems.'

Cousins were found to be so embarrassing and strange that they were even being denied by their own family, with a large majority of family members distancing themselves from their blood relatives indefinitely.

'I usually just say they're dead or that they're just related to me through marriage, citing some eejit who went rogue,' one man ashamed of his cousins told *WWN*. 'We like to call them the *Jeremy Kyle Show* side of the family, but to be honest, that's not really fair on the Jeremy Kyle guests, they're not that bad.'

The extensive report concluded that a staggering 50 per cent of cousins were as weird as fuck, with the remaining 50 per cent deemed to be 'up their own holes'.

HABITUAL Twitter user Eoin Kennedy is at a loss as to the source of his laconic and downbeat mood, rejecting all suggestion that it may have something to do with the fact that he spends day in, day out on Twitter searching out objectionable and abhorrent opinions and engaging in online squabbles with the owners of the aforementioned opinions.

MAN WHO SPENDS DAY ARGUING WITH STRANGERS ONLINE NOT SURE WHY HE FEELS SO MISERABLE

'No, that can't be it,' said a depressed-sounding Kennedy as the Twitter app on his phone seared discord, hatred and intolerance directly into his eyeballs for the 254th consecutive day in a row.

Devoting his time to trying to correct strangers online when they espouse barely literate expressions of xenophobic and misogynistic views, and often finding himself locked into weeks-long vitriolic exchanges, Kennedy is open to suggestions as to why he feels so miserable.

'I've analysed my habits and how I spend my time and I just can't figure it out,' offered Kennedy, failing to meet our gaze, his face glued to the constant torrent of negativity and acrimony on his Twitter feed.

'Yeah, maybe it's like you say – living in a state of agitation and aggression that comes with arguing with egg avatars could be it, but I dunno, maybe I just need to cut down on gluten or some shit,' reasoned Kennedy.

In a bid to change up his mood and navigate a path towards a more content way of living out his days and evenings Kennedy opened up his Facebook app on his phone to argue with strangers there.

DRINKING

LOCAL DOSE INTO THE WHISKEY NOW

LOCAL TRY-HARD Donald Ryan has announced to just about everyone he meets that he's now 'into the whiskey', following several painful years of promoting craft beer, wine, gin, basically any alcohol trend that was going at the time.

Desperate to disguise his habit under the label 'connoisseur', Ryan admits to never refusing the 'occasional shot' of whiskey in his favourite haunts, with the majority of Ryan's whiskey drinking occurring via the free samples given out by hipster barber establishments that look like they're trapped in an episode of *Peaky Blinders*.

'You can really taste how that cask finishing pays off in the end,' Ryan expressed at his latest barber

> **'Is it a bleedin' haircut ya want or just to talk bollocks about the free Jack Daniels knock-off ya got?'**

choice, conveniently chosen by the 'free whiskey' offer he saw online last month, 'although, the cooperage on those barrels is standard, you can really get the hint of the aged oak. And that extra long lyne arm they use to carry the spirit vapours to the condenser really pays off in the end.'

Now 'nosing' the last of his complimentary measure, Ryan's newly found barber ushered him to his chair.

'So what will it be this time, pal? Weren't youse here only last week again?' he asked his latest 'regular'. 'Is it a bleedin' haircut ya want or just to talk bollocks about the free Jack Daniels knock-off ya got?'

'Just a trim,' Ryan retorted, ignoring the hostility like a pro, familiar with

the tone that several previous barbers had who copped on to his penchant for free booze, adding, 'You do student discounts, right, chief? Christ, how did we ever drink those god-awful craft beers back in the day, ha-ha. Whiskey's where it's at now,' hinting at his empty glass with a nod. 'You're definitely one of the best barbers I've had, chief, keep 'em coming, man,' he said before being fucked out on his ear.

BREAKING NEWS

LOCAL MAN SITS DOWN TO PEE THESE DAYS

Predictions for 2022

The UK will opt out of the 2022 Eurovision after accepting that it's just a televised 'free sucker punch' that the Europeans get to throw at them every year.

DEFENDING a recent trip to the toilet in the early hours of the morning where he sat down to urinate, local man Mark Dalton blamed tiredness as the factor behind his new sitting routine.

Accidentally spotted at 6.36 a.m. by his son James, who was going for a 'normal stand-up pee', Dalton was left embarrassed and feeling a little less masculine when the unsuspecting 17-year-old opened the unlocked bathroom door, revealing his ageing parent.

'But why, Dad, why?' James reportedly screamed at his squatting father, urine tearing into the toilet water below like machine gun fire from a Vietnam War-era US helicopter. 'You're not even pooing, Dad, what the fuck are you doing sitting down there?'

The incident, which sparked a rather worried conversation among family members at breakfast time, was flagged by wife Deirdre Dalton as her husband sat down at the kitchen table.

'You know you can tell us anything, Mark,' she pried, unprepared for her husband's ground-breaking admission.

'I wouldn't dare sit down to pee during the day. That's not the type of person I am.'

'It's only early morning pees I sit down for, when I have to get up out of bed half asleep and my eyes are half shut,' the distraught 43-year-old stressed, now standing up and making a dash for the door, before turning around and screaming, 'I wouldn't dare sit down to pee during the day. That's not the type of person I am. I swear to God. Just leave me alone. You don't even know me. No one does.'

Despite repeated knocks on his bedroom door, Mark Dalton was not available for further comment on the matter, but family members have confirmed he has made at least two standing-up pees since this morning's incident.

More as we get it.

County Knowledge

Wexford

Wexford's Hook Head was named by someone who had clearly never seen a hook.

Would the 1798 Rebellion have been successful if Davy Fitzgerald had been in charge? Probably.

Shaving Ryan's Privates, the porn version of Steven Spielberg's epic war movie, was also filmed in Wexford.

BREAKING NEWS

YOUTHS PELTED WITH ROCKS BY EMERGENCY SERVICE WORKERS

DOZENS OF DUBLIN teenagers were hospitalised over the past few days in what authorities are calling a 'turn up for the books' after fed-up emergency service workers exited their vehicles and began pelting rocks and sticks at youths in retaliation for decades of abuse.

'I was just walking down the road waving my trusty iron bar at passing cars, minding my own business, when I got clocked on the head by a large rock,' *WWN* was told by one 14-year-old victim, who also admitted to having 23 previous convictions. 'Then a bunch of ambulance men and women ran over and kicked the absolute living shite out of me and my mate Cathal, and even took his collection of rocks from him.'

Fire crew members on the west side of the city were also reported to have used fire hoses on one gang of youths, leaving them dazed and extremely wet.

'We were only saying hello to the fire engine lads by sending a firework directly into their windshield, and then they just turned on us for nothing and sprayed us with the water yoke,' one eyewitness recalled, still very clean from the attack.

Frontline workers have vowed to continue pelting youths with rocks, citing 'fighting fire with fire', and have called on parents of young juveniles to continue ignoring their children's crimes and anti-social behaviour, as they found beating the little shits with rocks was actually quite therapeutic, and a great way of letting off years of built-up steam.

> **'We were only saying hello to the fire engine lads by sending a firework directly into their windshield, and then they just turned on us for nothing.'**

RELIGION

PRIESTS PERFORM SOCIALLY DISTANCED ASH WEDNESDAY SERVICES WITH INNOVATIVE 'FINGER ON A POLE' DEVICE

WORRIED THAT you were going to have to kick off your Lent without a reminder that you are but dust and unto dust you shall return? Well fear not, as a quick-thinking Waterford priest has devised a novel solution for administering ashes in a socially distanced manner.

'I call it the long finger,' beamed Father Augustus McNamara, proudly showing off an 'ashing device' made from four broom handles duct-taped together with a rubber index finger stapled to the end of it.

'I can ash a forehead from 20 feet away. The other end of it rests on a little claw thing like a snooker cue would, and the parishioner just steps up and bam – one cross, no fuss. Deadly!'

Joking that this wasn't the first long finger the church has put things on, Fr McNamara went on to discuss how he wouldn't be patenting his device, leaving it free for others to copy in a bid to ensure maximum ashage, minimum red tape.

'This is my gift to the world,' he exclaimed, while parishioners wearing suitable eye protection lined up to get their foreheads smudged.

'And yeah, it doesn't give you that nice defined cross that you could get

> **Without this, you wouldn't know where people would be getting ashes, or what was in them. Protestant ashes, you never know.'**

with your thumb, but it'll do for now. It cuts down on illegal, unregulated back-alley ashing, that's for sure. Without this, you wouldn't know where people would be getting ashes, or what was in them. Protestant ashes, you never know.'

Fr McNamara also took us through his prototype for a socially distanced baptism device, which currently consists of a water balloon filled with holy water and a lady's bra tied between two trees.

LOCAL MAN ADDS 'SURVIVED PANDEMIC' TO CV

WATERFORD MAN Mike Mahone, seeking something to make his CV pop out among the sea of other jobseekers, has added 'pandemic survivor' to his list of 'Hobbies and Other Interests'.

'I believe that my ability to remain Covid-free for almost two years shows that I'm a team player, that I follow rules and guidelines, and that I'm able to occupy myself and stay busy when asked to remain indoors for months on end,' said Mahone, when questioned why he bumped 'long walks' from its usual place on his résumé.

'I fully believe that no employer really gives a crap about what your special interests are, but on the off chance that someone glances at this section they'll see that I'm very capable of knuckling down in the face of the greatest medical emergency to hit the planet in over a hundred years.'

Elsewhere, other job hunters have taken quite the opposite approach to Mahone, and have boasted on their CVs about how they 'broke through the norms'.

'I've put on my CV how I managed to maintain a decent social life with plenty of house parties,' said one young woman we spoke to.

'This shows that I'm not afraid to challenge the rules in order to deliver a better experience for everyone all around. I'm not content to go with the flow. And now, all my grandparents are dead so employers don't have to worry about me taking time off for funerals or the like.'

Meanwhile, employers have admitted that they don't really care how you spent the pandemic; if you're willing to work shifts for minimum wage, then you're off to a pretty good start.

WHEN WATERFORD couple Caroline and William McIntyre are asked how their son Eric is getting on since he moved up to Dublin last year, they adopt a solemn tone and say that he succumbed to a mystery illness while travelling and passed away, rather than reveal the truth that their son is a would-be TikTok and Instagram superstar who trades under the handle 'Erickin' Ball', *WWN* can reveal.

'How can we expect our friends to understand what he does, when we

PARENTS OF INFLUENCER TELL THEIR FRIENDS HE DIED OVERSEAS

don't even know ourselves?' sighed 58-year-old Caroline, watching a clip of her son dancing to a Drake song wearing only a nappy to promote a brand of cheap electric razors specifically for trimming pubic hair.

'His dad was the first to tell people that Eric had contracted "super malaria" in America and died instantly, and I just went along with it.'

'He's my only son, so it was hard to fake-lose him to a fake illness so young,' added William McIntyre, wondering where his parenting skills had gone so very wrong.

'But it came down to either admitting that our kid is one of these fucking social media doses, or being able to set foot outside the house with our heads held high ever again. We made our choice.'

Currently the proud organiser of a YouTube channel that boasts almost 735 subscribers, 'Erickin' Ball' remains blissfully unaware of the fact that his parents have secretly killed him off, as well as remaining blissfully unaware of the public's perception of him, and indeed most things that happen in the world that he isn't directly involved in.

CRIME

GARDAÍ ISSUE 'STALE APPEAL' FOR MURDER INVESTIGATION

GARDAÍ in Dublin today have launched a 'stale appeal' for any information surrounding an unsolved murder that happened in the city centre in 2015, or 2014 maybe, they're not sure.

Detectives made the half-arsed appeal during a poorly organised press briefing, while sitting back tucking into some snacks, scrolling through old *Sunday World* news articles of the case on their phones.

'It says here some lad was shot on Dame Street, so it would be great if someone owned up to that particular crime or something. It would make our job a whole lot easier,' one detective pleaded, reading further, 'the victim was apparently known to Gardaí, but I have never seen sight nor sound of him to be honest', before

then asking his fellow detective if he knew the victim.

'Jesus, Tom, he looks familiar alright, but sure don't all them scutts look the same,' his partner replied, now turning the phone sideways, like that would make a difference. 'No, can't put my finger on the face, Tom, but yeah, if anyone knows anything give us a bell at the station early enough because we do be out spinning around during the day. Cheers.'

The stale appeal called on anyone in the country to come forward if they had seen a murder around 5–7 years ago in Dublin city centre-ish.

'The victim was fairly tall now, around 5 to 6 feet, aged around 20 or 30 and wore clothes and a pair of trainers or shoes. He wasn't saying much now, as he was fairly dead, but

we believe he was probably shot with a gun and involved in the drug trade because he had one of those short haircuts with the fringe, you know the type,' Gardaí concluded, before heading off for lunch.

HAVING MADE her way through the smooth online customer experience of her favourite clothing site in effortless fashion some three days ago, local woman Ciara Fahy has now been informed via an email in her spam folder that her order will land at her front door imminently within the next three working days, or at the turn of the next millennium.

LOCAL WOMAN'S ORDER FROM UK EXPECTED TO ARRIVE WITHIN 3 TO 478 WORKING DAYS

Citing 'Brexit-related delays', which the online shopping giant conveniently didn't mention when Fahy was putting in her card details, the 23-year-old faces an uncertain wait for her new clothes in a hammer blow that left Fahy stating 'could this bastarding, shit-chugging, pox of a lockdown get any worse'.

Online shopping, known to many as the only thing getting some people through this damned never-ending lockdown nightmare, has experienced significant changes since the onset of Brexit tariff and custom rules, leaving many to stare forlornly out the window for days with no delivery driver in sight.

For online retailers 'some Brexit-related delays' has become a catch-all excuse to rival 'my dog ate my

homework', sending customers everywhere into a frustrated rage.

'It's not fair, all I did was order fourteen dresses, five crop tops, eight sets of underwear, two bomber jackets, three pairs of boots and nine different pants that I'd probably return once I tried them on. Next-day delivery shouldn't be too hard,' confirmed Fahy, whose purchasing power rivalled that of a small country.

Elsewhere, a small number of 'Irish based, owned and produced' businesses are struggling to explain to customers how deliveries can be experiencing 'Brexit-related delivery delays' when their websites claim all items are handmade on the Blasket Islands by direct descendants of Peig Sayers and not in Bangladesh, as is now clearly the case.

CRIME

RAT BASTARD dogs working for Revenue have seized drugs worth over €50k at a Dublin parcel hub today, despite not being paid any money for their touting.

Snitches Bailey and Sam sat proudly as they uncovered two kilos of herbal cannabis and 10 kilos of cannabis-infused sweets, stating they will rat out anyone for the price of a doggy treat.

'Is using my addiction to uncover contraband to supply other people's addiction a bit hypocritical? Yes, but you've never tasted these dog biscuits, man,

they're trippy as fuck,' Bailey said, explaining his logic and crippling addiction. 'I almost piss myself when my handler pulls out that sweet-ass treat. I don't even know his fucking name, man. I just call him my dealer.'

Responsible for a string of major drug stings across the country, the dogs said they were not scared of any criminal repercussions over their blatant touting.

'They say snitches get stitches, but I've had my balls removed, dude,' Sam reveals. 'My fucking testicles were ripped off. Have you any idea how much that shit hurts and how frustrating

RAT BASTARD DOGS HELP SEIZE €50K DRUGS

it is? When you have your nuts chopped, you just don't care anymore. Just kill me already. I fucking beg you.'

Destined to continue ratting out parcels, people at airports and shipping containers for the next few dog years, Bailey and Sam said they look forward to retiring in their later life and

just eating as many treats as they can.

'I've heard from other dogs that they just get treats every day for doing nothing – that's the kind of life I want, man, none of this working-for-the-man bullshit,' Bailey concluded, taking a dump on the ground before licking his arse clean.

ROSCOMMON PLEDGE TO END WITCH TRIALS NEXT YEAR

ELDERS IN THE COUNTY of Roscommon have indicated that the archaic practice of accusing women of being witches and putting them on trial will cease as of next year, a decision welcomed by human rights groups.

'I think we can all acknowledge that this is an outdated practice from a bygone era of 2018, and times have moved on, but let's not rush into this. Willie Tracey's youngest was still able to work in the bank after getting pregnant – witch. Then the D'Arcys' youngest came back from college in Dublin with opinions – witch. So once the last few trials are out of the way, we'll be done with them for good,' explained one Roscommon elder.

Perhaps the most famous of Roscommon's trials involved Joanne Connell, who was burned at the stake after successfully passing her driving test in 1999,

> **'Look, we didn't get them all right, but you go and try to correctly guess who is and isn't a witch; it's not as easy as it looks.'**

something labelled by local men as 'wicked sorcery, the likes of which can only have come from the devil himself'.

Lasting just three minutes, the trial saw Connell attempting to explain how she had simply 'studied' and partook in 'driving lessons', but fearing she was reciting an incantation, the men covered their ears while tying her to a stake.

'Look, we didn't get them all right, but you go and try to correctly guess who is and isn't a witch; it's not as easy as it looks,' offered chief lighter of flames, Denis Hackett, who said the decision to end the trials had nothing to do with a man finally being accused of being a witch.

However, not all locals are happy about the phasing out of the trials.

'I've no problem in principle, but what am I going to do with all these stakes and kindling,' asked one local man who does a roaring trade in ducking stools but fears for the future of his business.

GARDENING

CHUFFED BEYOND his wildest dreams, father of five John Regis stared longingly out the front window at his freshly cut lawn, admiring his precise linear cuts and likening it to the work of a professional.

'I went a bit off towards the end, but the rest of those grass furrows are to die for,' he whispered to himself, slurping a nice mug of sugary tea. 'T'ah, you can't beat a good cuppa after 12 minutes hard labour – this must be what Wimbledon court attendants feel like after a cut.'

Hoping some family member would enter the front room to see his intense gaze, Regis relished in his simple achievement, before spotting a fellow resident and neighbour, Mark Shields, walking down the street.

'Watch now. He'll pretend not to see it out of spite,' Regis told himself, trying to use some form of telepathy to force his neighbour to look. 'Surely the

LOCAL MAN STARES LONGINGLY OUT WINDOW AT LAWN HE JUST CUT

blind bastard smells the fresh grass,' Regis said before speculating that 'he's probably afraid to look in case it reminds him to cut his own grass – yeah that's it – the lazy prick.'

Noticing an erect 'yellow flower thing' dead centre of the lawn, Regis began to panic.

'Ah, you weedy bollocks,' he shouted, realising the sitting room window was ajar and catching eyes with Shields.

'Oh! Hi, Mark!' he said, red in the face, 'no, no, not you – the weed I was shouting at, ha-ha. Yeah, no, I just realised I missed a bit, sorry, yeah, see you at the residents meeting Wednesday.'

Filled with shame at now being the talk of the estate, the humble 49-year-old grass cutter recoiled from his front window where once he stood proud, defeated once again by sporadic

flowered weeds, never to quite feel the same.

'Fucking weed wanker! I'll tarmac the lot!' he concluded, before sulking for the remainder of the day.

INVESTIGATION LAUNCHED INTO WHO TAMPERED WITH THE THERMOSTAT SETTINGS

GARDAÍ in Waterford have called on anyone passing Lismore Pines housing estate on Monday evening to report any suspicious activity around house number 79 after reports from the owner who found the settings on the family thermostat to have been drastically rearranged, *WWN* can report.

The alarm was raised at 6 p.m., after dad Gerard Power returned home from work to find the heating to be off instead of on, despite carefully spending nearly 'one fucking hour' timing the thermostat to come on at peak times in the house, mostly when he was going to work, home or bed.

'It couldn't have just changed its-fucking-self,' the irate father-of-four-

sheepish-looking-children explained at a press conference inside the family home today. 'I specifically remember pushing down the little white things on the dial so that the house would be nice and toasty by the time I got home

from work at 6, but now the whole time is wrong and a load of the white things have been pressed down, like some maniac was messing around with it.'

Forensic teams confirmed that no 'new fingerprints' have been detected on the thermostat, pointing to either a gloved intruder, or someone closer to home.

'We're investigating all lines of inquiry,' Garda Paul Monk told *WWN*, his eyes darting from family member to family member. 'We're looking into the possibility that the dial may have been turned at what appears to be 4 p.m., prime coming-home-from-school time,' he added, as one of the Power children shifted awkwardly in their seat.

In an unrelated incident, two unwashed cups were also left upside down in the family sink, and several damp towels were left on the bathroom floor.

EXCLUSIVE

TWO MANKY CHIMNEYS STILL CAPITAL'S MAIN LANDMARK SOMEHOW

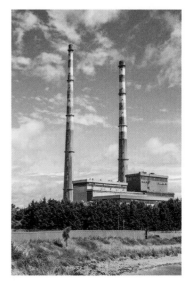

DESPITE a vast range of iconic landmarks to choose from, a manky pair of decommissioned chimneys from an ESB station have managed to somehow become Dublin city's most loved landmark, *WWN* can confirm.

The chimneys, which have no real relevance apart from featuring in a U2 music video once, have somehow crowbarred their way into the hearts of native Dubs.

'I don't think there is anything more representative of Dublin right now than two filthy unused exhaust pipes,' said one Dublin man, who is calling for the structures first built in 1965 to be 'listed'. 'It's our Eiffel Tower, our Taj Mahal, a magnificent piece of Irish structural engineering that dates back to the beginning of time itself.'

In a desperate bid to steal their thunder in 2003, the Spire was erected on O'Connell Street, yet it failed to fill the long, pole-like void in Dubliners' hearts.

'Give me red-and-white industrial power station chimneys any day over that modern piece of junk,' said another Dubliner, who is not a fan of any other supposedly 'iconic' landmarks either. 'Trinity College, Custom House, Molly Malone statue, Samuel Beckett Bridge, Croke Park, Leinster House, Dublin Castle, Christchurch; none of these even come close to those two ESB vents in my mind.'

The group behind a petition launched in 2014 that saved the towers from demolition are now calling for the city of Dublin to be renamed Poolbeg Towers instead.

'We would settle for the names Twin Pipes, Soot Holes or Pair of Pricks if people don't like our main preference,' the group concluded.

MAN WHO BOUGHT HOUSE FOR £20K THINKS SNOWFLAKE GENERATION HAVE IT TOO EASY

AS STUDIES at home and abroad continue to suggest that today's younger generations will be the first to regress in terms of key indicators of quality of life such as life expectancy, one local man of advanced years Michael Barton has taken the opportunity to say that the snowflake generation will complain about anything.

Barton, who bought his 4-bed urban home on his modest single salary as a postman in the 1980s and retired early, can't believe a generation locked out of owning homes and facing up to a second global recession in a decade amid a climate crisis would piss and moan like the snowflakes they are.

'I'd like to see them survive with what I had to deal with in the dark days of the '80s when I was their age,' Barton said of walking into a bank and receiving a mortgage hassle free for a property that has since increased in value twentyfold.

'It's all "poor me", I have "anxiety", the pension age will be 75 by the time

I retire or I'm "burned out". And it's all backed up by "empirical evidence". Jesus, all they do is moan, moan, moan,' said Barton, moaning once again about 'millennials'.

Barton, like many people his age, mistakenly talks about the hardship his own parents grew up with like it was actually something he went through, omitting the fact that his childhood was defined by relative comfort, affordable living, career stability and no major wars.

'Can't believe they give out when it was me and my generation that had to fight Hitler a week after the Titanic sank, smack bang in the middle of the Irish famine,' added the 65-year-old. 'They don't even post letters or know what a house phone is – too busy spending their life savings on avocados!'

'And the students have the cheek to give out about paying exorbitant fees for remote learning? They've no idea how easy they have it. In my day, Pangaea hadn't even broken up to form the continents!'

CRIME

INNER-CITY DUBLIN TEENS TO BE SENT TO NORTHERN IRELAND IF THEY DON'T COP ON

INNER-CITY Dublin teens involved in a number of anti-social incidents recently are being warned that they will now be rounded up and dropped into Northern Ireland's most troubled areas in a bid to show them 'what it's really like', *WWN* can confirm.

Following a series of incidents across the city that saw several scrapes and grazes administered and dozens of handbags scattered around the streets, Gardaí and the PSNI agreed to show 'the little scuts a real riot'.

'These little knob heads are only playing playground tag compared to our boys up here, so bring them on up to fuck and we'll see if they're man enough,' a spokesperson for

> **'These little knob heads are only playing playground tag compared to our boys.'**

the Carrickfergus division of the PSNI said. 'We'll drop them off in Newtownabbey with some free-stater signage around their scrawny necks. See them throw shapes and wave puny penknives then.'

The new initiative called 'So You Think You're Hard Enough' has already sent 30 inner-city youths to the heart of ongoing Loyalist violence with 100 per cent of them immediately pleading for their family members to help.

'I'll never do anythin' ever again, I swear ta God, please get me out of here,' shouted one Dublin teen as a petrol bomb landed beside him, while the distant sound of gunfire rang through the tear-gassed street. 'Mammy! I'm sorry, Mammy, please, I'll be good forever, I will. I'll never pretend I'm hard or nutin', please just help me … Waaaaah! Janey mack, Mammy, they've real guns an' all and they look like they'll actually kill us instead of just throwing a few slaps.'

EXCLUSIVE REPORT

IS IRELAND READY FOR AN INCLUSIVE UNITED IRELAND, OR WILL THE BASTARD PRODS RUIN IT? WE INVESTIGATE

AS A BORDER poll looks increasingly likely within the next decade, and debate about how the process of a shared island should be approached, *WWN* looks into how feasible an inclusive, welcoming and tolerant United Ireland is.

Soliciting opinion from across the island, *WWN* gained a clearer picture as to how that could be achieved.

'A shared island in which everyone can live in secular, tolerant harmony can't be taken as a given, and must be hard fought for, but we just can't do that with the Protestants here, so they'll have to go, sorry,' confirmed one committed equality and tolerance advocate.

'Aye, the difficulty of all this reunification business is over-egged if you ask me. It'll be a walk in the park after the last of the Prods head back to Britain,' one man we spoke to confidently asserted.

The more people we spoke to, the more we realised that the political establishments in Belfast, Dublin and London were behind the times; the people were ready and willing, and the time for open discussion and debate was now.

'Live in harmony with them lot? Sure they're savages!' confirmed one woman, who declined to specify which group she was talking about.

'We're looking at this the wrong way, if you ask me. Surely Loyalists and Republicans can be united in a shared suspicion and hatred of foreigners?' shared one man.

'I have this beauteous vision, so crystal clear, of hands united,

County Knowledge

Kilkenny

Should a musical number ever kick off in real life, Kilkenny is the place it will happen. The city is purpose-built for hordes of dancing chimney sweeps to emerge at any given moment.

The animation capital of Ireland, many of Kilkenny's residents are 2D and very sketchy.

Not just a hurling-obsessed county, Kilkenny is known for much more, including ... No, we're drawing a blank, sorry.

no longer living in fear. A bright emboldened future lies ahead, but if the Prods think they'll be staying I'll have them shot dead,' confirmed Republican poet laureate Éóín Ó Fáóláín, who plans on making his first-ever trip north sometime in the next century.

'This is about a mutual respect and patience for each other's cultures. You can't just discard one community and drive them out. No, you have to be much more subtle than that. Do it over time, day by day, maybe rename Church of Ireland, Church of England, that sort of stuff, then they'll get the hint,' shared one priest.

'Our lot might take the kneecaps off a lad, but they cut the crusts off their bread, the psychos,' offered another open-minded United Ireland advocate.

The people of the island of Ireland seem ready and disarmingly accommodating of differing cultures.

'You know, the Orange Marches, let them at it, just stand a few feet in front of them at all times laying down pictures of the Queen in the nip, like a breadcrumb trail, they won't even notice being loaded onto the boat and ferried over to England.'

Predictions for 2022

2022 will be the year when everyone in the world wises up to Vladimir Putin, and accepts him for the badass, take-no-shit living saint that he really is.

What Conflict?

JANUARY 2021

Syria? Palestine? Yemen?

Know your rubble

Catch up on what the EU was so concerned about it did nothing.

UN Condemns Wherever It Is This Week

MIGRANTS, ASYLUM SEEKERS OR REFUGEES
How to ignore them all

Free Palestinian Flag Profile Picture
To Show How Much You Really Care

10

Emergency charity appeals that are no match for your sociopathic detachment

Can't we just blame it all on Putin?
- The West

Your Favourite Genocides ranked

Uighur Muslims wins best ignored

Who to declare solidarity with

Your Weekly Stance Options

FREE THOUGHTS AND PRAYERS INSIDE

WORLD NEWS

GREEK IMMIGRANT WHO LIVED OFF WELFARE DIES IN ENGLAND

ONE OF ENGLAND'S most notorious welfare cheats has died at the age of 99, *WWN* can report.

Hailed as a hero among the welfare cheating classes of Britain, it is believed that the Greece-born welfare king has made millions out of his schemes, funding his lavish lifestyle, which included castles, yachts and cars, all on the taxpayer's dime.

'He tried to hide his immigrant status by anglicising his name, gaining people's trust after changing it from Battenberg to Mountbatten. He was clearly well versed in the art of conning,' confirmed one policeman.

Welfare officials confirmed it was hard to pin down Mountbatten, as he moved around a lot between his various properties acquired through his welfare scams. It is believed that

Mountbatten's four children, a product of his incestuous marriage to a blood relative, have adopted a similar lifestyle, and continue to rip off the British taxpayer to this day.

'I heard one of the kids is in big trouble with police, FBI involved and all,' confirmed one member of the public, who hates welfare scroungers.

'They are the poster family for all that is wrong with this country. He was known to be a bit of a racist, but maybe he should have gone back to where he was from if he didn't like it here. And his kids? Affairs, divorces, illegitimate kids, the works. It'd make you sick. Thank God Brexit will sort out stuff like this ever happening again.'

Questions will be asked of authorities as to how a man could evade them for decades while racking up serious sums of cash, but it has recently emerged that Mountbatten's wife used her connection with politicians to ensure laws that applied to everyone else never affected them.

ISRAELI MILITARY CONFIRM HAMAS ROCKET FIRED FROM IRELAND

RESPONDING to the news that the Irish parliament has discovered the correct definition of the word 'annexation', the Israeli military have revealed that their intelligence suggests a number of Hamas rockets are being fired from Ireland, possibly the Leinster House area of the island to be specific.

'And we have a right to defend ourselves against the terrorists of Hamas firing rockets out of the Irish parliament. If we total a building containing media offices or kill 66 children, well so be it, war isn't as black and white as Irish politicians make out,' confirmed one military official, pointing to satellite imagery of Ireland that had been crudely photoshopped to include thousands of rocket launches emanating from Kildare Street.

'This is fairly solid intelligence now, non-stop rockets by the looks of it coming from the Dáil. Is that Richard Boyd Barrett with a rocket launcher? Are you sure about that "annexation" business?' an Israeli military official questioned.

Israeli authorities were said to be so incensed at the news that a motion was passed declaring that the Israeli government's land grabs of Palestinian territories and displacement of Palestinian communities were 'de facto annexations', and that they were strongly considering forging Irish passports to carry out assassinations again.

'"Simplistic reading of situation", "baseless", "anti-Semitism",' continued an Israeli official reading from a 'condemning the condemnations' bingo card.

The Israeli military then politely asked if Ireland could expel all US military from Shannon Airport, as this would make their planned disproportionate response to Ireland that little bit easier.

BREAKING NEWS ━━━━━━━━━━━

IDIOT KID CRYING OVER DROPPED ICE CREAM NO IDEA ABOUT 40 ONGOING WORLD CONFLICTS

SOME IDIOT KID is reportedly crying over a spilled 99 ice cream on the ground, despite dozens of ongoing world conflicts currently taking place, *WWN* can confirm.

Darren Reilly, 4, is said to have begun wailing like a little baby outside Molly's ice cream parlour in Waterford city, forcing witnesses to slam the child's behaviour as selfish and totally tone deaf.

'I'd love to see what he'd do if his entire family was blown into chunks of steaming flesh, their body parts draped across the debris of what was once his three-bedroom semi,' offered eyewitness Tony Kent, who admitted to wanting to punch the little shit right in the face. 'The little inconsiderate arsehole probably wants another ice cream now, while there's children in

Palestine left licking the tears off their own dust-caked faces.'

Reilly's cries were also later criticised by experts in ongoing world conflicts, with many pointing out that there are currently over 40 wars taking place across the planet.

'I blame the parents for not sitting the brat down in front of LiveLeak and showing him all the brutality and violence being uploaded from conflicts,' one expert suggested. 'I can guarantee you that if they bothered to press play on a few ISIS beheading and torture videos, he wouldn't be too long whingeing like a little bitch over nothing.'

Unaware of the criticism, the mother of the child, Donna Reilly, apparently went back into the parlour to buy her little precious a tub of ice cream

with sprinkles instead, leaving many observers disgusted with her lack of empathy towards victims of war.

'People like her make me sick,' another expert concluded. 'Sometimes I wish we were at war here so that people like that would open their eyes and face the grim reality we're all in.'

'I can guarantee you that if they bothered to press play on a few ISIS beheading and torture videos, he wouldn't be too long whingeing like a little bitch over nothing.'

US NEWS

CURSE OF THE KENNEDYS: 104-YEAR-OLD MICHAEL KENNEDY JR DIES UNEXPECTEDLY

Historical Facts

'My wish is to terrify Irish primary school children, to cause them endless trauma when they thought they'd be out on a fun school trip' – Oliver Plunkett's dying declaration.

THE KENNEDY FAMILY curse strikes again! Michael Kennedy Jr has died unexpectedly today following a short illness that left him dead early this morning, *WWN* can confirm.

The 104-year-old was found lifeless by his wife, Jane Kennedy, and is believed either to have died suddenly in his sleep or to have woken up dead.

'He had his whole entire life ahead of him, and was always the life and soul of the party,' said a close family member, who admitted to being afraid

Predictions for 2022

Having seen it in a movie somewhere, Elon Musk begins work on a tunnel through the core of the earth from Ireland to Australia, just for the fun of it.

to carry the Kennedy name. 'We now live constantly in fear of dying. What have we done to deserve this?'

Michael Kennedy Jr also leaves behind five sons, two daughters and 15 grandchildren, many of whom are looking to change their names by deed poll.

'It's like having a dark thunder cloud following you around everywhere you go, waiting to strike us down with Kennedy-killing lightening,' said granddaughter Mary Kennedy, looking over her shoulder every couple of sentences in fear. 'I'm always extra cautious when I'm out and about and constantly double check whatever I eat. My mechanic thinks I'm stone mad, as I

get my car brakes and wheels checked every month. I don't even dare to fly or take the boat.'

The famous Kennedy curse has taken dozens of lives over the years, most famously John F. Kennedy and his brother Bobby, who were both assassinated in the 1960s.

> **'We now live constantly in fear of dying. What have we done to deserve this?'**

'Oh, Jesus no, we're not related to them at all, sorry. We're the Kennedys from Longford, not the Yank Wexford lads,' Jane Kennedy added. 'I suppose the curse still stands though, as Michael's brother Davy died last year, and he was only 96? Like, both brothers were taken too soon, so it's definitely the curse of the Kennedys, right?'

TRUMP LATEST

DERANGED TRUMP FOUND SCRAWLING TWEETS ON WALL OF OVAL OFFICE

AS HOUSE DEMOCRATS in America keep themselves busy by introducing articles of impeachment for the outgoing president, a shivering and sweating Donald Trump is still struggling with social media withdrawals, having been banned from Twitter, Facebook, Instagram, Pinterest, Twitch and Bebo.

Finishing his latest offline tweet posted via big black sharpie on the Oval Office wall, Trump's small hand began seizing up after hours of all-caps scrawling.

'Haven't had any insurrection issues! JUST

ASK MELANIA!' Trump scribbled, presumably in response to reports that Trump-supporting domestic terrorists are plotting more attacks on Capitol Hill, according to DC police.

'SO UNFAIR! Twitter will have low ratings without me,' scrawled Trump in a feverish flurry of fury, condemning the social media giant for limiting his

means of communication to just the White House press room and taking questions from the world's biggest media outlets.

It has been reported that Trump's children are growing frustrated by their father hovering over their shoulders any time they browse Facebook on their phone, begging for five minutes of social media time.

'This time out in the bold corner from Twitter has given the president time to reflect, reflect on how right he is about everything, and that inciting violence is no big deal,' shared one aide, who has been forced to write numbers of likes and

retweets below each scrawl on the Oval Office wall.

'BIG ELECTION WIN! NO VIOLENCE! What next? Blaming 300,000 covfefe deaths on me, so stupid!' Trump hand-tweeted, his scrawl finishing halfway across a portrait of Andrew Jackson.

While the desecration of the Oval Office is nowhere near the damage wrought by his supporters on Capitol Hill several days ago, those officials who have yet to resign to save their own skins believe it is best to let Trump continue scrawling.

'Just let him tire himself out. It's either this or he starts asking about the nuclear codes again.'

BREAKING NEWS

DONALD RUMSFELD IS IN HEAVEN, INSISTS CIA REPORT

DESPITE little to no evidence that such a thing is possible, leading figures within the CIA have insisted that former secretary of defence Donald Rumsfeld is currently in heaven following his permanent neutralisation at the age of 88.

Mr Rumsfeld, who always claimed to have created a 'more stable and secure world' by invading Iraq in 2003, created a more stable and secure world by passing away, thus ensuring he would not be able to serve under any more US presidents other than the four he already had.

'Just as Mr Rumsfeld was confident that Iraq had weapons of mass destruction, we are confident that he has gone to his eternal rest in the glory of heaven,' stated a CIA spokesperson today with authority.

'We are certain he is not in hell, as there is no evidence of that area being rich in any sort of fossil fuels. And yet, there are many unpatriotic Americans who believe that the murder of almost half a million Iraqi people is something God would even consider when deciding who gets into heaven or not. God wouldn't consider that kind of death count to be anything in light of the security and wealth it brought to the US and its allies.'

Meanwhile, the UK government has announced that if the CIA says Rumsfeld is in heaven, that's good enough for them, despite an incident where a respected heavenologist outlined reams of data proving that Rumsfeld was nowhere near the place, before subsequently killing himself out of nowhere.

TEARFUL NETANYAHU HANDS OVER KEYS TO PALESTINIAN DEMOLITION EQUIPMENT

OUSTED Israeli premier Benjamin Netanyahu has relinquished control of his fleet of heavy construction equipment to the country's new prime minister-elect, Naftali Bennett, urging him to 'take good care' of the machines he used to demolish Palestinian homes during his 12-year reign.

'Mind the JCB, she sticks a bit in third,' said Netanyahu, who leaves office after the nation's bitterly fought election which has seen a multi-party coalition led by Bennett emerge.

'And if the bulldozer doesn't flatten a Palestinian two-bedroom apartment in one go, just back it up a bit and give it more of a run-up. She'll get the job done, I promise.'

With increasing sadness at the fact he wouldn't be the one to finally eradicate the region from 'those bothersome Palestinians', Netanyahu issued a tearful farewell to the deconstruction staff he had championed for so many years and assured them that their new boss would 'get the job done'.

'Look, I know that there's a lot of apprehension about the somewhat very right wing, somewhat barely centrist, bit-of-this, bit-of-that gang that have landed into government, but one thing I know for certain is this: they'll want that sweet $3.8bn in military aid every year,' said Netanyahu, as IDF soldiers wept like Palestinian schoolkids.

'So they'll be as eager to "protect Israel" as we were, and as quick to retaliate with airstrikes and demolition orders and what have you. You've served me well, everyone. Farewell.'

Netanyahu will now live the rest of his life devoting himself to humanitarian causes, or possibly by remaining a key figure in Israeli politics with a mind to reclaiming his rightful place as leader of the powerful nation.

EXCLUSIVE

DELAY IN RUPERT MURDOCH DYING DUE TO HELL REFUSING TO TAKE HIM

ALREADY OVERSTAYING his welcome here on earth, media mogul Rupert Murdoch's current life status remains in the balance again this year as opposite factions of the universe refuse to take him post-death.

A spokesdemon for hell confirmed the sanctity where evil souls are subjected to punitive suffering, often torture, as eternal punishment after death will not be available for the 89-year-old hanger-on, citing a clashing of entities with the Dark Lord, Satan.

'It would be like God taking in Buddha, or Jesus moving in with the prophet Muhammad. It just wouldn't work in the long run, as they'd just end up hating each other for eternity,' a fiery charcoal-laced statement read.

Mr Murdoch, whose vast empire of newspapers and 24 news stations has been responsible for decades of human anxiety, misinformation and propaganda, causing numerous brutal wars and toppling of regimes on all sides of the East and West divide, has been somehow allowed to remain on the earth, accumulating billions in wealth and imposing his influence on every aspect of society.

'He puts Lucifer to shame, so I guess he doesn't want to lose his position down there in the underworld,' a spokesangel explained. 'God obviously doesn't want him either, but he understands the predicament all

> **'God obviously doesn't want him either, but he understands the predicament all sides are in. Neither heaven nor hell wants him.'**

sides are in. Neither heaven nor hell wants him.'

The dispute first arose in 2018 during a near-death yachting accident, when Mr Murdoch almost died, having suffered broken vertebrae, which required immediate surgery, and a spinal haematoma, which is said to have increased the chances of paralysis or even death.

'It was the first time God and Satan spoke in a while, but they both agreed to call off the death for another few years before they come up with a solution.'

Conspiracy Corner

Getting the figs in Fig Rolls is actually a fairly straightforward process involving a very basic production line set-up, and is in no way as complicated as they make out.

US NEWS

DEREK CHAUVIN DEFENCE TEAM DEMAND RETRIAL IN THE 1950S

THERE HAS BEEN a fresh twist in the trial of Derek Chauvin, the former police officer charged with the murder of George Floyd, after his defence team moved for a mistrial and the swearing in of a new jury.

Defence for Chauvin sought to alert the judge to a creeping sense that there was a clear 'bias' among the current jury as they appeared the type to judge all men equally, with one lawyer stating that the jury were likely to possess a contemporary attitude towards the victim, his humanity and the circumstances of his murder on account of their living in 2021.

'We ask your honour to accede to our request to have the defendant judged by a jury of his peers and thusly, we see no other option than to swear in a jury from 1952. Alabama, if we could proffer a switch in location too, but if the judge sees fit to swear in a 1930s or 1850s or even 2016 jury, we may be open to it,' shared one of the attorneys on Chauvin's legal team.

Further elaborating on what it described as an 'untenable insistence' that the jury should process and absorb the evidence like their client's innocence wasn't a foregone conclusion, on account of the race of the victim, rendered the trial 'a farce'.

'Your honour, we only ask that the judge allows for an "originalist" reading of racism. How is our client's behaviour, which is rooted in the 1950s, expected to be understood, if no one currently living in the 1950s is on the jury? We motion for a mistrial immediately,' added the attorney.

The defence team also asked that a new judge be assigned to the trial, preferably one who is going to be late for his tee-off time at his local whites-only golf club if this thing isn't wrapped up quickly.

'Such a judge should still be easily procured in 2021,' concluded the attorney.

> **'How is our client's behaviour, which is rooted in the 1950s, expected to be understood, if no one currently living in the 1950s is on the jury?'**

County Knowledge

Antrim

Facing stiff competition from around the world, Antrim holds the record for most incomprehensible accent on earth.

Disappointing and tricking American tourists with deceptive promotional pictures that make the Giant's Causeway rock formations look humongous remains Co. Antrim's most popular ruse.

Portrush is what Tramore could look like if it was arsed.

MIDDLE EAST

'WE THOUGHT IT WAS FREE TO TAKE': ISRAEL APOLOGISES AFTER MISUNDERSTANDING PHRASE 'FREE PALESTINE'

TAKING TIME OUT from recent deadlocked elections, Israeli officials admitted to being left red-faced this week after finally realising the term 'free Palestine' did not actually mean it was free to take, citing an embarrassing misunderstanding on their part.

For years, Israeli settlers had apparently thought they were doing Palestinians a huge favour by taking the land off their hands, and always wondered why the people were so aggressive about them helping, but it has all started to suddenly make sense.

'No wonder they were wailing at us all the time and lobbing mortar rounds at us,' revealed Isaac Feinstein, who admitted to being so embarrassed over the whole thing that he nearly gave back the 10 acres of land he acquired via a bulldozer and armed members of the Israeli army. 'It's actually hilarious now I think back on it. What a complete and utter cock-up on our part,' he said, adding, 'So all those "free Palestine" signs are really saying "give it back"? Hilarious! Oh well.'

Much like when a piece of furniture is left outside someone's home with the sign 'free couch', successive Israeli governments, who do love a nice freebie when they see one, apologised to the Palestinian people, before insisting on continuing their land-grab regardless of the obvious mix-up.

'We started, so we might as well finish the job,' explained a government official. 'No point in taking it off their hands in a half-arsed, leave them a tiny bit of land way. No, no. Best just go full hog and be done with it.'

𝔚aterford 𝔚hispers 𝔑ews

| VOL 1, 20156136 | WATERFORD, SATURDAY, JUNE 26, 1954 | 3p |

Thousands of Italian Chippers Appear Overnight

TOWNS and cities across the country were left perplexed today following the sudden and abrupt erection of what is estimated to be thousands of Italian-owned fast-food takeaways, all opening simultaneously and bearing the first name of the owner.

'What's peculiar is that these restaurants are selling what appear to be fried Irish potatoes cut into chips back to the Irish people and they're scoffing them like pigs at a trough,' one observer said of the phenomenon. 'Seriously, what the hell is a battered sausage when it's at home? Or a scallop? Give me tripe any day over this muck. It will never catch on.'

'Yesterday my entire extended family were all lounging around in the hot Mediterranean sun, drinking beautiful red wine and eating the healthiest of foods when my brother Gino just stood up out of nowhere and said – "hey, guysa, letssa all mova to a colda and dampa Irelande and sell them some fatty fried foodsa for the rest of our livesa." So we all then agreed at that moment to do exactly that,' recalled owner of Tony's takeaway, Anthony Marconi, who is still adapting to the English language after only having landed in Ireland last night.

Within 24 hours, the group of Italian entrepreneurs landed in Ireland before dispersing to every town and city to set up their chain of chip shops, immediately retaining a wide range of customers. 'They're like part of the furniture already,' insisted local Garda Thomas Lyons, who was tucking into his seventh snack box of the day. 'Nobody is objecting to them either, which is strange considering

we're usually a bunch of pricks in that regard,' he added, before concluding with a wild thought:

'Next thing you know we'll be letting the Chinese sell us food ha-ha, or worse, the Indians!'

UK NEWS

WHAT HAPPENS IN THE UK WHEN* THE QUEEN DIES?

*We first must acknowledge that a recent survey revealed that 97 per cent of the British public believes the Queen is immortal and will simply refuse to die, so for Britons it's strictly an 'if' rather than a 'when' scenario.

Despite this, plans are in place for the eventuality, and *WWN* had a sneak peek at what's in store:

- Every man, woman and child will be placed at half mast.
- All UK citizens will be sent a 10-litre jar, which they must cry into and return as proof of their intense mourning and grief.
- The British will begin an hourly 21-gun salute that will last 21 years.
- Anyone who thinks about tweeting about how Britain should explore becoming a 'republic' has their hands pre-emptively chopped off.
- The Queen's corgis will act as pall-bearers, which will lead to an epidemic of 'paw-bearer' puns from middle-aged men.
- After a brief period of mourning for four months, Britain will still refuse to return to normal.
- Boris Johnson intends to throw himself into the open grave while screaming, 'why God, why? Why not take all the poor people instead?'
- The BBC will interview 4,000 Royal Correspondents across BBC channels 1, 2, 3 and 4 to tell everyone how, despite the fact that the Queen had servants to apply toothpaste on her toothbrush at night, she was just like us.
- The BBC will also specially set up BBC 5–99 to play the same coverage on a loop. The official BBC Mourning channel will just feature people crying.
- Prince Andrew won't be able to avoid those calls from the FBI anymore.
- Elton John will be kidnapped and kept in a cell until he writes a moving ballad befitting the Queen.

FIRST-EVER IRISH GARDENS OPENS IN JAPAN

TOKYO HAS OPENED the world's first-ever 'Irish Gardens', featuring an array of Ireland's most common park features, and marking a milestone in Irish/Japanese culture, *WWN* has learned.

The Irish Embassy in Tokyo welcomed the new addition to the Japanese capital, with a spokesperson stating that the park, which will cost in the range of €2 billion to recreate, was 'like a little piece of home in Japan'.

Shortly after opening, the Irish Gardens filled with pale white people donning sportswear or see-through leggings drinking cans and bottles of beer, as more well-to-do middle-class people circled its perimeter in needlessly large jeeps while sipping skinny mocha lattés and scoffing at the garden's questionable population.

'This could be anywhere in Ireland,' pointed out one Irish reveller working as an architect in the area, who admitted to feeling a bit uneasy, but at home all the same. 'Jesus, where did these scuts even appear from? Anyway, I suppose it's spot on as an Irish Gardens all the same, very similar to home.'

Much like Japanese Gardens here, with their array of beautiful flowers, shrubs, plants and trees, the Irish Gardens in Tokyo was awash with seasonal dandelions, thistles and several tonnes of dog shit.

'I even sat on a syringe,' one Japanese worker having his lunch pointed out. 'And I've never seen so many unmuzzled pit bulls in my life being led around by topless young men with tribal tattoos, drinking tonic wine, washing their jocks in the fountain and shouting at each other for no reason.'

RELIGION

GOD SORRY NOW HE FORGOT TO INCLUDE BIBLE PASSAGE ABOUT HIM BEING BLACK

'WHEN I THINK back on it now, it probably could have made a huge difference to the way humanity treats one another,' God said in an emotional interview with *WWN* ahead of publication of his book *The Newest Testament*, due for release next month.

During the course of promoting the latest update of the Bible, God has surprised followers with his first public appearance, which revealed he's actually of African descent, proving a jaw-dropping moment for many.

'It's not something I really thought of, considering the whole human race descended from Africa,' God explained, referring to scientific consensus on the origins of man. 'You do know I made man in my image, right?

'And if the first man and woman were just that, then I would have assumed you idiots would have known I was black – next thing you'll be saying my son Jesus was some blonde-haired, blue-eyed white boy ha-ha,' he added.

Released on October 12th, God's updated edition of the New Testament will go on sale across the world, hoping to 'right a few wrongs' along the way in a bid to keep up with an instant-information world.

'To be honest, you people don't have long left to read it, so I'd say get out there and buy the book ASAP,' God said, hinting at a possible future ending for his next book. 'I've included the part where I'm black, bisexual and love a good pork chop now and again, so I'm sure this edition will go down as well as the previous ones, hopefully without all the violence this time.'

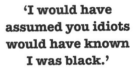

> **'I would have assumed you idiots would have known I was black.'**

County Knowledge

Clare

The Cliffs of Moher were chiselled by Clare people a thousand years ago, to give the country a more menacing, 'tough guy' appearance.

Formally adopted by Munster in 1639, fellow Munster counties are still suspicious of the Connacht blow-in.

Clare people are known nationally for their propensity to look at their own video feed while on Zoom calls.

EXCLUSIVE

FRUIT FLIES INTERDIMENSIONAL, CERN SCIENTISTS FIND

FRUIT FLIES that just appear out of absolutely nowhere have now been found by scientists working at the CERN facility to be in fact 'interdimensional', after finding thousands of them in the Hadron Collider, *WWN* can confirm.

Following their latest particle accelerator test in Switzerland, staff at the facility discovered fruit flies appearing out of thin air, with scientists later speculating that they must have come from a parallel universe somewhere.

'We asked the question how they could just appear like that from nothing,' said Professor Hans Reinstein, who first found dozens of flies whizzing around the collider. 'Their tiny quantum-like size must be something to do with it too, and we are actively researching how they move from one dimension to the other.'

For years, people have speculated as to the nature of fruit flies and their ability to just turn up out of nowhere, with the CERN lab now happy they have discovered one of the first living organisms to appear, or indeed, disappear on command.

'We've suspected in the past that odd socks, teaspoons, pens and earrings have interdimensional properties, as they just seemingly vanish into thin air, but this fruit fly

> **'We've suspected in the past that odd socks, teaspoons, pens and earrings have interdimensional properties, as they just seemingly vanish into nothing.'**

discovery is a new one for us, and very exciting.'

UPDATE: CERN scientists have since retracted their report on fruit flies and apologised after finding a rotten lemon wedge dropped in the CERN canteen to be behind the source of the fruit flies, and not their ongoing experiments.

The Year in Numbers

150mn – the number of times Irish men fell asleep on the couch before 7 p.m. while watching TV.

RELIGION

IS THIS GOING TO BE A CARTOON OF MUHAMMAD OR DO WE VALUE OUR LIVES?

AS HUMANITY ENTERS its 5,220th consecutive year of trying and failing to reason with religious extremists of all shapes, sizes and creeds, *WWN* is weighing up whether this is going to be a cartoon of Muhammad or something else, as we contemplate the fragility of our own existence, which could be snuffed out at any moment.

Is this blank page going to become a cartoon or, after careful consideration, which reveals preferential treatment to the sanctity of our bodies, born of a desire to continue breathing, maybe it could be a really nice picture of a tree or something?

A kitten caught mid-sneeze? Or Emmanuel Macron crying because no one will buy his cheese?

Or maybe we could have the best of both worlds with a Schrödinger's Muhammad in this black box:

Is it a cartoon of a religious figure inside the box, or is it an image of something mean about Taylor Swift? And which will result in even more death threats?

Or maybe it's a picture of a hologram of Robert Kardashian? Or will we again lean towards showing considerable bias for remaining alive and reveal that it is and always was a few puppies instead?

Oh, like you could do better? Fuck you! That's pretty decent for a quick five-minute effort. What were you expecting, da Vinci doggos? Everyone's a critic. At least we're still alive.

GINGER LAD HAD SEX AGAIN

A BRITISH MAN with red hair has confirmed on Sunday that he is after having sex again, resulting in a second baby with his wife, *WWN* has learned.

Harry Windsor and his wife Meghan officially announced the news online, sparking hope and anticipation among the ginger community across the world.

'Fair play to him, he's after giving a lot of people some faith in themselves,' said one 'auburn'-haired man. 'His wife must be a bit of a saint in fairness, allowing that to happen. That's twice now, I hear, which is mental when you think about it.'

The couple, who married in a lavish ceremony in 2018, had a son in May of the following year, with many speculating the ginger had sex in September of 2018, probably the same month as his most recent intercourse.

'Harry's birthday is the 15th of September, so I'd say he got the sex off her then, which is really sweet of her,' said another woman following the incredible news. 'It's simply great to see them get a bit, ya know? Those poor ginger lads get an awful time, and I suppose they will take all they can get when it's there.'

The bright-ginger-haired man has not yet revealed if and when he will have sex again, but was commended for his 100 per cent record so far.

'He had sex twice and now has two babies! A bit of a ginger legend if you ask me,' concluded another online commentator.

TRUMP LATEST

YOU'D MISS TRUMP ALL THE SAME, FINDS STUDY

THE KICK-OFF of the impeachment trial of former US president Donald Trump has brought with it a welcome burst of 'Trumpy-ness' that has been missing from life since Trump left office in January, research has shown.

The Senate took to the floor yesterday to vote on whether or not Trump's second impeachment was constitutional, and featured the arrival of a new character in the Trump saga: lawyer Bruce Castor, who lit up social media in a manner not seen since the 'good old days' of three weeks ago.

'This is what has been missing since Trump left office and was booted off Twitter, just a good old-fashioned pile-on while Republicans outdo themselves in the "Jesus Christ did they just say that out loud?" stakes,' sobbed one anti-Trump campaigner, who admits that every day without his former nemesis feels emptier than the last.

Other people who took part in the study admitted that, while Joe Biden is their chosen president, he doesn't bring that daily dose of 'oomph' to their lives that Trump, much as it pains them to admit it, brought in spades.

'What am I supposed to do with all the spare time I have now that I don't have Trump on Twitter to reply to and lash out at?' stated one bored Democrat, uncertain about whether or not Biden even has a Twitter.

'Life is all just so … meh. No covfefe. No easily debunked lies, no hornets nests being kicked. Should I just go back to living a normal life with my family? It's not so easy after doing the same thing for five years.'

Many more Trump addicts have admitted that his impeachment trial will suffice for now, but add that they wouldn't mind the glimmer of hope that he'll run again in 2024 and give them something new to bitch about.

MEDIA NOT SURE WHERE MONEY-GRABBING BITCH MARKLE GOT IDEA THEY HAD IT IN FOR HER

COUNTERING Meghan Markle's experience of the media's barely disguised, racially motivated hatred of her, the British media insisted it has no idea how the money-grabbing bitch, who should consider herself lucky the likes of her was even allowed within 50 miles of a palace, could have got that impression.

'Haven't the faintest clue,' said one Fleet Street editor, while throwing darts at a picture of the former actress with one hand and typing up a 'Did Meghan Eat The Wuhan Bat & Cause Covid?' article with the other.

'Meghan, bless her, has just misread some signs, which in fairness is typical of "them lot", isn't it? Smaller brains than us – actresses I'm talking about, obviously, wink wink, nudge nudge,'

confirmed another editor, batting back claims of a targeted and unrelenting hounding of the woman who married Prince Harry.

'Oh, so now it's "racist" to say the royal bloodline should remain racially pure?! Give over, what a pair of snowflakes,' confirmed one *Daily Mail* correspondent, who had a coronary and demanded the death penalty for Markle for that time she ate an avocado.

With fevered reaction to the explosive content of the Oprah interview having the effect of temporarily turning England into the largest open-air asylum in the world, it is believed that it will be several centuries before the public realise a glorified incest factory is not

inherently better than them, nor the nation's 'rightful rulers'.

Elsewhere, the media remains uninterested in both Prince Andrew's Pizza Express trips or the revelation that the Queen sent her private solicitor to lobby the government into changing a law to help her hide her private wealth from the public.

UK NEWS

OUTRAGE AS UK CLAIMS RACISM AGAINST TRAVELLERS AS THEIR OWN

THE ENTIRE POPULATION of Ireland was left reeling today following news that the UK has once again claimed an Irish trait and pastime as its own.

UK holiday firm Pontins has agreed to change its working policies after it was revealed it was operating a blacklist against Gypsy and Traveller families, enraging Irish racists here.

'Only we're allowed to be racist against the Travelling community,' shouted dozens of people along the eastern shores of the country, hoping the UK could hear their bitter words. 'How dare you claim our racism as your own, you shower of inbred, tribal-tattooed, buck-toothed, big-eared bastards?'

> **'How dare you claim our racism as your own, you shower of inbred, tribal-tattooed, buck-toothed, big-eared bastards.'**

An investigation by the UK Equality and Human Rights Commission found that the company had been using the blacklist of mainly Irish surnames as part of a policy of refusing bookings by Travellers to its holiday parks, with no indication if desirable Irish settled families were included in the ban.

'I'm torn here really. Fair enough, they have to do what they have to do to be openly racist, but I'm just wondering if they refused me that time over my surname,' pondered local settled man and non-Traveller John Anthony O'Reilly-McDonagh-Stokes, who admits to understanding the ban, but not when it affects him and his family personally.

Meanwhile, a mixed group of Irish hoteliers and publicans have launched a €10 million lawsuit against Pontins, claiming the company has plagiarised its Traveller policies, word for word.

71

US NEWS

'POPPA JOE AND COOL AUNTY KAMALA' ROUTINE GOING TO GET OLD AFTER FIRST DRONE BOMBING OF CHILDREN

THE WAVE of relief felt by many with the instalment as the 46th president of the United States of America of Joe Biden, who, alongside his vice-president, forms the 'Poppa Joe and Cool Aunty Kamala' duo, could become startlingly old if and when targeted drone strikes obliterate innocent civilians abroad, in an as-of-yet-unknown location.

As America's Grandpa restores the soul of America with the help of history-making Harris and reverses the damaging legacy left behind by Donald Trump, experts have warned that the public may be getting way ahead of themselves.

'Plenty of people are going to dislocate their spines trying to bend over backwards to find a way to justify the "collateral damage" of dead women and children whenever Yemen, Syria, Afghanistan or wherever get a taste of American drone freedom,' shared John Johnson, an expert with previous knowledge of America.

'Those backed into a corner may find themselves saying "but the Paris Accord", "re-joining the WHO", "equality" before giving way to the inevitable "well at least it's not Trump doing the bombing, it would be worse then", and "well, he's just keeping America safe",' added Johnson.

If such hypotheticals come to fruition, the sad, sombre faces who will order such atrocities will belong to Democrats, and, it is argued, will therefore be much easier to agree with and make excuses for.

'Yeah, but now the military personnel operating the imprecise drone strike that could slaughter innocents could be transgender,' explained one defender.

'Harris doesn't strike me as the type who would stand for any of that,' argued one voter, who has already forgotten that Harris is the same politician who said she believed Biden's sexual assault accusers right up until the second she was asked to become his pick for VP.

'Yeah, but …' continued the voter.

FRANCE

RIOTS KICK OFF IN FRANCE FOR NO APPARENT REASON

FRENCH PRESIDENT Emmanuel Macron has called for calm today following a sudden riot yesterday that left dozens injured and resulted in hundreds of thousands of euros worth of damage, *WWN* has learned.

Protestors took to Paris streets on Friday before erupting in violence, but no one knows exactly why, or what they are protesting.

'It just kind of kicked off. I'm sure it's over something really important,'

one man explained, throwing a Molotov cocktail at riot police.

It is understood that the French propensity for protesting and rioting has advanced to the point that the nation's residents have simply fallen into an automated state of uprising.

'I suppose it has become a bit of a pastime,' explained one expert in social behaviour. 'It's got to the stage now where we just riot for no particular reason. The police here just expect it. C'est la vie.'

Since the beginning of 2020, over 3,789 riots have taken place in France, with a large majority of the protests having no real purpose, having been carried out only for the sake of rioting.

'It's just a bit of fun now. It's great to meet up with mates and get out of the house for a bit,' another looter concluded, before smashing a storefront window with a headbutt and picking up a brand-new 50-inch TV.

THE GAMESTOP WALL STREET STUFF EXPLAINED BY THAT LAD IN WORK

SHORT SELLING. r/wallstreetbets. Hedge funds. Market manipulation. Robinhood app. Melvin Capital. Memes you don't understand. What does it all mean? No matter your lack of questions on the big GameStop stock furore that has shocked Wall Street, Ian in sales is only happy to answer them while you're waiting for the boss to jump on the video call and start this meeting about redundancies.

'It's like that bit with Margot Robbie in the bath in *The Big Short*. Can't remember anything she said, but it's like that,' confirmed Ian, the office's self-appointed explainer of internet subcultures and Wall Street trading.

'Do you reckon actors are actually in the nip when they film stuff like that? They're probably wearing a flesh-coloured bikini or something, right? Yeah, that's what I thought,' Ian added, further informing everyone who had already muted him on the company-wide Zoom.

'Funny thing about all this stuff is that I actually had the idea to, like, not have hedge funds, like, make so much money. It's basically my same idea from years ago,' added Ian,

who has previously claimed he had the idea for *The Matrix* movies, the internet itself and brunch long before they were created.

'I think to crash the stock market technically you need a stock market driving licence, but these wallstreetbets guys haven't taken the test, and Wall Street is pissed.'

'The Wall Street guys "shorted" stuff, but you should just keep things at their natural length. That's what my therapist tells me when I say I've nearly got the money for the experimental surgery down there.'

'No, that's not it,' Ian said, ploughing on through and ignoring a pretty concise and correct summary of the events by Alice in accounting.

'Obviously, I understand every aspect of this saga wholly, but for all your benefit I'll dumb it down – rich people got fucked over, and that's

like a thing that never happens, so it's pretty cool. It's hard to say what direct role I played in it all, but I did buy a second-hand PS3 from GameStop back in the day. Should I be entitled to some stock? Probably.

'I dunno, I reckon Margot Robbie was for real naked in that bath.'

US NEWS

BILL COSBY RELEASED UNDER CONSERVATORSHIP OF JAMES SPEARS

AFTER another fantastic day for women saw Bill Cosby walk free and Britney Spears fail in her bid to remove her father as conservator, yet more details are emerging from the two high-profile cases.

While some people initially presumed a monumentally stupid legal mix-up saw the judgments for the 'Free Britney' and 'Free Cosby' cases switched, it turns out that they weren't far off, as James Spears has been granted conservatorship of Bill Cosby.

The use of Spears as the conservator overseeing Cosby's life initially appeared an acceptable choice, as Spears was deemed a reliably overbearing and controlling influence who could eliminate any possibility of

Cosby being able to do what he wants, but the judge's wisdom in the case has been questioned.

'It's that controlling nature that might find the two men bonding, especially when they realise they have a particular passion for it when it comes to women,' remarked one justice activist.

While Cosby's quashed sentence had been for a maximum of 10 years, Spears' conservatorship of his daughter was only meant to last a brief time, something Cosby's legal counsel are wary of.

'When it comes to someone being forced to do something to someone against their will, I think we know what side of the line our client

wants to be on,' Cosby's lawyers confirmed, chuffed to see their client walking free.

'When we said we wanted criminal justice reform and a reduction in the number of black men in prison, we didn't mean this,' an exasperated American public remarked as it took in the news of Cosby's release.

Predictions for 2022

Elon Musk will be beaten to within an inch of his life by a gang of cryptocurrency investors who have become sick of his bullshit tweets, sending Bitcoin crashing to its lowest price yet.

BIDEN URGES ISRAEL TO ONLY USE $3.8BN IN US MILITARY AID FOR 'NICE STUFF'

US PRESIDENT Joe Biden has condemned Israeli airstrikes on Palestinian civilians that have resulted in the deaths of children in the strongest possible terms by urging Israel to use its annual US military aid of $3.8 billion for 'nice things' only.

'When we gave you that military aid with no strings attached and our implicit support for your human-rights abuses, illegal occupation and apartheid, we honestly thought you'd use that military aid for something nice like flowers for your soldiers,' explained Biden, intent on continuing America's long-treasured unconditional support of the indefensible.

With the vast majority of world leaders turning a blind eye to the Israeli government's policy of a thousand eyes for an eye, Israel is free to continue launching nine-hour missile bombardments every time a Palestinian farts, safe in the knowledge that only Hamas is to blame, always.

Pre-empting the events yet to come as tensions and violence escalates, White House press secretary Jen Psaki confirmed that 'whatever the Israeli military is about to be accused of, it didn't do it'.

Elsewhere, wailing Palestinian women lost to grief and mourning their dead children have apologised for interrupting your mindless internet

scrolling and TV watching, but confirmed there is nothing to worry about, as the media will lose interest and move on to something else almost instantly.

NEW ZEALAND

NEW ZEALAND PRIME MINISTER Jacinda Ardern has ordered the army to source nuclear bombs from somewhere and detonate them in key locations in a last-ditch attempt to wipe out Covid-19 for good, *WWN* has learned.

The new measure comes after three people were found to be infected with the highly contagious UK variant, initially forcing the PM to call a 72-hour lockdown, before then issuing an all-out nuclear strike.

'It's the only way to beat the virus,' the 40-year-old leader told citizens in an emotional televised address, showing a map where strategically placed nuclear weapons will have to be detonated. 'This will be quick

'IT'S THE ONLY WAY': JACINDA ARDERN CALLS TO NUKE NEW ZEALAND AFTER UK VARIANT FOUND

and painless for all of us, but more importantly, it will stop Covid-19 for good, which will be a massive win for us in the long run.'

Ardern's zero-Covid strategy gained media attention across the world last year for its hardline approach in combatting the global pandemic, which proved highly effective. However, many have since come forward to criticise this latest measure as a bit over the top.

'It just seems a bit extreme to vapourise everything and everyone

> **'This will be quick and painless for all of us, but more importantly, it will stop Covid-19 for good.'**

on the island over a virus, but look, if it means we don't have to hear about this bloody thing for as long as we live, then I'm all for it,' said one New Zealand man we spoke to.

Despite New Zealand being a strong supporter of the Nuclear Non-Proliferation Treaty and agreeing to never acquire nuclear weapons, Ardern insisted this was a special circumstance, pointing out it will only be this one time and promising never to do it again.

Housing Ladder Tips

Many people move into a mobile home while saving for their house. Bet you haven't even considered that. Jesus, what, do we have to do everything for you?

EXCLUSIVE

DAD RECALLS OWN CHERNOBYL AFTER 1985 VINDALOO

STILL VISIBLY SQUIRMY at the painful memory, 56-year-old dad Gerry Cody recalls the catalogue of horrors from a 1985 incident that rocked him to his very core, likening it to his own, personal Chernobyl.

Admitting to repressing memories of the bowel movement until now, Cody opened up about that fateful day in December 1985 to his now grown-up family, finally getting everything off his chest.

'Arse like a throbbing Japanese flag, it was,' the emotional dad of four

recalled, his eyes focused on his memory zone. 'I've always said it since: if it's burning you going in, it's sure as hell going to rip that arse of yours to shreds on the way out. Like passing a salted barbed-wire fence hooked up to a tractor battery, is the only way I could describe it.'

Sparked by commemorations of the 35-year anniversary of the Chernobyl disaster in the Ukraine yesterday evening, Cody shook his head in disbelief as the gruesome details re-emerged on the family's TV screen.

'At least that reactor blew,' he added, almost rubbishing the event that killed hundreds, if not thousands of people. 'My reactor had to just put up with the meltdown and grin and bare it. I swear I saw God himself that

morning as I clutched the side of the bath and toilet bowl with my hands. Give me a swift kick in the balls or having to give birth to triplets any day over another vindaloo.'

'We didn't even have wet wipes back then to put in the fridge. All I had was coarse old-fashioned toilet roll and the will to live,' the dad concluded, his eyes vacantly staring out a thousand yards past the TV screen, unaware of its content as his flashbacks slowly subsided.

GOODBYE!
NUMBER 254 – JUNE 2021

"We're down to our last 10 mill"

"I DON'T WANT TO TALK ABOUT MY FAMILY ANYMORE, BUT ..."

HERE'S WHAT WE'VE LEARNED FROM THE LAST 305 MEGHAN & HARRY INTERVIEWS

WE THOUGHT YOU TWO HAD FUCKED OFF?

LEAVING: THE DICTIONARY DEFINITION, FOR THOSE THAT NEED IT!

"Nan had mum whacked"

"I'll gut that bitch like a pig" — we put words in Kate's mouth for the craic

ENTERTAINMENT

CINEMA

ALMOST A FULL WEEK PASSES WITHOUT RELEASE OF SUPERHERO MOVIE

FEARS ARE GROWING for the future of the movie industry, after a six-day stretch without the release of an AAA tentpole blockbuster featuring either a well-established comic book superhero or indeed a slightly lower-budgeted adaptation of an obscure superhero's origins.

'This could be us fucked lads,' said David Harrinan, owner of the Waterford Omniplaza cinema.

'For years we've had a very set schedule of releases that have kept us in business; a big sequel to a superhero movie series, or a reboot of an older property with enough call-backs to the original to keep parents happy while the kids sit and eat popcorn for two hours, and then two or three smaller $150 million sequels or spin-offs to tide us over for the rest of the week. And now we're being told that there's going to be at least one week with none of that? Ah here.'

Further troubling rumblings surrounding the superhero movie bubble emerged after it was revealed that not only would there be nothing along the lines of *Iron Captain 4: Smashes of Lightning* released this week, there wasn't even the release of a superhero movie trailer.

'Normally we like to see superhero movie trailers when we sit to watch our superhero movies, or at least have

them to view on our phones while we're waiting on the latest episode of a superhero TV show to show up on our streaming services,' said Allan Dohan, a virgin.

The cruel superhero movie drought is set to be broken next week with the release of *Corkman: Legend of the Insufferable Dose*, the disturbing tale of a deranged Middleton man who thinks being from Cork is a superpower.

GAMING

PS5 NOT FILLING VOID IN LOCAL MAN'S LIFE LIKE HE'D HOPED

EAGER 38-YEAR-OLD gaming fan Charles Marrington has made certain to snag himself a PlayStation 5 console before some pesky parents looking for one for their kids could buy them all, admitting he thought the sleek new purchase would bring him some sort of momentary pause from the loneliness that is his life, maybe even some spark of joy, anything.

'I remember the joy I got when I received a PS1 for Christmas when I was 12, or when I spent a summer collecting glasses in a pub so I could buy a PS2 when I was 19,' mused Marrington, looking at the €500 console he bought with wages from his big-boy job.

'PS3 when I was living at home, PS4 when I moved out and got a place of my own. So many memories attached

to each console. I really did think I'd feel at least a bit of that *Vice City* buzz, those *FIFA* tingles. Instead, I'm just very aware of how I'm nearly 40 and I've got so little.'

In an attempt to make himself feel even a little smug, Marrington rang up his old pal Derek Henson to slag him off for buying Microsoft's rival console, the Xbox Series X.

'Turns out he hasn't turned on his old Xbox in years, and didn't bother with this new one,' sighed Marrington, unmoved by the supposedly stunning 4K gaming experience unfolding in front of him.

'He did say he had a Nintendo Switch, so I was going to laugh at him for having a kid's console, but then he told me that it actually was his kid's console. I keep forgetting all my

friends have kids now. Ah well, but do they have the house to themselves so they can curse as loudly as they want during *CoD* deathmatches? Nope! Fecking losers the lot of them!'

MAN SUES BRYAN ADAMS IN HISTORIC EAR ABUSE CASE

A DUBLIN MAN has today launched the world's first landmark ear abuse case against a singer, which could see thousands of similar lawsuits flooding the courts, *WWN* has learned.

A legal team representing 42-year-old Mark Jennings has claimed that the Bryan Adams song '(Everything I Do) I Do It for You' caused their client undue stress over a 16-week period in 1991, stating that the power

ballad left Jennings with crippling flashbacks, causing decades of anxiety issues every time the song was played in his vicinity.

'When I hear those lyrics, I'm just left paralysed in terror, especially at the "There's no love like your love" part,' a dishevelled-looking Jennings told the court, his face visibly haunted with the memory of those four long months during his delicate teenage years.

'Even when someone mentions Robin Hood, the song slithers into my head like an earworm.'

Despite several medical brain procedures to try to pinpoint and destroy the area of the brain responsible for the memory, the plaintiff continues to cringe deep down inside at the mere thought of the song, which he said ruined his childhood experience.

'Back then we only had long-wave radio Atlantic 252 to listen to for decent music, which was notorious for repeating popular tracks,' Jennings went on. 'But when Adams' song kept being played, over and over again, every day for 16 fecking weeks – it just destroyed all my love for music, and left me feeling dead inside for decades after.'

The song, which featured in the 1991 film *Robin Hood: Prince of Thieves*, is said to be responsible for thousands of ear abuse claims, with the singer now expected to be bombarded with similar cases against him.

'We just want justice,' explained another man whose ears were also abused in the early '90s by Adams. 'That monster needs to pay for what he has done to music lovers worldwide.'

CELEBRITIES

BILL AND MELINDA GATES IN BITTER BATTLE TO SEE WHO GETS THE MICROCHIPPED KIDS

ONCE BELIEVED to be the golden couple of the Illuminati-led secret worldwide cult that controls our every action, Bill Gates and his wife Melinda have announced that they are to part ways after 27 years of marriage, prompting speculation as to who will gain control of their ever-growing horde of mind-controlled children around the world.

'Bill and Melinda will both want to be the ones with their hand hovering over the 5G kill command when the day of reckoning happens,' said one online observer we spoke to, who has spent an extraordinary amount of his time on this earth following every move of the Microsoft billionaire.

'And it's not just the thousands of microchip-implanted kids that they'll want to hang on to. They'll also be contesting for year-round use of the deep-earth laser that triggers tsunamis, and their control over NASA that continues this dumbass myth that earth is some sort of globe, and not the flat disc that it clearly is.'

The Gates' divorce may hit a further snag, as there currently doesn't seem to be a court big enough to handle a case of this size. With $145 billion, a space ark that will ferry them off the planet if an asteroid shows up, and a shared Spotify account at stake, Bill and Melinda may actually have

to purchase an entirely new legal system if they want to part ways.

Meanwhile, the newly single Bill has expressed disappointment that 'none of the lads' are available for a session on the beer with him. 'All henpecked, ha-ha, I remember that!' said Gates, in his one-bedroom apartment with his sweet stereo system that he can play as loud as he likes.

𝕸𝖆𝖙𝖊𝖗𝖋𝖔𝖗𝖉 𝖂𝖍𝖎𝖘𝖕𝖊𝖗𝖘 𝕹𝖊𝖜𝖘

VOL 4,785   WATERFORD, WEDNESDAY, APRIL 1, 33 AD   1 GOLD COIN

Police Raid House Party

A NAZARETH man was arrested tonight and charged with organising an illegal house party after an informant outed the ringleader by kissing him on the cheek, *WWN* can confirm. Understood to be a cult leader, the 33-year-old man was charged with organising the event, which broke all leprosy lockdown measures, as well as with trying to start a new rogue religion, and will be brought before a special sitting of Pontius Pilate court in the morning.

'Ironically, he said that this would be one of many suppers to come,' eyewitness Judas Iscariot confirmed, who also attended the supper but left soon after to tip off the police, 'he was blabbing on about how he was the king of the Jews and started breaking bread claiming it was part of his body and all the other lads at the table were totally sucked into his bull. He also had this weird fetish where he wanted to wash all of our feet – I was out the door after he started that shite.' Under current Jerusalem leprosy laws, only two people from separate homes can meet up at one time; however, the man claimed he did nothing wrong while being arrested in an open-air garden in Gethsemane, in the Kidron Valley on the Mount of Olives. 'We arrested Jesus Harold Christ in the garden at Gethsemane at 7.12 p.m. for a number of social distancing violations, sorcery on the Sabbath, exorcising people by the power of demons and generally inciting rebellious, religiously unorthodox behaviours,' stated arresting temple guard of the Sanhedrin, Ramous Stickus. 'Christ will be remanded in custody while a file is sent to the DPP (Director Pontius Pilate).'

Meanwhile, the 11 other men found at the scene were released without charge. 'Never seen the lad before in my life,' insisted one attendee at the garden who goes by the name of Peter, as a rooster crowed in the distance, 'mad as a hatter I'd say, best crucify him.'

MUSIC

HOZIER ANNOUNCES NEW CONCEPT ALBUM ABOUT FIRST TRAFFIC LIGHTS IN LEITRIM

THE WORLD-RENOWNED, chart-topping Bray singer is to tackle his most ambitious project yet with the recording of a new concept album, *WWN* can reveal.

'It's just always intrigued me, and I could never do the subject justice with a single song, hence the eight-CD, 50-song album,' Hozier tells *WWN*, outlining his intention to record a concept album about the introduction, in 2003, of Co. Leitrim's first set of traffic lights.

'Red, amber and green, the people couldn't believe what they'd seen,' Hozier sang into a microphone during a studio session *WWN* was privileged to sit in on.

While some artists could be drawn into producing a concept album about the Celtic Tiger years, the stain of shame left on the country's soul by an oppressive church, or the Mayo curse, Hozier, a true artist, has chosen to sink his teeth into a much weightier subject.

'I've got the heavy metal track "What The Fuck Does Green Mean?" opening the album, and I think that speaks to the panic and uncertainty probably felt in Leitrim at the time. Indeed, what does green mean to any of us?' mused Hozier, who has also written a plaintive ballad, 'Right of Way to My Heart', a duet with Enya.

On 'We Hardly Knew Ye', a weeping

> **'I've got the heavy metal track "What The Fuck Does Green Mean?" opening the album.'**

Hozier sings about the subsequent removal of the traffic lights due to locals believing them to be 'witchcraft'. He considers

this sombre 18-minute epic to be the emotional heart of the album.

Lights in Leitrim is out next week, and Hozier takes his *Lights in Leitrim* tour on the road next year, starting with a 10-night sold-out run in Madison Square Gardens.

CELEBRITIES

AS RUMOURS CONTINUE to swirl about the fate of her relationship with Kanye West, reality TV royalty Kim Kardashian and her team have urged the press to respect her right to maximum publicity at this difficult time.

'It is at this difficult time that Kim asks for wall-to-wall coverage, and for her privacy to be disrespected,' read a section of a brief statement from Kardashian's representatives.

Kardashian's people stated that in due course they will have a comprehensive list of all the locations at which she will be available for photographs.

'Kim will be out in public and available to photographers for a

KIM KARDASHIAN ASKS FOR PUBLICITY AT THIS DIFFICULT TIME

range of photos, including "tired and stressed", "hitting the gym", "flaunting famous curves", "not wearing wedding ring" and "out with mystery man" in due course. We trust the media can be relied on to honour Kim's publicity.'

Her representatives said they would inform the media of the identity of her new beau once the committee had selected the successful candidate.

'There has already been a lot of interest, and we're just trying to work through applications. Ultimately we will go with what works best for Kim's brand. She's not ruling out a female partner if the publicity is right. We ask for patience, and Kim's fans need not worry; Kris has had the TV cameras rolling on all the drama for the inevitable new reality series,' explained a member of her team.

Housing Ladder Tips

It's important to let politicians easily pit you against your neighbour by allowing yourself to be convinced that 4.5 million single mothers are living in palatial mansions, rent free.

LEONARDO DICAPRIO RECEIVES GOLDEN GLOBE NOMINATION FOR BEST MEME

AMERICAN ACTOR and humanitarian Leonardo DiCaprio has welcomed his nomination for Best Meme with the ever-popular *Django Unchained* still of him holding an alcoholic drink and laughing snarkily at his own joke being the odds-on favourite to win and become one of the most popular internet memes this year.

'The Best Meme category is probably the most prestigious award any human being can get right now, and people are already placing huge bets on whether DiCaprio finally wins a Golden Globe Meme Award,' a member of the Golden Globe academy explained. 'No one wants to hear about Best Film, Actor or Director anymore. It's all about the memes, and this year has some strong contenders.'

The nomination comes alongside the versatile Bernie Sanders' inauguration meme, the Mike Pence

fly meme and a homosexual-themed *Tiger King* meme, with meme experts tipping DiCaprio to steal the award.

DiCaprio pointed out that this is probably his best holding-a-drink meme, stating that his *Great Gatsby* meme came close to stealing the 2015 Best Meme Award, but came second to the one-doesn't-simply-walk-into-Mordor meme, won by Sean Bean.

'I've spent years crafting my drink-holding techniques, and it's only now that all my work is finally paying off,' the 46-year-old DiCaprio told *WWN* earlier today. 'I think this year is my year. Winning Best Meme at the Globes would mean a lot for my career, and I hope it will be an inspiration to young actors everywhere, that becoming a meme can be achieved if you simply pull the right facial expression or make the right gesture.'

EXCLUSIVE

LOCAL MAN ALMOST FORGOT TO BRING BUCKET AND MOP FOR THAT WAP

'I never thought that there would be a song that would be dedicated solely to the subject of very, very wet vaginas.'

'I WILL TELL YOU one thing that you can take as fact. If your girlfriend destroys the back seat of your Nissan Sunny with that WAP, then you will never forget to bring a bucket and a mop with you the next time you meet her,' advised Waterford man Declan O'Canlon, leaving his house with two armpits full of Lynx, a wallet full of Durex and his mam's Vileda supermop.

O'Canlon continued on his way to collect his on-again off-again girlfriend Sinead Mara, owner of the aforementioned WAP, after her Intermediate Ladies GAA match outside Dungarvan, with dreams of a pleasant seafront drive on his mind, and perhaps even a chance to park his big Mack truck right in that little garage, if you get his drift.

'Sex is what I'm talking about. If you didn't pick that up. But of course, you have to make preparations for Sinead's explosive female ejaculate,' said O'Canlon, sending a 'b Rite there, didnt 4get bkt n mop' text.

Although they believed their 'have sex, mop up' ritual was unique to them, the young lovers were surprised to hear their exact circumstances described in the Cardi B x Megan Thee Stallion shanty 'WAP', which also speaks of the adversity faced by ladies who are moist of vagina.

'When Megan sang "get your boots and your coats for this WAP", I felt that,' smiled Mara, as she joined O'Canlon for their date.

'I never thought that there would be a song that would be dedicated solely to the subject of very, very wet vaginas. It's like they wrote it just for me.'

Classifieds

Warning

Whoever hit me a sly dig in the back of the head at Bon Jovi in the RDS in 1995, I haven't forgotten and I will find you.

Tom in the white Bon Jovi T-shirt – you'll know when you see my fist.

BREAKING NEWS

ARMED TO THE TEETH PAT KENNY READY FOR LAND WAR

SPEAKING OUTSIDE his south Dublin home today, veteran broadcaster Pat Kenny has vowed the total annihilation of his latest land enemy, developer Bartra Properties, stating he is locked and loaded and ready to roll.

'If these motherfuckers want a land war, I'll give them a land war to end all land wars,' voiced Kenny, brandishing an array of automatic and semi-automatic weapons, and with camo army paint on his burst-blood-vessel face.

Mr Kenny is fighting plans for a 104-bed nursing home beside his house, saying it is akin to stuffing an 'Ugly Sister's foot into Cinderella's delicate slipper', quickly pointing out that he

has nothing against ugly women, just ugly prick developers attempting to cross his turf.

'Do you know how much Semtex it takes to level a nursing home like that? Very little,' Kenny stated, gently stroking a terrified badger, one of dozens of native badgers living on the proposed site to be demolished. 'You don't want to see a big bad smelly nursing home being built on your home either, do you, Badgy?' the 73-year-old whispered to the now urinating creature, forcing Kenny to release him.

'Don't worry, young Badgy, Uncle Pat will sort that shower of bastards out,' he added.

Loading several 5.56-millimetre rounds into his AR-15 rifle, Kenny expects this latest war to be quick, advising Bartra Properties that he has already laid down dozens of landmines in the area that also have remote detonation capabilities.

'If I even see one digger moving onto that site it's goodnight Irene,' he concluded before letting off several rounds into the air, sparking a mass barking of local dogs.

County Knowledge

Waterford

A flawless county. Truly the jewel of Ireland.

Ireland's cheapest city to live in until a few more Dubs move down and fucking ruin the place.

Waterford is a second cousin removed of Hollywood actor Harrison Ford.

ROYALS

ALL THE SHOCKING REVELATIONS FROM MEGHAN AND HARRY'S INTERVIEW

THE EXPLOSIVE OPRAH interview revealed that the royal family were worried about the potential dark skin colour of Prince Harry and Meghan Markle's children, but that's not the only revelation contained in an interview that sent shockwaves through fans of *The Crown*:

- Harry and Meghan were the only two people unaware that Meghan was marrying into a backward, racist, vindictive, outdated institution that is slavishly defended by the tabloid press.
- Prince Andrew was actually very nice to Meghan upon meeting her, and offered to take her to Pizza Express in Woking.
- At public engagements and small family gatherings, the Queen would blame Meghan any time she broke wind.
- Upon asking for a Coke during one of her first Royal dinners, Meghan

was asked 'Is Pepsi okay?' Meghan believes this is the moment where the 'air got colder' around the palace for her.
- Passive-aggressive behaviour was constant, with Kate Middleton always spelling Meghan's name 'Megan' in the royal family WhatsApp group 'Fuckingham Palace'.
- Harry confirmed the palace's decision to no longer financially support him and his wife, leaving the couple destitute millionaires.
- Prince Philip asked Meghan at least 15 times if she was related to Nelson Mandela. On many occasions, Philip begged Meghan to smother him with a pillow. 'Let this end,' he would croak.
- Although she put it down to 'some royal thing' at the time, Meghan now believes it was quite odd

for the Queen to spend all their meetings together dismantling and cleaning an assortment of shotguns.
- Meghan recalled that the Queen would always wake her up at 2 p.m. by drawing the curtains in her room and opening the window in a passive-aggressive manner.
- MTV Base was always pin-locked on the couple's Sky Digibox.
- Although he left active military service many years ago, Harry laughs and admits that sometimes he still liked to take his attack helicopter up for a spin and blow up a few Middle Eastern people.
- Meghan's 'Sassy Lil' Princess' mug that she always drank her tea from showed up smashed on the kitchen floor one day. Although she can't prove it, she has her suspicions as to how that happened. 'Accident my ass,' she stated.
- In response to Meghan's admission that the claustrophobic, prison-like existence of being a royal made her suicidal, a palace spokesman confirmed, 'Yeah, that was sort of the idea.'

Conspiracy Corner

Joe Dolan is still alive and driving across Route 66 in a campervan with Elvis.

MUSIC

EXHAUSTED SPOTIFY TEAM WORKING THROUGH THE NIGHT TO COMPILE LOCAL MAN'S DISCOVER WEEKLY

'FOR CHRIST'S SAKE, Darrell, Aiden doesn't even listen to experimental industrial noise anymore, since the perforated eardrum incident in '08. He's going to hate that track,' scoffed Spotify team leader Cheryl Lyons, tasked with overseeing local man Aiden Grimshaw's latest Discover Weekly playlist. 'We've got to get this right, people, otherwise he might drift off again to the same five albums he's been listening to the last 15 years.'

Frantically searching for the most obscure, Aiden-type genres of music, the dedicated group of 22 researchers were left bewildered by a sudden appearance of 'Californication' by the Red Hot Chili Peppers.

'Ah fuck, he's gone back to his Time Capsule playlist. Now we have to hear those assholes next door gloat for the next week,' pointed out head monitor of Aiden's live streaming, Mark Johnson. 'If he play's Nirvana's unplugged album next we're all fucked.'

Calling for calm, and a five-minute pizza break, supervisor Lyons took the opportunity to remove herself from the now 13-hour shift, which was going nowhere.

'Okay, let's not panic here. All our jobs may be on the line, but if we panic now, we're going to end up like last month, and suggest something he actually goes to the effort of clicking "dislike",' she added, referring to former Aiden Discover Weekly researcher Tony Ryan, who was fired for suggesting Sia classic 'Chandelier', reminding Aiden of his ex, Shauna, who used to say it was 'their song'.

'I've got it – how about we send him some remixes, cover versions of songs he already likes?' interrupted new guy to the team, Bill Martin.

'Oh my God, Bill, you're a fucking genius!' Lyons rejoiced. 'We can just plant these poor suggestions we come up with today at every second song … but just for this week, guys, I know we're all tired!'

Following some rearranging of tracks, Aiden's latest Discover Weekly playlist was finally uploaded just two minutes before deadline, saving the Spotify team for yet another week.

'Great job, guys, we should probably come up with an algorithm for this someday,' Lyons concluded, before turning around to point two fingers in jest. 'Psych! Ha-ha got ye!', leaving the whole team in fits of laughter.

CELEBRITIES

'I HAVE UTTERED MY LAST MOTHERFUCKER': SAMUEL L. JACKSON CONFIRMS SWEAR-FREE LIFE

'NOW JUST SEEMS the motherfucking time for some discreet, polite communication in my roles and my life. Aw shit, ain't that a motherfucker! I've done it again,' a frustrated Jackson explained, as he reset his 'it's been X minutes since my last motherfucker' timer back to zero.

Evidently, it's early days, but Jackson is confident that the retirement of his oft-used curse word will be easily done.

'Sure, the first few days the itch is like a motherfucker, but as long as motherfuckers like yourselves stop bringing it mother-the-fuck up, I'll be fine in the long run,' an irritable Jackson added.

Clinical psychologist Brenton Harris has been helping ease Jackson into his motherfucker-free life, and

admits that Jackson's insistence that he retire the phrase means aspects of the iconic actor's life will never be the same again.

'If Samuel is to make a success of this, he will have to avoid certain trigger points, such as banging his toe off the coffee table – that's a guaranteed motherfucker right there,' explained Dr Harris.

In addition to the coffee table, Jackson will have to avoid being cut off in traffic by anyone, refrain from watching his favourite teams play sports, and never, ever watch the news again.

'And avoid annoying motherfuckers like you,' added Dr Harris, who admits that one drawback of working so closely with Jackson on this endeavour has meant he has picked up a penchant for the curse word himself.

'Motherfucking ironic or some shit,' added Dr Harris, before adding, 'don't you dare, motherfucker' in Jackson's direction as his lips quivered and spasmed before losing control.

'Motherfucker, it's hard! What do you expect, motherfucking miracles? I'm not about to start calling motherfuckers fathersuckers after all these years, am I?' Jackson barked back in defiance.

AMERICAN MOVIE STAR Vin Diesel has confirmed he has changed his name via deed poll to Vin Electric over increasing taxes targeting environmentally unfriendly surnames, *WWN* has learned.

VIN DIESEL CHANGES NAME TO VIN ELECTRIC TO AVOID CARBON TAX

Vin Diesel

Citing huge income tax bills, Mr Electric is set to reduce his tax contributions by a staggering 8 per cent, sparking a flood of similar name changes across the world.

'It's a no-brainer really,' began local man Thomas Briquette, who applied for a name change today. 'I think it's really important to do your bit for the environment, and if it involves changing your whole identity then so be it.'

Carbon tax has become a huge factor in combatting climate change over the past two decades, and has been proven to be solely responsible for the hole in the ozone layer healing.

'Even the sheer mention of carbon tax sends the climate shaking in

its boots,' insists Ireland's Green Party leader, Eamon Ryan. 'Taxing carbon is the way forward in tackling environmental issues, and we welcome Mr Electric's decision to dump his smelly old Diesel name.'

The 53-year-old actor said in a brief interview that he was now happy to keep the Electric name, but hoped he doesn't have to change it again.

'I was originally named Vin Petrol, but then the environmentalists said petrol was bad, so I changed it years ago to Diesel,' he confirmed. 'Let's hope they don't change their minds again about electric, as this could all get very confusing for my career as a big-name Hollywood actor.'

CINEMA

RANKED: WORST IRISH ACCENTS IN HOLLYWOOD MOVIES

SPARKED by the unspeakably twee and diddly-eye-ness of the newly released trailer for *Wild Mountain Thyme* and the accents therein, which are surely crimes against the Irish people, *WWN* has produced a definitive list of the most awful Irish accents ever to emanate from the screens of Hollywood movies.

The Field

The Field? Do we all live in fields then, the Irish? Honestly, who writes this offensive shit? Eh, right, so Irish people are so obsessed with land they'd be driven to murder over it? Has this talentless hack ever even been to Ireland? And the actor and his hammy accent? Don't get us started. Irishman Sean Bean just about rescues this movie.

The Wind That Shakes the Barley

Sure, we buy that lads from Cork would argue over absolutely anything,

the sour shites, but in *The Wind That Shakes the Barley* we're just not buying US screen legend Eddie Murphy's cousin, Cillian, in this one. The Cork accent grates like nails on a chalkboard – zero points for effort. AND IT'S DIRECTED BY AN ENGLISH PRICK NO LESS!

My Left Foot

Ah, it's stereotype bingo with this infamous movie. An Irish mother whose love for her children is never ending and full of sacrifice? Have they ever met an Irish mother? Poorly

County Knowledge

Laois

Nobody is quite sure when Laois snuck into the country; it just appeared one night. No nametag, nothing. Ireland meant to rehouse it, but just got used to it after a while.

Thanks to the Electric Picnic festival, Laois's Stradbally serves as the world's largest abandoned children centre in the world.

Ironically, Laois is the only county in Ireland where you don't need to keep your dog on a leash.

researched, but what do you expect from Hollywood?

After watching this offensive portrayal of an Irish mother, viewers knew exactly where they wanted to shove their left foot, up the backside of whatever Hollywood honcho thought we'd be fooled by this. Not a convincing Irish-sounding syllable out of actress Brenda Fricker, who we presume was flown to and from LA to do her scenes each day.

Brooklyn

The stereotype here is inexcusable. What? This gangly, handsome Gleeson Yank is supposed to pass as 'Irish'? Give us a break. Brooklyn may be many things, but devoid of offensive stabs at Irish accents it is not. He didn't even have the decency to dye his hair red, for feck's sake. And 'Domhnall'? Really, what is that, a Greek name? Barely a freckle or piece of dirt on him as well? Do they take us for fools! The 'Enniscorthy scenes' were filmed in Palm Springs too. Charlatans, the lot of them.

The Snapper

The Snapper failed to gain a cult following in Ireland, and it's easy to see why. Not only is the accent offensive to Dublin people (it's too thick by half), but was there really a need to use extensive prosthetic make-up to increase the size of Hollywood star and *Star Trek* actor Colm Meaney's head so it's a 'more Irish head'? Bordering on xenophobic here lads. The worst of the lot.

MUSIC

NEW INITIATIVE AIMS TO HELP WOMEN AVOID DATING MUSICIANS

A NEW GOVERNMENT-BACKED INITIATIVE has been launched in a bid to help women avoid the ignominy of dating men who label themselves 'musicians', *WWN* can reveal.

'If I can help one person avoid dating a man who wears a beanie and insists on writing love songs about the woman he's dating, I'll know I've done some good,' shared Dierdre Lacey, a spokesperson for There Are Other Options, a group set up to help women date non-musicians.

'It may seem like a rite of passage, but trust us, they're all just massive self-important arseholes,' confirmed Helen Hickey, member of another

advocacy group, Why Not Date Someone Sound Instead.

Urging women to date other cohorts of men that they will later regret having dated in years to come instead, the push to avoid musicians has now become a nationwide campaign.

'From shite buskers to a lad who says he played the trombone on that one song by Hozier, no matter the quality or calibre, just fucking don't,' added Hickey, who said she had to replace her bathroom mirror after a musician ex left her and ran away with his own reflection.

Information evenings are being organised in

every county, and will see women persuaded to see the advantages of not falling for the romance of dating a 'tortured musician' who is 'in touch with his emotions'. Female musicians will not form part of the awareness campaign, as they've more cop on than to make 'rock star' their only personality trait.

'Look, we're not saying there's better options out there, but there certainly isn't worse, and no one else is going to ask you to take moody black-and-white photos of them alone in a field for a never-to-be-released EP called *Raining In My Heart* or some shite,' warned Hickey.

PODCASTS ▬▬▬▬▬▬▬▬▬▬▬▬▬▬▬▬▬▬▬▬▬▬▬▬

NEW SCHEME THAT PAYS PEOPLE NOT TO START A PODCAST UNVEILED

Historical Facts

The Celts arrived in Ireland around 2000 BC after hearing about the generous welfare system and liberal attitudes towards gender and race.

A NEW ARTIST FUND will encourage a variety of artists, including comedians, actors, radio DJs, TV hosts, musicians and sportspeople, to agree not to start a podcast in exchange for money.

County Knowledge

Down

Down is the only county in Ireland that has its own convenient handle, allowing it to be picked up whenever necessary.

In order to play Co. Down in easy mode, simply input Up, Down, Up, Down, Up, Down on your PlayStation controller.

Atop Co. Down's Mourne Mountains, an otherwise beautiful view is ruined by the sight of Co. Louth to the south.

'We just can't take it anymore,' confirmed the public, which has pumped money into the fund in a bid to bring an end to the constant deluge of podcasts clogging up the internet, and music and streaming apps.

In this 'name your price' model, any washed-up talent or new kid on the block can submit a funding application, which takes the form of a solemn oath not to attempt to start a podcast in exchange for whatever sum of money they demand.

'Whatever format you were thinking of, be it "interviewing a celebrity", "interviewing your mates", "funny concept" or "mental health", just please, don't,' added those operating the fund, who have estimated that in Ireland you are now never more than six feet from someone who has a podcast.

'Look, you can say you're launching it for all kinds of altruistic reasons and breezily claim "hey, just think of it as a couple of people having a chat, giving you a welcome break from this crazy world", but we see right through you. Please just take the money and put away the selfies of you next to a big elaborate microphone set up in your spare room,' added a spokesperson for the fund.

The fund has already made great strides by entering into a high-profile deal with Marty Morrissey, who agreed to abandon plans for his Marty's Sharty Party podcast, which would have seen him interview whoever passes for a celebrity in Ireland about the times they sharted themselves.

MUSIC

LOCAL MAN LEAVES WORK EARLY AFTER DEVASTATING DAFT PUNK NEWS

DOZENS OF WORK colleagues gave their deepest condolences to local man Gary Foley this afternoon following the devastating news that his favourite dance duo Daft Punk are to split up after 28 years, *WWN* has learned.

Openly weeping at his desk shortly after watching an eight-minute video titled 'Epilogue' depicting the newly announced split, Foley wailed in agony at the thought of never again having the chance to see the French music producers live.

'Christ, he's really having a moment there,' voiced Trisha in sales, who was tasked with purchasing a mass card for the bereaved 43-year-old adult for everyone to sign.

Still sobbing like a child, trying to find his breath through the pain, the brave but busted HR manager gathered himself, before delivering an emotional address to staff at Macey Ryan and Co. Printers.

'I'd like to thank you all for your condolences and well wishes,' Foley began, standing on his desk and putting his fist up to hide his now quivering mouth, 'I just … sorry, this

is very hard for me … obviously I'll be taking some time off to get over this, but I just want to say that I have no feelings of resentment towards Thomas Bangalter and Guy-Manuel de Homem-Christo, as I'm sure they have their reasons … sorry, I'm choking up here again, ahem … but I will get over this news and I want to organise a little Zoom tribute tonight if anyone's interested. Thank you all.'

Before taking the rest of the day off, a now standing-proud Foley hushed the office, turned his Dell monitor's external audio speakers on and began playing a 1997 BBC essential mix on full in some form of memorial.

'Goodnight, sweet princes … goodnight,' he was heard saying under his breath, wiping a single tear from his cheek while several young interns asked quietly, 'Who the fuck is Daft Punk?'

FORMER *GOOD MORNING BRITAIN* host and professional gammon Piers Morgan has today defended his claim that Meghan Markle was lying about being suicidal in a recent Oprah interview, stating he misses the good old days when traditional media could ruin someone's life for good without facing any consequences.

'There was a time when you could simply oversee the hacking of royal oppressors' voicemails and totally destroy their character using newspaper headlines we sold to morons,' stated Morgan, who was editor of the *Daily Mirror* during a time journalists engaged in hacking.

'Now it's all "mind people's mental health this" and "basic human decency that". The world has gone mad with this humanity bollocks – it's time to go back to basics,' added Morgan, the demon spawn of arrogance and an angry tomato.

Leaving the world with a horrible sick feeling that he probably planned this dramatic exit all along, speculators believe Morgan

PIERS MORGAN LONGS FOR DAYS WHEN YOU COULD HACK SOMEONE'S PHONE AND DESTROY THEM

is expected to take up some kind of position in a new Fox-like news station called GB News.

'If you believe that hungry prick simply left an ITV salary like that, then you obviously have no clue who Piers Morgan actually is,' a close friend of Morgan pointed out. 'He's a horrible human being who thrives on trolling and belittling people who make him feel uncomfortable, so he will make a great host on whatever right-wing TV job he can get.'

Elsewhere, middle-aged dads everywhere confirmed that Piers Morgan voluntarily quitting a show in a childlike temper tantrum after receiving mild criticism is cancel culture gone mad.

TELEVISION

'I ALWAYS FOUND ELLEN DEGENERES TO BE VERY KIND AND CARING': SATAN DEFENDS PAL

SPEAKING from the fiery depths of hell, the Dark Lord, Satan, has broken his silence regarding the ongoing bullying allegations relating to chat show legend Ellen DeGeneres, stating that the 62-year-old was by far one of his kindest and most caring friends.

'You guys have heard of my buddy Hitler, right? Well, Ellen is way nicer than him,' Satan explained. 'She's even kinder than Saddam and that ISIS leader they keep killing and sending back down here. I can't understand why people would say she's an awful person. Ellen is sound as a pound.'

Satan is one of literally tens of high-profile celebrities to publicly defend the American comedian, along with Jay Leno, Ashton Kutcher, Katy Perry, Kevin Hart and North Korean dictator Kim Jong-un.

'All pals of mine too. It's great to see all the gang defend El, and it's an absolute honour to have been the lucky devil who bought all their souls,' Satan added.

Meanwhile, employees at DeGeneres's talk show have been told that steps are being taken to improve their work environment following reports of 'toxicity'.

'All staff will now have to wear earplugs and blinkers, and will be given a free frontal lobotomy to help protect them from further torture and torment,' a statement from producers read.

As replacement rumours swirl, it is not yet clear who would be favourite to take over from DeGeneres, but rumours suggest James Corden.

'Holy fuck, talk about jumping from the frying pan into the fire,' Satan later commented. 'You people sure love punishing yourselves.'

> **'You guys have heard of my buddy Hitler, right? Well, Ellen is way nicer than him.'**

Predictions for 2022

The Royal Windsors have it out on a special return of *The Jeremy Kyle Show*, where DNA results prove Harry is not Charles's son, sparking a specially arranged mud fight between Kate and Meghan.

FRIENDS

WE HAND-PICKED THE WORST POSSIBLE SCREENSHOT OF MATTHEW PERRY FROM THE FRIENDS REUNION SO WE CAN PUBLICLY SPECULATE ON HIS HEALTH FOR CLICKS

AFTER hours of debate over what exact frame to use of Matthew Perry from the *Friends* reunion, *WWN* has carefully selected the worst possible screenshot we could find in the hopes that it will spark some form of speculation about the actor's current state of well-being with our readers.

Not happy to leave Perry's historical substance abuse issues in the past where they belong, we believe his slightly warped facial expression here may be just subtle enough for our sterling publication to get away with, without any accusations of shaming or unfair gaslighting towards his appearance.

Known for our heroic stance when it comes to our campaign against body shaming female celebrities, our editors and sub-editors agree that this screengrab is potential click 'gold' when it comes to inciting unfounded rumours, leaving it to our followers to hypothesise on whether he may be still secretly necking tablets on the sly, driving our social media engagement wild.

We contemplated headlines that transferred the blame onto you, our reader, such as, 'Viewers Point Out Matthew Perry Speech Was Slurred', thus distancing our flawless publication from any wrongdoing or malice. Instead we decided to go with the worst possible image of him we could find, with a reverse psychology headline like 'Doesn't Matthew Perry Look Great In The *Friends* Reunion?', a move we also like to do when body shaming female celebrities when paps take unflattering images of them.

Despite our cunning ability to twist and skew news and media in our favour for unwarranted kudos, we would also like to promote recommended articles that totally contradict everything we were just trying to hide, because hey, we really don't give a fuck what harm we do as long as we generate revenue from you dumb fucks.

The Year in Numbers

44mn – the number of lives saved by the innovative Covid-19-busting, Irish-invented technology known as the €9 substantial meal.

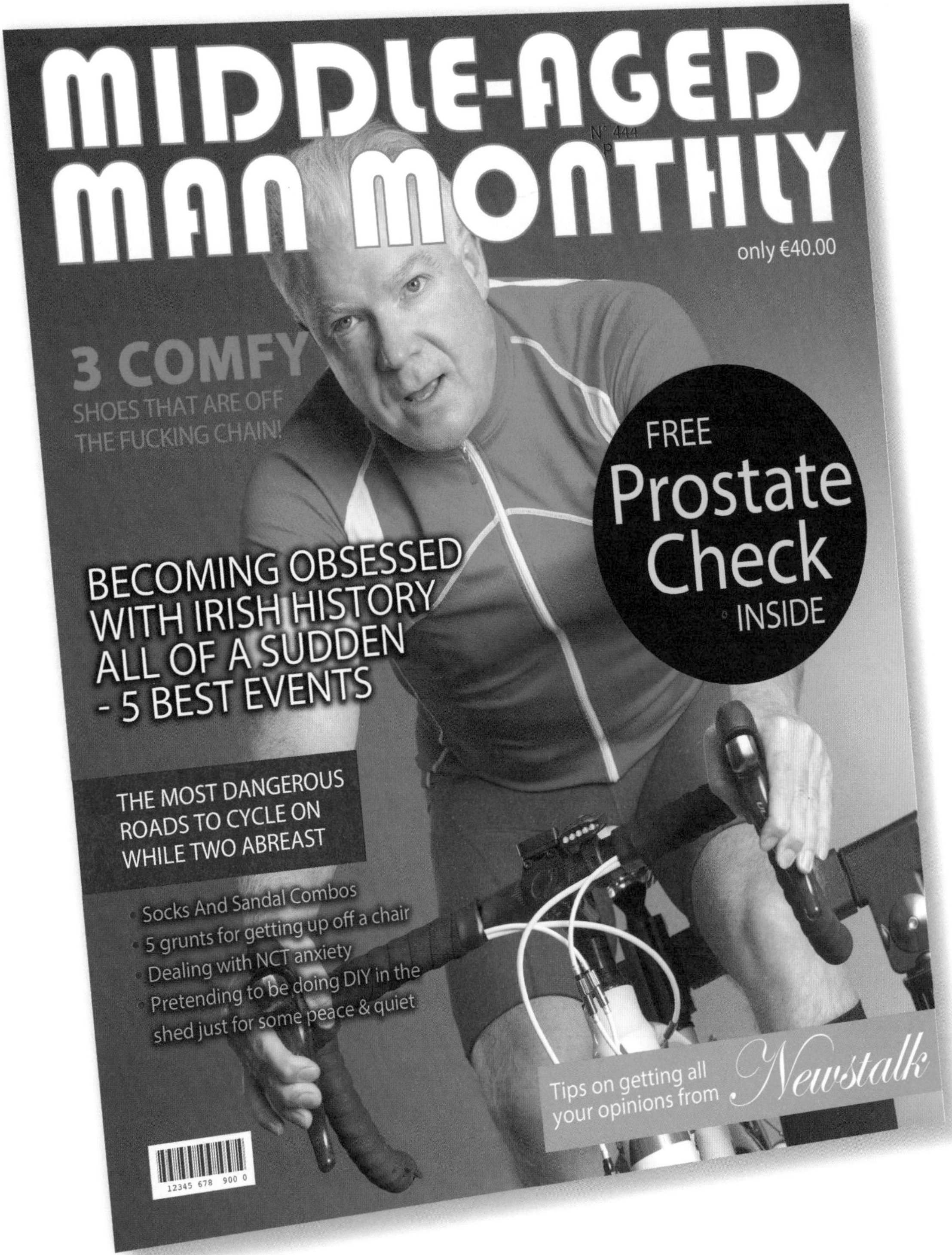
MIDDLE-AGED MAN MONTHLY
N° 444
only €40.00
3 COMFY
SHOES THAT ARE OFF THE FUCKING CHAIN!
FREE Prostate Check INSIDE
BECOMING OBSESSED WITH IRISH HISTORY ALL OF A SUDDEN - 5 BEST EVENTS
THE MOST DANGEROUS ROADS TO CYCLE ON WHILE TWO ABREAST
Socks And Sandal Combos
5 grunts for getting up off a chair
Dealing with NCT anxiety
Pretending to be doing DIY in the shed just for some peace & quiet
Tips on getting all your opinions from Newstalk
12345 678 900 0

LIFESTYLE

WWN GUIDE

DOING JUST ENOUGH HOUSEWORK TO ENSURE YOU CAN'T BE GIVEN OUT TO: A GUIDE

CHIPPING IN around the house is a sure-fire way to keep the lady in your life off your back, but you don't want to make it a regular thing. Follow us room by room to find out how you can earn a day of doing nothing by tidying the absolute bare minimum.

Bedroom
Cleaning an entire bedroom is hassle you don't need, so sidestep any accusations of laziness by simply making the bed when you get up in the morning. A quick flick of the wrist will do the job, and it'll show you're not utterly useless on a day-to-day basis. It'll also get you out of more heavy-duty bedroom cleaning, such as hoovering, dusting, weird stain removal, etc.

Laundry
Do your part laundry-wise by loading the washing machine every two days, and then putting it on a spin afterwards. This will absolve you from emptying the machine, putting clothes on the line, taking them in, ironing, putting clothes away … It's not your fault you got to the easy job first, is it?

Cooking
Be a star in the kitchen once a week by declaring that tonight is a take-away night, on you. Although this may seem expensive, it will allow you to kick back and get a hot dinner handed to you on the other six nights of the week.

Gardening
Unlike the day-to-day grind of housework, gardening isn't really all that pressing. It is, however, easy to do, soaks up a whole day and can be done while listening to podcasts, drinking beer and otherwise having a fairly enjoyable time. And again, it will give you enough collateral to sidestep jobs you don't really want to do, such as hoovering. You can't be expected to hoover twice a week when you spent a Bank Holiday Monday in the garden a month ago, can you?

Toilets
Remove the worst skid marks from the bowl with the toilet brush as and when they occur; do not let them harden like Weetabix. That should keep everyone off your case.

GRANDDAD WON'T BE HAPPY UNTIL HE BREAKS HIP

'Hey, you, Shawn Michaels, would you get down off that fuckin' ladder,' pleaded an exasperated Ruth O'Rahallan, shouting up at her 87-year-old father, who seems bound and determined to break one or both of his hips today.

Seamus O'Rahallan, not known for acting his age or being a man who gives a bollocks all that often, will frequently act in the manner of a much younger man, and dismiss the notion that a person nearing 90 shouldn't be up a wobbly ladder clipping trees in a crosswind.

'He's the only one of his few remaining pals who hasn't 'had the hip done', and I think he feels like less of a man because of it,' said Ruth, watching her dad play football with his grandkids and going in for actual sliding tackles here and there.

'We sat him down the other day and said, hey dad, see the way you just sit down and get up, no problems? Wouldn't it be nice to still be able to do that next year because neither of your hips were broken? Also, I know you don't appear to care whether or not you have a stroke, but I'd rather not, for the love of God. Don't have my blood pressure up this high all the time.'

Mr O'Rahallan was unavailable for comment, as he was up a tree trying to poke a football out of a higher branch with the handle of a broom, causing a 150 per cent increase in swearing from inside the house.

JUST YOU AND YOUR AUNT ON FACEBOOK THESE DAYS, FINDS REPORT

DATA RELEASED TODAY has shown that Facebook's once-dominant market share has dwindled to just you and an aunt on your Mam's side, along with a local taxi firm that has been closed since last year.

'This is super not-great,' said Facebook CEO Mark Zuckerberg, looking at a red-line graph that dropped off the bottom of the page and continued down the wall.

'Where did the couple of billion people we had every day go? Now it's just women in their advancing years sharing uplifting memes and lads in sunglasses sharing conspiracy theories. I mean, we can still monetise it, but it's just not as cool as it was, guys. I thought we were the cool guys, no?'

A team of analysts attempted to convince Zuckerberg that years of next-to-no moderation of dangerous right-wing politics on the platform appears to have chased off the majority of users, but the billionaire had other ideas about how to win his audience back.

'Let's overhaul the look of the site again, change it up on desktop so nothing was where it used to be,' said Zuckerberg, alive with what he believes is creative energy.

'So users will still see just the same five people over and over again, but now they'll be in a different part of the screen. Remember, if they can't find what they're looking for, they'll spend longer on the page looking for it. Either way, we can keep selling ad space for stuff based on what we hear people mention within earshot of their phones,' he added, before turning his attention to fucking up Instagram as well.

FAMILIES

FRIEND'S OLDER BROTHER WONDERING IF YOU WANT TO SEE A DEAD BODY

YOUR FRIEND'S older brother, who could be anywhere between 18 and 40, is wondering if you and your fellow 13-year-old friends would like to see a dead body.

'Ah, the guards will find it eventually. It's horrible, some auld lad or something, he's up beyond the way in a bush. I'll take yiz if you like,' said the older brother, whose full-time job seems to be sitting around the house

and bothering his brother's friends anytime they're around.

Not a phenomenon restricted to just you, it seems that the nation has had experience of an idle older lad who is

available to give his younger brother and friends their first smoke, drink, joint, dirty nudie magazine and other odd things.

'Yiz can all poke him with a stick like, the body, it's not like he can do anything about it now, the poor fucker. Was mad though, he was just there in a heap, found him when I was doing my daily outdoor shit,' confirmed the older friend, in a sentence he thought sounded perfectly normal.

Always on hand to absolutely brutalise you in a game of football on the green or to encourage you and your friends to punch each other in the face to see who is the toughest, the older brother, normally called Dave or Mick, shows no signs of just leaving you to it and getting his own friends, which he definitely should have.

'Ah it's only a dead body like, don't be a chicken,' Dave/Mick confirmed as he insisted the corpse was really a must-see.

'GET OVER IT' SAYS MAN STILL HOLDING MULTITUDE OF DECADES-OLD GRUDGES

TAKEN ABACK by how fixated his wife has become following a minor disagreement in work with her boss, local man Eddie Boylan has implored her to simply 'get over it', despite himself being an avid cultivator of countless decades-long grudges over the most trivial matters.

'Love, so what if he's made you work two late shifts, being petty gets you nowhere,' Boylan told his wife, Elaine, despite the fact that he still curses the name of a former friend called Sean Roland, who once scribbled on a drawing he was doing in senior infants some 35 years ago.

'Take a leaf out of my book Elaine, and just let that stuff go,' added

Boylan, a man who drives 5 km out of his way to a Centra, all because Fionuala Carey, who runs the corner shop a 100-metre walk from his house, once short-changed him by 20 cent in 2015.

Boylan, who at last count has put a hex on and cursed out approximately 413 people, continued to encourage his wife to let some of his zen-like calm and good vibes rub off on her.

'Hang on, is this the boss that was in front of us at the cinema that time, with the popcorn?' Boylan inquired, to which his wife said yes.

'Fuck sake, he was chewing away like a pig at a trough? What is it with people and their disgusting and

annoying munching? Was he raised by his parents at all, or did they outsource that to wild animals? Big ignorant head on him too,' raged Boylan.

'Right, Elaine, there's nothing for it but to quit. I'll type up your notice letter. Don't think I won't put "has the table manners of a caveman eating shit through a straw" on it as well.'

LATEST RESEARCH

THERE'S ALWAYS FUCKING SOMETHING, FINDS STUDY

NEW EVIDENCE discovered by an Irish-funded scientific study has concluded that 'there's always fucking something', proving at long last that when things seem to be going your way, some absolute crap pops up to ruin your day.

The study, which focused on 1,000 people over a 10-week period who claimed they were having a good spell of luck, discovered 98 per cent of the subjects soon experienced some form of dilemma, tragedy or unwanted person in their life.

'We discovered there was always something popping up to wreck the buzz,' explained lead researcher Prof Tadhg Hennessey. 'Most of the problems were to do with some prick in their lives saying or doing something that sparked a family feud, rumour or financial problem, and usually came in waves of three and lasted for several weeks at a time.'

Some of the most common problems ranged from the insignificant self-tangling of electrical wires, such

> **'Most of the problems were to do with some prick in their lives saying or doing something that sparked a family feud, rumour or financial problem'**

as earphone cables, to the most serious of problems, like a family belonging to a drug cartel moving in next door.

'Many subjects reported that when they were in a rush to go places or late for something a farmer in a slow tractor would suddenly appear in front of them on a road,' said Hennessey, whose own study was suspended for three weeks after his wife ran off with the postman. 'Other people reported that when they had some savings in their bank accounts, the timing chain

in their car would break, costing them a fortune, or they would suddenly find a pain in their tooth that ended in a root canal.'

The study concluded that, if you are at a stage where you think your life is going okay, snap the hell out of it, as it's only a precursor for certain disaster.

'My advice is to make sure your life is just mediocre and a bit shite, always making sure to create some problem for yourself so the cosmic joker doesn't come along to mess up your life,' the professor advised, shortly before falling down the stairs and breaking both his legs.

Housing Ladder Tips

If you don't get a home of your own, relax, all is not lost. The government's new one-metre-square co-living pods will make sure you have a place to stay while working yourself to death.

TALENTED AND BEAUTIFUL YOUNG STUDENT REMAINS ALIVE AND WELL, MUCH TO DISMAY OF TABLOIDS

TABLOID EDITORS have expressed their profound sadness at the discovery of a blonde-haired, blue-eyed young student from a wealthy background who remains alive and well in a stroke of horrible misfortune.

'These are the days you dread in the business,' said one editor, frankly livid that the D4 resident student didn't even go missing for the briefest of times.

'I can think of nothing worse for us than a beautiful girl "with her whole life ahead of her" failing to fall foul of some great tragedy. It's unfair, we could have got 15 front pages out of her at least,' said another doleful editor.

'Sure that's great for her family and friends, but has anyone considered us hacks, who now can't write really exploitative tragedy porn about a young woman taken from "us" too soon?' shared one reporter, who sadly has no idea when they will next be able to doorstep a grieving family and hound them for quotes.

Sighing heavily and thinking of what could have been, tabloid editors lent on each other for support, their bodies shattered by the lack of tragedy.

'We've been robbed of a life of headlines through which we could have driven "I bet the father did it" speculation, then we could have

ruined the life of someone wrongly accused by us and us alone, and of course if ever there was a slow news day, we could have published a bullshit "hope of breakthrough in X's case". But we'll never get any of that,' said one editor before breaking down in tears and insisting no more questions, please.

60 DEAD FROM HYPOTHERMIA IN IRISH OUTDOOR DINING TEST EVENT

TRAGEDY HAS STRUCK during routine preparations by local councils looking into the feasibility of conducting a summer of outdoor dining in Ireland, as 60 participants in a test event died of hypothermia amid cloudless skies and blazing Irish sunshine.

'It was all going well. They were getting the full force of sweltering single-digit temperatures, but minutes after ordering brunch they crystallised into giant ice blocks and shattered everywhere,' explained one council official.

The worrying development comes as councils announced the pedestrianisation of numerous streets and further outdoor dining grants for cafés and restaurants ahead of the reopening of outdoor dining at the start of June.

'I don't think this is as big a setback as everyone is making out. Diners in June will just have to wear shorts, shades, sun cream, winter jackets, hot-water bottles and waterproof skin,' countered another official, striking a more optimistic tone.

Several other measures are being considered amid Ireland's bid to embrace a continental European style of outdoor eating.

'We're ugly as sin as a people too, and we don't want to put people off their food, so Irish diners will be replaced by specially flown-in sallow-skinned Spaniards and Italians,' added the official.

Similar test events on the west coast resulted in 14 people drowning due to torrential rain, while several more were taken skyward by gale force winds, never to be seen again.

SHROOMS

LOCAL MAN WALKING AROUND TOWN REALLY REGRETS TAKING THOSE SHROOMS

'FOR CHRIST'S SAKE, Mark, you're in the middle of Main Street now tripping absolute balls, what are you going to do?' Waterford man Mark Denny asked himself, realising that he may have taken way too much magic mushrooms to be simply walking around town, now peaking outside Penneys.

Forgetting once again the sheer overwhelming power of the simple Irish mushroom he picked and dried last October, Denny was hit with a whole galaxy of anxiety as he pulled his baseball cap down over his sunglasses like blinkers, opting to also throw on his Covid-19 face mask in a bid to hide himself from reality before taking it off again due to fogging up his shades.

'Ah fuck, fuck, fuck … I hope I don't meet anyone I know,' he muttered, his face now pressed against a shop window in terror, spiralling further into his trip. 'How do you always forget how strong these things are, Mark, you clown, they're not a walking around the town on a sunny day type thing. Shit! Is that Claire from work across the road? Fuck, hide!'

Now hiding beside a bin, the great-grandson of eight began praying to the heavens, despite being a proud atheist just two short hours ago.

'Please, whatever you are, just get me home out of this madness to my safe, people-free home so I can curl up into a ball and die,' Denny begged, as a passing stranger dropped a euro in front of him on the ground thinking he was looking for change.

'Ah for fuck … now I look like a homeless person or something … Great idea, Mark, take some shrooms and head into the city centre for a nice happy walk in the sun – I've had better nightmares than this, you gobshite.'

Manoeuvring through the least populated streets and laneways, Denny sprinted

> **'Please, whatever you are, just get me home out of this madness to my safe, people-free home so I can curl up into a ball and die.'**

the last 500 metres home, before slamming the door in celebration and rummaging for sugar, vitamin C, whatever the fuck will help get past his peak.

'Right, I'm definitely getting a tattoo on my forehead to remind me to never ever do that kind of shit again,' he falsely concluded.

BREAKING NEWS

MAN ASSUMES HE MUST HAVE SUPERHUMAN REFLEXES AFTER CATCHING THING AS IT FELL

The Year in Numbers

978 – the number of times Tánaiste Leo Varadkar was called 'Taoiseach' in the Dáil since handing over office.

WOULD-BE WATERFORD NINJA Steven Barten has taken the afternoon off to marvel at the cat-like reflexes he exhibited earlier today, which prevented a mug from shattering on the floor after he accidentally elbowed it off the kitchen table.

Barten, 37, has no previous experience in moving quickly or exhibiting good hand-eye coordination,

making his rescue of an almost-full mug of hot liquid all the more amazing – something he is very keen to tell everyone about.

'It was like it was all moving in slow-motion. My hand just shot out and bam! Caught that sucker in mid-air!' he told his wife, Elaine, for the fourth time since the incident occurred.

'You should have seen it. I wish I'd been recording it. We must install cameras in the house in case it happens again. It's almost certainly faster than anyone has ever moved in their whole life,' he told his dad, ringing him for the first time in over a month to tell him the story.

'Did you ever catch something as it was falling? I did earlier, you wouldn't believe it. One in a million shot, just pure superhero reflexes altogether,' he told a call centre worker, who was beginning to regret ringing to see if the Barten family were happy with the monthly price of their gas and electricity.

Meanwhile, Mr Barten has reacted badly to a complete swing-and-miss when attempting to catch the TV remote that his wife threw to him, claiming that he 'wasn't ready for it' and that it 'doesn't count'.

County Knowledge

Mayo

There's not a day goes by that the people of Mayo don't regret building their county on a Native American graveyard.

They mocked Mayo man Henry Loftus when he said he wanted to put a bar in his castle, but look at it now!

Each Mayo newborn is now tattooed with 'Mayo for Sam' on their foreheads in a sure sign the county hasn't gone mad.

DRINKING

DELICATE LITTLE PETAL NEEDS A FEW BEERS AFTER MINOR STRESS

A POOR SENSITIVE little petal has tonight vowed that enough is enough in regard to his midweek sobriety after a minor altercation with a family member forced his hand into buying six of his favourite beers, all in the hopes of quelling a minor stressful experience, *WWN* has learned.

With this, his 12th excuse since promising himself 'not to touch alcohol on a school night' three weeks ago, Michael Hennebry pointed to unforeseen circumstances as the latest cause for turning to his favourite go-to stress reliever, ignoring the fact that he's just a total savage when he's gasping for a drink.

'Fucking brother acting the bollocks again,' Hennebry said, vaguely alluding to his sibling, while his own mouth salivated at the thought

of tasting the cold frosty suds about to touch his parched lips. 'Taaaghh, Jesus, that's better now. I'm like a new man. Why does it taste so good?'

Having already polished off his first beer, Hennebry compartmentalised his guilt by dishing out the blame,

with the grandson-of-four once more cursing his brother Eamon for making him do this.

'Balls on it anyway, I should have bought eight beers – I'm flying through them,' he barked at himself for underestimating his thirst and the level of minor stress he was put through earlier today. 'I can't believe my brother would ask me to give him a lift to the bus station out of the blue like that. God, he's such an inconsiderate dick.

'Yeah, I get that his car broke down and he was really stuck, but he knows I'm really busy on Mondays, and he totally wasted 24 minutes of my time,' Hennebry stated, adding, 'At least I'm all okay now. Sure, I can always knock it on the head now until Friday night … yeah, that's a promise, liver.'

DELUSIONAL MAN BUYS MEDIUM-SIZED T-SHIRT

DESPITE REPEATED PURCHASES online resulting in dozens of ill-fitting clothes now lying in the bottom clothes drawer, Darren Mackey has once again chosen the 'M' option for his €49 T-shirt choice, reassuring himself that this time the top will fit perfectly.

'If it's too small it can go in the drawer with the rest of the new tops I bought until I lose some of this weight,' he told himself, for the 11th year in a row, unaware that his wife Julie has already given away most of the previous new T-shirts to charity.

Denying the fact that he may be now more a large size than a medium, the 33-year-old decided to also add a 34-inch waist pair of skinny jeans to the online cart, knowing full well that he was more a 38 now, and sometimes 40.

'The great thing about jeans is that they can stretch,' the now delusional son-of-two convinced himself, compartmentalising a previous encounter with a new pair of 34" Tommy Hilfiger jeans in a store last year when he met with a

loud laugh from Julie upon exiting the fitting room.

'Sure, God love him, he still thinks he's in his mid-twenties, the big eejit,' his wife explains. 'He's been wearing the same three T-shirts now for the last five years, because he continually buys clothes that are too small for him.'

Experts believe that ageing men reach a stage of denial in their 30s and 40s when it comes to how Dadbod-afflicted they really are, before moving on and succumbing to tucking their T-shirts into their jeans in a misguided attempt to appear slimmer.

RELATIONSHIPS

'I DID WARN HIM': MAN STABBED FOR CALLING INTO FRIEND AFTER 9 P.M.

WATERFORD DISTRICT COURT has heard that the stabbing of a 34-year-old man in the city centre last year was 'unpreventable' after the victim called to the defendant's home at 9.45 p.m., without so much as a text or call.

Solicitor Eamon Mahoney stated that long-time friend of Dermot Hantigan, James Martin, 'cold called' his client by simply pressing the doorbell, giving Hantigan an awful fright and a sense of anxiety, forcing him to retrieve a large kitchen knife before answering the door.

'I opened the door and there was James smiling like a big fucking idiot at the door saying, "Well, what you up to, lad?",' Hantigan told the court. 'I was like, "What are you doing calling after nine o'clock", and he had the cheek to say he was just popping over

for a chat, so I had no other option but to stab him several times in the stomach – I did warn him before about that calling late craic.'

Taking over seven months to recover from his wounds, which left him unable to urinate without

a bag, Martin told the court he was sorry he called so late, and that if he could turn back time, he would have at least rung his friend first before calling over.

However, Judge William Holden quickly pointed out that calling before texting was also a crime in itself, explaining that he should have texted his friend first to say that he was about to call him on the phone to ask if he could physically call to his house, and urging Martin to brush up on his social etiquette.

The stabbed man apologised to his friend and the court for calling unannounced, before the judge sentenced him to two years in prison, with the last year suspended under the clause that he would attend a 'cop-on course' while inside.

A NEW REPORT has revealed a long-running rivalry among mobile phone customers in Ireland, with many people under the impression that their choice of signal carrier somehow makes them a higher class of people, *WWN* can reveal.

087 PHONE USERS THINK THEY'RE BETTER THAN EVERYONE ELSE, STUDY FINDS

'Although service providers in Ireland are now all mostly as shit as each other, there was a time when certain carriers were considered more "premium" by customers, and their mobile prefixes are now held as a badge of honour,' explained Dr Visjan O'Neill, head of Snobology in Trinity College Dublin.

'So you have people who still have the same 087 number they've always had, who now look down on the late-to-the-market 089 prefix, which due to its cheaper tariffs is considered a lesser service and indeed, suitable for only a lesser class of person. Even though pretty much all networks cost the same and all have loads of dead spots around the country, 087-ers think they're top dog.'

Speaking to an 087 user who did not wish to be named, *WWN* drilled down on just what it is about his prefix that makes him better than everyone else.

'Back in the day, 087 was the best coverage, but the 085 numbers were much cheaper,' we were told.

'So even though your mates had phones, you could never contact them, cos they had no bars. So yeah, even to this day when someone says they're on 085, I think, "You dumb, short-sighted bastard". Even if they only bought the phone last week.'

Meanwhile, 086 users remain in the doghouse due to that prefix beginning life as Esat Digifone, and the ill taste that whole thing leaves in the mouth.

`PETS`

'LINDA, STOP, I CAN'T UNDERSTAND YOU, I'M A FUCKING DOG'

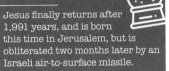
'LINDA! Once again, I'll stop you there,' barked pet dog Smudge, interrupting owner Linda Moran, who was minutes into delivering a detailed breakdown of her day to her dog, who remains unable to understand human speech.

'Sure, intonations and tones I can pick up on to a degree, but I'm a fucking dog at the end of the day, Linda, so all these stories are wasted on me, you eejit.'

Despite Smudge's protestations via the medium of barks, Linda ploughed on with her lengthy run-down of the day, complete with boring observations, endless rants and idle gossip, all delivered in a cheery sing-song tone in an effort to gain her dog's attention.

'And then what did Mammy do? I told Joan in accounts I didn't fucking get that email, did I? Cus Mammy was on two days annual leave, wasn't she? Yes, she was, Smudge, Joan's a complete bint, isn't she? Yes, she is! That's right, and she's having an affair with Tom in the warehouse, yes,' explained Moran, an idiot who somehow believes Smudge has the cognitive ability to understand her speech.

'You're a laughing stock, Linda. Imagine if another human peered in the window now and saw you trying to engage me in meaningful conversation. A joke, an absolute joke,' barked Smudge, who was now making his way to the sitting room window, seeking help from the outside world.

'Honestly, Linda, you're just embarrassing yourself now at this stage. I'm no human expert, but you're in your pyjamas from 6.30 p.m. every evening, glued to the couch. What, if anything of interest, would you be telling me anyway?' added Smudge, before losing his mind the second Linda said 'walkies' out loud.

> **'I'm no human expert, but you're in your pyjamas from 6.30 p.m. every evening, glued to the couch. What, if anything of interest, would you be telling me anyway?'**

BREAKING NEWS

MAMMY NEEDS SOME WINE

Conspiracy Corner

Deranged motorists insist there's a mysterious flashing light on cars that you can flick when turning off a road.

RESIDENTS of the O'Riordan household in Mallow, Co. Cork, have been advised that the mother of the house, Tina O'Riordan, needs some wine, *WWN* has learned.

The statement, issued at around 7 p.m. this evening, was short and concise, yet managed to convey her message without any retort from her immediate family.

'Mammy needs some wine,' reported the exhausted 36-year-old, who spent the entirety of Saturday changing beds, washing and drying clothes, before making dinner for her children to half eat.

Following the announcement, the remaining O'Riordan family members retired to their bedrooms, knowing now not to disturb the young mother, but yet somehow still unafraid to ask for certain items of nourishment.

'Mam! Water!' bellowed seven-year-old Katlin O'Riordan, while playing *Roblox*, before receiving the reply, 'Go get it yourself, Katlin, there's plenty in the tap.'

The weekly ritual was marked by a familiar howl of laughter, as O'Riordan laughed with her girlfriends online, before then checking on her three children.

'Mammy usually starts apologising for shouting at us during the day for not cleaning our rooms,' 10-year-old

The Year in Numbers

3,789 – the number of days it takes for a government scandal to reach tribunal stage.

Jonathan O'Riordan said, explaining pre- and post-wine mammy. 'But then in the evening she's all nice and silly and gives us big hugs and nice things and even lets us stay up late!'

Meanwhile, in the sitting room, Mammy confirmed to friends via text that she is not looking forward to tomorrow morning's existential dread, while insisting that it will be totally worth it.

FAMILIES

DESPITE HER DAUGHTER being up since 7 a.m. to get the children to school before starting a full day's work at 9, local grandmother Doreen Hegarty relentlessly called her eldest in the hopes for a quick 60-minute chat, *WWN* has learned.

Frantically calling her daughter for the seventh consecutive time in a row, the now put-out Hegarty opened with her usual dig in the hopes of offloading on the work-from-home customer care worker.

'Oh, finally, Charlotte! Did I wake you, pet?' the 63-year-old began, settling into her favourite chair for

'DID I WAKE YOU?' MOTHER ON PHONE ASKS AT 3 P.M.

chatting in before exaggerating, 'I've been trying to ring you all morning.'

'For the love of Christ, Mam, I'm working and taking calls here. If I don't answer the first time, just take it that I'm on a call, okay?', said the daughter of two, furious at the suggestion that she'd been lying in bed all day.

'Well, no need to bite my head off. I was only calling to see if you were okay,' Hegarty said, relishing in the negativity. 'You've your father's temper. Is everything okay at home? I hope he's treating you right over there, you can always tell your …'

'Mam! I'm working from home. I've told you this already – I can't drop everything when you ring,' Hegarty's

daughter shouted, now angry at herself for getting angry.

'Okay, pet. Your poor old mother here just wanted a chat is all. I'll leave you be,' a now rather satisfied-with-herself Hegarty ended the call, wondering which of her daughter's four siblings to call next and ruin their day.

'Hmmm, Gerry said he had that big important construction meeting at half three – I'll call him,' she thought to herself, looking at her watch before laughing maniacally at her own deep-set deviousness sparked by years of torment from raising children. 'Mwahahaha, winding these little bastards up is way too easy … Oh, finally, Gerry! Did I wake you, pet?'

NOT CONTENT with having just one guardian angel by her side, local alternative medicine dose Heather Partridge has claimed that a multitude of celestial beings are looking after her after successfully avoiding a minor road traffic accident, *WWN* has learned.

Barely missing an oncoming car while texting a friend, Partridge swore to family members and anyone who would listen to her that she was somehow 'blessed', escaping certain death and proving once again how special she must be.

'My angels are looking after me. Otherwise I wouldn't have heard the car beeping and flashing its lights at me for being on the wrong side of the road,' the 53-year-old said, recalling the incident and desperately trying to convince herself that she has a greater purpose in life. 'It was divine intervention, and only for they were looking after me I'd be stone dead.'

Citing a small collection of healing crystals hanging from her rear-view

EGOTISTICAL ASSHOLE BELIEVES SHE HAS MULTIPLE ANGELS LOOKING AFTER HER

mirror as another possible reason for her miraculous escape, Partridge speculated that the €4.99 rose quartz may have also played a part in keeping her on earth.

'The crystals may have channelled all my angels at once, forcing them to drop whatever they were doing and save me. It's probably not my time yet, and I have a lot of work still to do here,' concluded the unemployed actor, artist, singer, dancer and faith healer. 'God and his angels obviously have big plans for me.'

UPDATE: Heather Partridge was tragically killed after being struck by a truck while failing to look up from her phone crossing the road, presumably while her angels were on lunch.

PARENTING

IDIOT KID ON CLIMBING FRAME WAVING BACK LIKE HE JUST CONQUERED MOUNT EVEREST OR SOMETHING

AN IDIOTIC CHILD on a local playground climbing frame still insists on waving back at his parents every few minutes, like he has just conquered Mount Everest or something, *WWN* has learned.

'He just keeps looking over at us to see if we're watching him climb the thing,' mum Tina Roche explains, half-heartedly waving back at her son Fiachra. 'Like, he's not even at the top of it, he's only halfway up and still expects some kind of praise for that?'

Desperate for even more attention, the seven-year-old began shouting at his parents, who were just six feet away, to continually pay attention to him.

'Why is he even shouting – we're right here,' dad Thomas said, slightly

embarrassed at his son's poor effort and needy attitude in general, before suggesting to his wife to take turns staring at him. 'I can't even look over at him, Tina. Give him a wave or something there, shut him up.'

Finally making it to the top of the playground climbing frame after several agonising minutes, Fiachra Roche let out one last cry for attention, forcing both parents to react positively to his lame achievement.

'Well done on climbing the same frame you've been climbing for the past three years, Fiachra. Amazing feat, kid, you'll go far,' both parents laughed to themselves, now pretend-smiling and saying what a great boy he was.

𝔚aterford 𝔚hispers 𝔑ews

Issue No. 2,563,254   WATERFORD, WEDNESDAY, SEPTEMBER 15, 1954   24p

Marilyn Monroe 'Mortified' After Breaking Wind During Photo Shoot

AMERICAN actress Marilyn Monroe was today left reeling following a photoshoot which depicted the young star breaking wind, blowing her cocktail dress wildly in the air.

Ms Monroe, who admitted to eating several bowls of chili at a New York restaurant before downing four pints of beer, apologised to colleagues and fans for the faux pas, stating that the burst of flatulence just crept out during the filming of *The Seven Year Itch* on Lexington Avenue.

'I was standing around all day and had no option but to just let her rip,' the 28-year-old said, recalling the incident, 'I suppose one good thing was there was no follow through as I necked the coffee into me that morning too. I was absolutely

dying from the night before, so a huge lesson learned on my part: never trust a fart.' Such was the build-up, Ms Monroe's dress fluttered in her own gases as staff and fellow actors re-coiled in horror and retreated from the set on 53rd Street.

'It was definitely brewing up there for a while, I'd say, like it made a proper 'furp' sound too, which was odd to hear coming from such a sweet little ass,' one male extra from the movie confirmed.

'It smelled like rotten cabbage mixed with that putrid eggy fart smell. The director Billy Wilder literally had to call off the whole scene until she passed everything, her dress was like a candle blowing in the window,' he added.

Continued on Page 2

PETS

DOG FED UP FINDING OWNER'S HAIR ALL OVER COUCH AND BED

'IF I'VE TOLD HER once, I've told her a thousand times,' howled frustrated four-year-old dog Max, as one of his owners plonked herself down on the couch in a towel, insisting she dry her hair and covering the couch in the process.

Not meaning to sound ungrateful, Max made sure to state that he loved humans, but while charming in nature, they certainly had their drawbacks when it comes to keeping the house tidy.

> **'I tell ya, I don't even set foot in the bathrooms and toilets. I can't even look at them, the absolute state.'**

'Have you tried to get human hair off a couch? Pain in the hind legs, fucking animals the lot of them,' explained Max, fed up of walking into a room only to find his owners draped across the couch.

'Ah here, Dave! What have I said about eating on the couch,' Max barked as one of his owners dropped Bolognese sauce on a couch cushion.

'Ah fuck sake, I've to go here, sorry, he's after barrelling into the kitchen there, off to cover it in his ginger pubes too no doubt,' Max said, chasing down his owner and barking angrily at him as he placed his plate in the dishwasher.

County Knowledge

Kerry

Outside Kenmare exists a massive glass jar, in which all of the nation's small change is deposited at the end of the day.

Stunning and picturesque, Kerry's famous Inch beach is the second smallest on the island, next to Sligo's Millimetre strand.

Horse rides around the Ring of Kerry can vary in price from €50 to €500, all depending of course on how gullible you are, where you're from and if you've any relatives there at'all at'all.

After calming down briefly, Max spoke about how it's a constant battle to keep the house in anything resembling decent order.

'I tell ya, I don't even set foot in the bathrooms and toilets. I can't even look at them, the absolute state. Sure, I let them think they don't let me in there, but I think if I ever saw the sink or shower drain, I'd whimper like they'd stepped on my paw,' concluded Max, giving Siobhan the death stare as she left her hairbrush on the couch.

PARENTING

FATHER STILL WAITING FOR THAT 'WOW' MOMENT FOLLOWING BIRTH OF SON 16 YEARS AGO

'IT WAS MEANT to be the best moment of my life,' said Damien Reynolds as he recalled the birth of his son, now looking at his 16-year-old, stropping around his home like a wet hanky. 'Just look at him, moping around the place, eyes rolling every time he's asked to do something. Is this it? Is this what all the fuss was about?'

Reynolds is just one of millions of fathers across the world suffering from 'Disappointment Syndrome', which leaves parents feeling empty inside when looking at their unremarkable kids.

'To be fair, he did win that spelling contest in Junior Infants that time, but it's all gone downhill from there,' added the full-time dad, staring at his son scrolling through his phone, his greasy fringe covering one whole side of his face like a mop. 'The fucking state of it, like, the sooner he gets a job and the fuck out of here the better for all of us.'

Disappointment Syndrome experts believe that thoughts and feelings inspired by Hollywood movies and TV programmes have given sufferers preconditioned expectations before having kids, with peers in fatherhood also creating a false 'wow' moment post birth.

'The doctor handed me my son after he was born and I was like, "meh",' said another father suffering from Disappointment Syndrome, who also has a teenager. 'Some sick bastard previously told me that it's the best feeling of your life and everything will change. Well, he was right there, everything did change, mostly my finances and social life.'

Despite the chronic condition, the majority of sufferers still state that they wouldn't change anything if they had the chance to go back.

'They're handy excuses for getting out of things all the same, like when you're asked out by people you don't like – "Oh no, I have to mind the little fella" – which is basically the only reason for not going back in time and telling myself to pull out,' concluded Reynolds.

DUBLIN CITY RESIDENTS TO BE FITTED WITH COLOSTOMY BAGS

Conspiracy Corner

The filming of *Star Wars* on Skellig Michael was just a cover-up; the crew were actually building a Kerry-based death star known locally as a Healy Death Rae, which will be unleashed on 'them up in Dublin' any day now.

GOOD NEWS as an emergency meeting of Dublin City Council's (DCC) Anti-People Committee has thrown up a number of sensible measures that could see the capital become even more unwelcoming to residents and visitors.

In response to scenes of packed crowds drinking amid a lack of people-friendly outdoor spaces, the city manager and his crack team of anti-socialising advisers have been busy brainstorming.

'You're lucky to get what we give you. I voted for sealing up your orifices with cement and covering every inch of the city in a white-water rafting facility,' confirmed one team member, at the unveiling of new plans to fit Dubliners with colostomy bags and bins.

'You think we'd install toilets? Ya joking me? We can't trust you animals to use a toilet. Just piss and shit in bags and empty them when you get home unless you live in a tent, in which case we've probably already

> **'You think we'd install toilets? Ya joking me? We can't trust you animals to use a toilet.'**

ripped that apart with a JCB,' added the DCC official.

Asked if the removal of benches and bins in recent years, along with the failure to install toilets and public spaces, has created a city landscape hostile to people who don't view themselves as just ATMs for the city's businesses, DCC rejected the assertion outright.

'Sadly, people still come into the city. If anything, we're not doing enough to show contempt for the presence of people who don't spend money in shops, cafés and pubs,' said a DCC spokesperson, installing anti-people spikes on South William Street.

County Knowledge

Cork

Cork's annual 'Cork Festival' lasts all year round and is best avoided.

Cork City residents are evolving to develop gills to cope with routine flooding and huge, out-of-proportion mouths from gloating about Cork.

Native Cork skin is 50 per cent thinner than the rest of the country's, making them susceptible to all forms of jokes and mockery based around Cork. Over 10,000 Cork people die every year from Cork-based slaggings.

PARENTING

IRISH COUPLE'S GENDER REVEAL PARTY CANCELLED FOLLOWING CALLS TO 'COP ON'

A MORTIFYING DISASTER of epic, reputation-ruining proportions was avoided by a Waterford couple after friends and family intervened to successfully reason with them, *WWN* can reveal.

Sarah and Michael Corkley (both 26) had circulated the idea that they intended to have a 'gender reveal party' following the happy news that Sarah was pregnant with the couple's first child. However, the idea was labelled at best 'a load of American bollocks' and at worst 'would you two eejits ever cop on to yourselves before you ruin the Corkley name for

> **'I flat out pretended I've never heard of that awful "reveal" shite when they told me.'**

generations to come' by those closest to them.

'I flat out pretended I've never heard of that awful "reveal" shite when they told me. I told them I'd march straight into the hospital and steal the scan and tell them the baby's gender if they didn't wise up,' Sarah's mother Jackie explained to *WWN*.

Jackie conceded that, while she was all for keeping the baby's sex a surprise, the proposed plan of revealing it in a lavish ceremony by splashing blue or pink paint all over the Cliffs of Moher was 'a step or four thousand too far'.

In an intervention, all those who know the couple made it clear that they would be disowned for life if they did a gender reveal party, 'like they were some fucking influencer or YouTuber', and that they would be, according to Michael's father Richard, 'influenced into a tube and shot from a canon into a nearby wall'.

'Jesus, would Michael not do what his father and me did, and just think I was putting on a bit of weight until giving birth on the toilet nine months later like a normal person,' added Michael's mother Grainne.

'The fuckin' notions on this generation, I tell ya,' added the happy grandmother-to-be.

County Knowledge

Longford

Longford was formed by joining together two short fords end-to-end.

Longford is the only Irish county without a famous celebrity.

Longford has lovely trees.

RETURN TO NORMALITY AS MAN GETS HAIRCUT HE DOESN'T LIKE BUT DOESN'T WANT TO SAY ANYTHING ABOUT

LOCAL MAN Eric Downing felt his first signs of post-lockdown normality yesterday after receiving a haircut from his reopened barbers that was somehow worse than it had looked when he walked in with five months of shaggy growth on his head.

'Ah yeah it's grand, thanks,' said Downing as his barber showed him the back of his head with a mirror, despite the job not being grand, and despite Downing not feeling thankful.

'Deadly job, cheers,' he added, before paying way more than the cut was worth and leaving with a sense that he had somehow been cheated by the entire hairdressing industry.

Elsewhere, the return of barbers and hairdressers afforded many the

opportunity to flex their tongue-biting muscles, as their pals emerged with new hairstyles that looked absolutely shocking.

'It's hard to believe it's been over a year since I had to lie to someone and

say, "Your hair is gorgeous, it really suits you",' said one Waterford woman we spoke to.

'Amazing when you think of it. During lockdown, if you saw someone with a shaved head or a pure tangle of bushes on their head, you could just be honest and laugh and get along together, you know? You knew they were just doing their best in the circumstances. Nobody thought they were looking great or anything. But now, it's back to people with hairstyles that they paid actual money for, and we're back to lying to their faces to pacify them.'

WWN would like to take this opportunity to tell you all that you look great, it really suits you.

A LOCAL LAD driving around in an '08 blacked-out BMW 5 series thinks he's some kind of drug dealer, *WWN* has learned.

The man, in his early to mid-20s, has been seen driving aimlessly around his local town acting suspiciously, despite having no real connections to the underworld drug scene, or any real friends at all.

Occasionally revving his 1.6-litre engine, the lad is believed to be

LAD IN 5 SERIES PRETENDING HE'S A DRUG DEALER OR SOMETHING

harmless enough, but secretly wishes he had a bit more of a reputation to go along with the exterior look of the car.

'God love him, he's probably after taking years to save the few bob to buy

the car,' said one onlooker. 'Look at him there, all mysterious and hiding his face with his shoulder as he drives past with one hand on the wheel. Bless his little heart.'

Parking up beside a similar 13-year-old car in a local supermarket car park, the lad continued to stare at passing cars and people like he was up to no good, hoping Gardaí would one day search him and give him the kudos he desperately needs.

'Nah, drug dealers don't drive cars like that anymore. They're not that dumb,' Sergeant Martin Reynolds explains. 'He'd only love it now if we stopped him, so he could tell all his little friends, but we know from the reg that he has all his discs up to date, like a good boy.

'The poor lad's insurance probably costs more than the car.'

PARENTING

MORTO! THIS KID'S PARENTS ARE STILL TOGETHER!

REPORTS CIRCULATING a Waterford community this afternoon have confirmed that some little loser still has both his biological parents living in the same house together like some kind of fully functional family, *WWN* has learned.

Davey Lynch, 12, was branded a little freak by peers after slipping up and stating that his parents were still together, like mother and father.

'He just said it like it was nothing,' an earwitness to the news, teacher Alan Murphy, told *WWN*. 'We were all mortified for him when he realised

what he'd said, and now the poor little fella is getting slated in class for being such a little freak.'

Born in 2008, Lynch was coached by his parents into not revealing their current marital status, telling him that other little boys and girls in his class wouldn't understand.

'It's his own fault really,' mum Irene admitted, now looking for a new school to send Davey to. 'It can't be easy for him now being the odd one out, so we have no other option but to send him to another school.'

'That's what he gets for gloating,' added the boy's father. 'If he messes up again and spills the beans, we'll have no other option but to do the right thing and split up – it's just not fair on him or the rest of the kids.'

MINIMUM ALCOHOL PRICING HAILED A SUCCESS AS YOUNG PEOPLE TURN TO €5 YOKES

'WHY DIDN'T WE THINK of this sooner,' a frustrated-with-itself government said of the impending introduction of legislation implementing minimum alcohol unit pricing in retail settings.

'We did it, we solved Ireland's drink problem! We cracked how to wean young people off alcohol, while as a

small bonus imposed a stealth tax on everyone,' confirmed a spokesperson, mistakenly thinking young people weren't going to just turn in greater numbers to €5 yokes than they were already doing.

'Statistics suggest young people are drinking less and less, and indulging in recreational drug use more and

more, so naturally making alcohol even more expensive won't in any way incentivise spending on yokes, bravo,' confirmed one young person.

'I'd rather chew my jaw than chew a hole in my wallet,' shared another young person, who clearly doesn't understand the magic of being charged €10 into a nightclub, €2 for the cloakroom and €7 for a pint.

Explaining the rationale behind implementing an increase that will hit low-wage earners the hardest, the government spokesperson stated, 'There's only one type of acceptable alcohol abuse, and that's when a ruddy good bottle of pricey plonk is consumed in a nice restaurant or at a home with a respectable postcode.'

In a bid to further encourage people back into pubs and away from off licences, the government announced a pilot programme that, once pubs reopen, will see anyone attempting to enter an off licence sucked up into a giant tube that transports and spits them out into their local.

SOCIALISING

NEW RETRAINING SCHEME UNVEILED TO HELP IRELAND LEARN HOW TO PUB AGAIN

THE BIGGEST RETRAINING scheme ever undertaken by the Education and Training Boards in cooperation with SOLAS is set to take place in the coming months, as Ireland receives a refresher course in essential pub skills.

Aware that the public's pub-based skills have all but evaporated during extensive lockdowns, the government is set to meet the demand for retraining once-seasoned drinkers in the event that pubs reopen in the near to medium future.

The areas in which the public will be retrained include:

- How to secure a table for your mates even though they're all late and people keep asking 'Can I take this chair?' This segment will be taught by Israeli Special Forces.
- Nodding techniques to attract the bar man. Depending on the level of attractiveness of participants, those on the uglier side will be taught a high level of patience.
- Pissing all over the toilet seat. With people urinating at home for so long, many men will have completely forgotten how to hose down a pub toilet seat like they were trying to put out Californian wildfires.
- Practising phrases like 'When you're ready', 'I've one in the pot', 'Do you have a Samsung Galaxy charger by any chance?' and 'Get your fucking hands off me, I'm grand' will be essential in repubbing patrons.
- When permitted to have groups in rooms again, the course will carry out group assignments that teach people the correct sarcastic tone of wild cheering when a glass is dropped on the floor.
- Making best friends with someone in the women's toilets is on the list too. Women will, after repeat lessons, manage to form an incredibly powerful bond in a matter of 12 seconds over something as small as a dress or eye shadow.
- Older trainees will be provided with a number of boring and offensive stories to once again tell uninterested people as they prop up a bar.
- In group lab sessions, the public's nostrils will achieve full Guinness fart immunity via an air-administered vaccine that contains a small dose of the worst farts Irish pubs have ever been exposed to, building up resistance levels in the process.
- Bouncers will be given absolutely no training to get back to being ornery pricks to absolutely everyone.

MEET THE WOMEN GETTING RULER TATTOOS ON THEIR ARMS TO BRING AN END TO BULLSHITTING MEN

SEVERAL ENTERPRISING single women have begun to revolutionise the face of dating with the help of a simple, solitary tattoo.

We meet the women who, long since fed up with the tall tales men tell regarding penis length, got a to-scale ruler inked onto their forearms.

'If lads had an inch for every time they claimed it's "like a baby's arm holding an apple", their dicks could serve as a ladder to Mars. Once I got the tattoo everything changed,' single-and-fucking-done-with-mingling Anna Pollock told *WWN*.

'When we're in the bedroom and I reveal the tattoo, you'd want to see some of them. They turn white as a sheet, some faint, some jump out the window, but the bullshit ends there and then,' added Pollock.

'Give men an inch, and they'll claim eight inches for the rest of their lives. When Anna showed me her tattoo, I ran off to get one myself, and it's made my life so much easier,' Rebecca Hodges explained.

'And when you catch them out, they give it the "Oh, you were using the imperial scale? I meant 12 millimetres, I can see why you're disappointed now",' continued Hodges.

'It just saves a lot of bullshitting. Now, admittedly, they do a lot more crying and whimpering, all "Your ruler must be wrong",' added Ciara Morgan, the ink not yet dry on her arm.

Bravado-led exaggeration among men in regard to their manhood is now down 20 per cent, with worrying reports of some men purposefully getting similar tattoos with centimetres incorrectly marked as inches.

STOP MOVING THE FUCKING EGGS, SUPERMARKETS TOLD

A COLLECTIVE OF SHOPPERS from around the world have today published an open letter to supermarkets in a bid to stop them constantly moving eggs and other vital produce around their stores, forcing shoppers to lose countless hours of their lives.

The letter, entitled 'Stop Moving the Fucking Eggs', called out big brands for the practice, stating that they know what they're up to, and told them to stop it immediately, or else.

'We're not saying we're going to do anything harmful to them, but just stop with the moving shit, okay?' stated an irate spokesperson for the

group, who estimated he has spent at least a week of his life searching for eggs over the sporadic moving. 'We know what ye're at, trying to get us to buy other things, and it's not on. Just leave the bloody eggs where they are and there won't be any trouble, okay?'

Supermarkets have since denied the allegations, claiming they only move the popular products around for logistic reasons, and not in some kind of conspiracy to put other products into the customer's line of sight.

'Ah, we wouldn't be that sneaky,' insisted one store manager we spoke to, glancing at the hidden camera in the store's advertising screen to watch people's movements. 'We just like mixing up the aisles, nothing else. You'd hardly think we'd be that crafty,' he finished, before asking for €2.99 for a box of own-brand corn flakes this reporter had no recollection of picking up.

SOCIALISING

PEDESTRIANS PLAY GAME OF CHICKEN TO CLAIM THEIR SIDE OF FOOTPATH

WITH MORE AND MORE people walking in a bid to break up the monotonous day, the Footpath Safety Authority (FSA) has warned that instances of head-on collisions between pedestrians are spiralling out of control, with 160 people already injured so far this year.

'Footpath etiquette has gone out the window, and people are becoming more adventurous when claiming their side of the walkway by playing games of mental chicken and not backing down,' a spokesperson for the FSA told this reporter.

Taking to the street, I donned cheap Lycra pants, an epilepsy-inducing reflective jacket and trainers before heading out for a nice stroll along a local ring road, making sure to keep right on the footpath, adhering to the rules of the road.

However, it wasn't long before I was met with the first challenge of the evening: an oncoming couple walking abreast, on my side, with their dog.

'I'm not backing down,' I found myself thinking, realising the couple had now cleverly switched their mutt to the inside path – my side.

Pretending not to see them, I stood firm, tensing both shoulders, my heart now beating from the adrenaline of it all, preparing for impact.

'Excuse me, sorry!' the man stopped dead, now rightly forced into single file behind his partner, before continuing on like a little bitch.

'Yeah, keep walking, pal,' I said under my breath when the pair of chancers were far enough away not to hear me.

'That's where it starts,' the FSA spokesman later told me. 'Once you make one person move out of the way, it becomes addictive and you keep doing it until you meet someone, just like you, who won't back down.'

Predictions for 2022

Cork becomes fully submerged after a series of floods and a rise in sea level, leaving the rest of the nation slightly relieved to be honest.

Accepting the FSA's challenge, I decided to take to the left side of the path on my walk, in a bid to prove I'm not some lame-ass chicken, scared of crossing the footpath.

It wasn't long before my next challenger came to the fore: an elderly lady pulling a little tartan trolley. With the words of our FSA friends still ringing in my ear, I wasn't going to let this innocent, frail woman get in my way.

Briefly looking up as she approached, the cunning pensioner caught my eye with a sympathetic stare, one only a sweet old grandmother could give, turning my legs to jelly, and my heart to mush.

Images of ambulance crews working on her limp torso played out in my mind, while spiralling newspaper headlines like 'Woman Killed In Head-On Walking Collision' flashed before my eyes, before I was suddenly hit full whack in the face with a tartan trolley, finding myself

Housing Ladder Tips

When you think about it, 30 years isn't that long to be paying half your wages into a house that your children will sell off when you're dead.

being beaten down like a rabid dog.

'Stick to your own side of the path, you little prick. Have some respect,' I recalled the words of my unknown assailant to Gardaí, followed by my detailed description. 'She was a big woman now, probably a body builder. On steroids, I'd say.'

Concluding my investigation, this reporter learned his lesson – playing footpath chicken is a dangerous game, and tartan trollies pack quite the punch. Expect the unexpected, stick to your side and you'll be okay.

This was a safety message from the FSA.

SPIRITUALITY

SIGNS THAT YOU'RE AN OLD SOUL

DO YOU FEEL like you're far more psychologically advanced and emotionally stable than your peers, but can never put your finger on just why you are so great and superior to others? You could be what cosmic researchers now call an 'Old Soul'!

The world contains only a handful of these incredibly special people, who are so clued in that they continually click into informative articles on the internet detailing how fantastic a human being they are. Quite simply, an Old Soul is a person who feels a lot older than they physically are, and are usually prone to empathy, intuition, gullibility. They just love reading about themselves being portrayed in a higher form than other, inferior-minded people. You are so special, so you are. Amazing.

Being an Old Soul, you constantly find yourself trying to blow out the lightbulbs in your home instead of hitting the light switch. You insist on calling your car after a 19th-century horse, and tell it to 'giddy up' when driving uphill.

You sometimes recoil in terror when someone turns the TV on, and you scream for someone to help the people trapped inside. You have already broken numerous phones off the wall because the noise startled you, and you just wanted to make it stop.

At night you constantly cry out for your loved ones, who are all dead for centuries now, and you insist that your current partner wear a condom made of goat skin during sex.

As an Old Soul you have by now reported several people for witchcraft for riding past your dwelling on electric scooters. You still insist on defecating in the garden shed outside, forcing the local council to intervene with a court order, threatening to remove you from the area.

You insist on rowing your currach to work along the city canal and will only speak to colleagues in fourth-century Gaelic, which no one understands. You've been cautioned numerous times by local authorities for killing and eating the swans in Stephen's Green, which you call Albert Green, so named after the death of Prince Albert in 1814.

You carry a portable sundial with you, which never works in this blasted country.

You continue to debate the fact that Newgrange wasn't a patch on 'Oldgrange', much to everyone's bewilderment.

You're never afraid to tell people what you think of them, as your ageing soul is so exhausted from returning back to earth to deal with these complete morons every single time.

In fact, it's like some kind of god-awful punishment, forcing you to keep reliving the same life pattern of asshole partners calling out your personal hygiene over and over again until you somehow get it right, but you never do and that's why your soul is so old and tired of everyone's bullshit. All you want to do now is remain dead forever, and you would be happy to never see another prick soul ever again.

SOCIAL MEDIA

MAN WHO NEVER READS PAST HEADLINE ON ARTICLES OFFERS HIS OPINION

ONE LOCAL MAN whose totality of current affairs knowledge is garnered solely from a quick scan of a handful of headlines insists on unloading his opinions on everyone, *WWN* can reveal.

Suffering from overexposure to dopamine hits from a variety of social media networks that are structured in such a way as to provide quick, surface-level hits of amusement or outrage has left Anthony Campbell's brain resembling a shrunken prune; however, this has not stopped him from challenging absolutely everyone on the issues of the day.

'I haven't read a full paragraph of any actual news since back in college, when I used to devour a *Ulysses*-sized selection of newspapers every day, but I'm pretty sure everyone needs my poorly researched opinion on anything and everything,' explained Campbell, already lecturing a friend on Instagram about a variety of subjects.

'I saw he's been posting a few things about transgender this or that, housing, doping in sport and Israel, so I let him know in no uncertain terms that, according to the headline I half read there from a news app push-notification today, he's talking out of his arse,' said Campbell, talking out of his arse.

Recent research suggests Campbell, along with a small band of like-minded news skimmers, are responsible for 98 per cent of the total comment output on the internet under news articles.

'Sure, it's important to be right, but it's more important to be loud and confidently incorrect,' concluded Campbell, before letting rip at someone in the comment section of *The Journal*, who also had no clue about the geopolitical conflict they were talking about.

UPDATE: Campbell has written 'You're dead right, seen plenty of these "only reads the headline eejits" online myself' as a comment under this article, which he failed to read.

STUPID FUCKING PLATE IN SINK A BASTARD OF A THING TO SCRUB CLEAN

LOUDLY SWEARING while declaring an inanimate object her mortal enemy, mother-of-three Teresa Lanigan has had enough of this prick of a plate in her sink, which, if Lanigan's loud cursing is anything to go by, is a 'complete bastard of a thing'.

Abandoning all cleaning utensils in favour of manically scratching at a stubborn bit of food debris clinging onto the plate for dear life with her nails, Lanigan was desperately close to throwing the plate in the bin and starting a new life in South America, such was her frustration at the situation.

'Bastarding little shit of a thing. Fucking clean, will you?' snarled Lanigan at the plate, which had the remnants of yesterday's lasagne on it.

Stopping short of getting the power washer out of the shed and blasting the plate into oblivion, Lanigan continued the futile pursuit by scrubbing faster and faster with increasing fury.

'That fancy scrubber down in SuperValu was a fiver, but oh no, Teresa, you had to go for the old cheap pack of 10 for a euro in Dealz. Well look at you now, you fool,' Lanigan said to herself as she battled the plate.

TRANSPORT

UNDERCOVER DART GARDAÍ TO WEAR SPECIAL UPHOLSTERY CAMO TO AVOID DETECTION

GARDAÍ HAVE CONFIRMED that a new undercover squad will be dispatched to tackle a spate of anti-social incidents on DART lines in recent months, and that they will wear a specially designed DART camo to avoid detection, *WWN* can confirm.

Tested over the past two weeks, the new camouflaged unit will blend into the background unnoticed, hoping to catch dozens of young offenders creating trouble on Dublin's city and coastline train service.

'We've had a few instances where people have accidentally sat on the guards, but that's to be expected with such sophisticated camouflage,' stated Garda Commissioner Drew Harris today, unveiling the €345 project, the biggest investment into An Garda Síochána in the State's history.

Mr Harris then thanked the people who embroidered the new uniforms for all their hard work.

'We hired dozens of elderly people in old folks' homes to stitch on the DART upholstery, and we're really happy with the results,' Harris added. 'Apart from the smell of snack boxes off their breath, our new undercover team are virtually undetectable, and we expect to catch any young scutts terrorising passengers on the DART line and create a safe environment for commuters.'

Gardaí have called on the commissioner to create working-class shop assistant camo in a bid to infiltrate the ranks of protesting former Debenhams workers and thereby help the liquidator and multibillion-euro-revenue-generating multinational KPMG reclaim stock from received stores.

Conspiracy Corner

Jim Corr is responsible for miles of Jimtrails made up of effluent which can be seen across the vast expanse of Irish social media.

County Knowledge

Louth

Known as the little county, Louth is one of the only municipalities on earth that is classed as a choking hazard.

Plans to fuse Drogheda and Dundalk together remain stuck on a debate whether to call the resulting town Drogdalk or Dunheda.

Louth is one of the few words in which Irish people pronounce the 'th' correctly.

BABIES

CONFIRMED: NEW BABY JUST A FUDJI-WUDJI-BUDJI WIDDLE THING

CONCERNS over whether or not six-day-old Rhea Marrison is a little dote have been cast aside following an assessment by her grandmother, who has confirmed that the infant is, in fact, 'just too precious'.

'Oh, she's an angel, just a little angel,' said Nanna Marrison, much to the relief of Cathal and Deirdre Marrison, who up to this point had feared that their newborn was some sort of dog-faced gremlin.

Further inspection by Nanna Marrison, real name Greta Marrison, has confirmed that the newborn has the correct number of fingers and toes, is appropriately sturdy, and even has 'a mighty head of hair'.

'Phew, it was like watching your car go through the NCT,' sighed Cathal Marrison, as his mam gave her new grandchild the final checks before confirming that she's a good baby, yes, she is, yes, she is.

'We knew Rhea was special, because Deirdre's mam had already given her a preliminary check for cuteness, but to hear it from my own mam is a relief. Deirdre was planning to take Rhea into where she works next week to see all her workmates, but you couldn't trust those people. They're just going to tell you what you want to hear. My mam, on the other hand … she'll cut a kid to the quick if it isn't a sufficiently cuddly bundle of joy.'

Meanwhile, Grandad Marrison has yet to offer an opinion on his new granddaughter, other than to say she's 'very good' and turn back to reading his paper.

CONCERNED for his privacy, Co. Waterford man Mark Lacey has group texted everyone in his immediate circle of friends to inform them that he will be deleting his WhatsApp account, and that they can now find him on Signal, *WWN* can confirm.

The Facebook Messenger user, who also uses Viber, Snapchat, TikTok, Instagram and, more recently, Bebo to communicate with friends, delivered the latest piece of important news like Moses on a hill, proud in the knowledge that he was now free from all privacy breaches.

'WhatsApp are forcing everyone to accept their new data settings, and I'm not going to bow down to their BS,' Lacey told several more friends through Facebook Messenger, oblivious to the irony. 'Signal is where it's at now when having highly confidential conversations.'

Cursing the move, sources at WhatsApp have expressed their

'I'M DELETING WHATSAPP OVER DATA CHANGE SO FIND ME ON SIGNAL', ADVISES REGULAR FACEBOOK MESSENGER USER

disappointment at Mr Lacey's cunning move, begging other users not to follow in his footsteps.

'Oh please, don't go. Your texts are so important to the world. How are we supposed to spy on the organisation of your mate's stag do, or see all those non-PC memes you send each other,' a very not-worried-looking WhatsApp source said. 'How are Interpol supposed to keep an eye on your closet homosexual videos of lads with big dicks that you send each other now? Or those mutilated people in car crash images,' the source added, before concluding, 'This could be the end of WhatsApp as we know it.'

SOCIALISING

WATERFORD LAD MISSES FIGHTING OUTSIDE PUBS

A CO. WATERFORD MAN has admitted today that he misses kicking the face off strangers outside pubs and chippers in the early morning, stating he would give anything for a good old-fashioned row right about now, *WWN* reports.

Jayo Lonergan, who has 57 convictions ranging from assault to drug dealing, said he'd 'gladly dance on someone's head' if given

Housing Ladder Tips

Small, simple steps can help: stop eating to save extra money, self-identify as a vulture fund, be born into a land-owning family – or, if your second job isn't earning you enough, just get a third one.

the chance, pointing out that fighting with friends and family members at home wasn't nearly as good as beating a total stranger to a pulp for simply looking at him.

'Der's only so many digs ya can giv a mate,' Lonergan pointed out, shaping up to this reporter. 'See you now, I'd batter de fukin' hed off ya no bodder boi an leave ya far ded, but der's no fun in dat coz we're not drunk outside de chippers an dat, j'know wha' I mean?'

With bars closed for the majority of the past 11 months, Lonergan's street cred has slipped several points on the scumbag stock exchange, leaving it up to him to come up with more creative ways of maintaining his 'hard bastard' reputation.

'Slapped a Tesco security guard in de face, I did, coz de little rat woz

tellin' me to put on a mask,' he added, recreating the proud moment by almost hitting this reporter in the head with his open hand. 'Hit him wit de palm of me hand like dis, I did, but I missed and hit his thick hed. Cunt woz lucky I didn't smash his nose inta his brain – he got off lite, so he did.'

Concluding the conversation, Lonergan called on anyone who was brave enough to meet him outside 'the chippers' any time after 2 a.m., as he now spends his time waiting for someone to start.

'You'd pick out a few stranglers walkin' home from sessions an' dat, but I'm mad for a good row if anyone wants der go,' he finished, before spitting onto the ground and walking off with his arms swaying out like a menace.

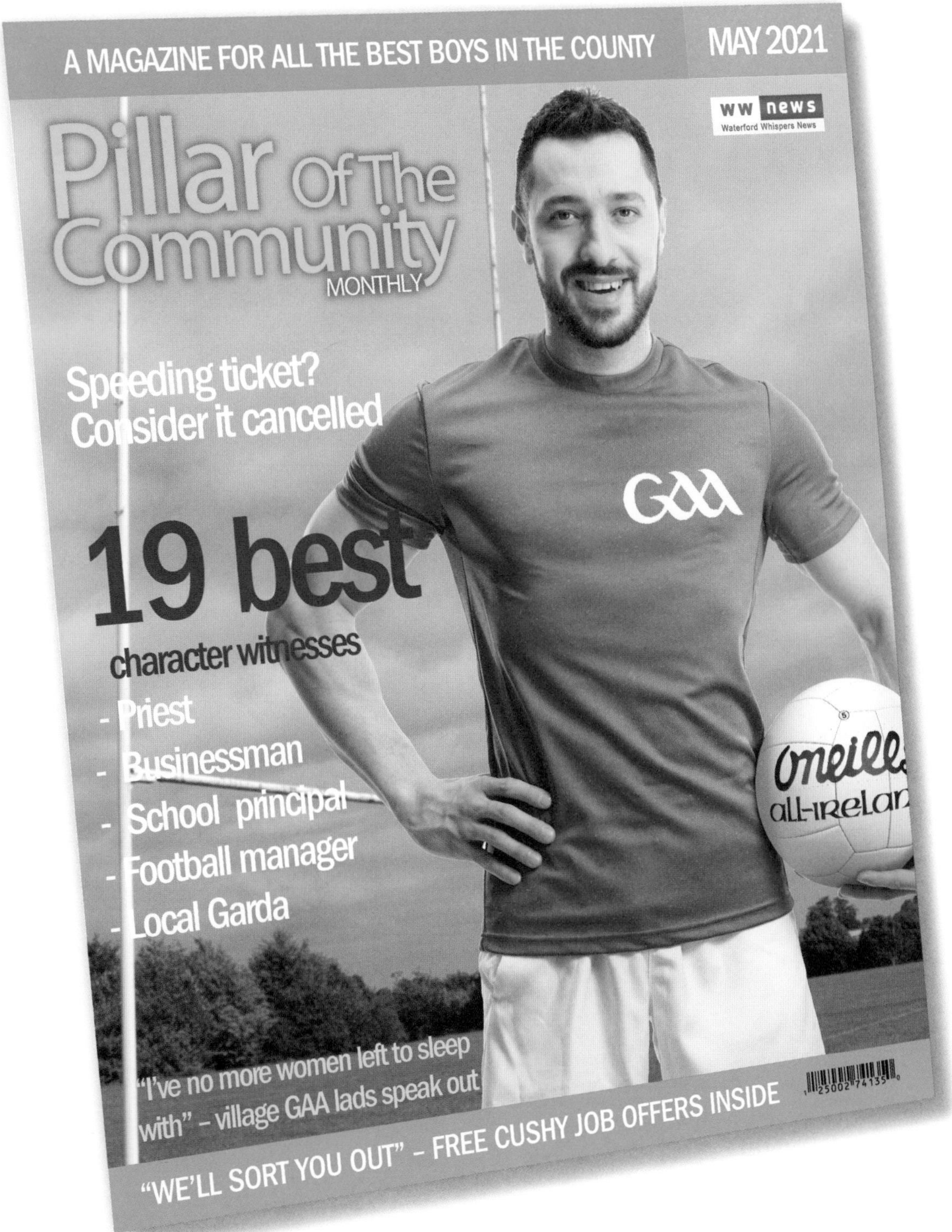

A MAGAZINE FOR ALL THE BEST BOYS IN THE COUNTY
MAY 2021
ww news
Waterford Whispers News
Pillar Of The Community
MONTHLY
Speeding ticket? Consider it cancelled
19 best
character witnesses
- Priest
- Businessman
- School principal
- Football manager
- Local Garda
GAA
"I've no more women left to sleep with" – village GAA lads speak out
"WE'LL SORT YOU OUT" – FREE CUSHY JOB OFFERS INSIDE

SPORT

FOOTBALL

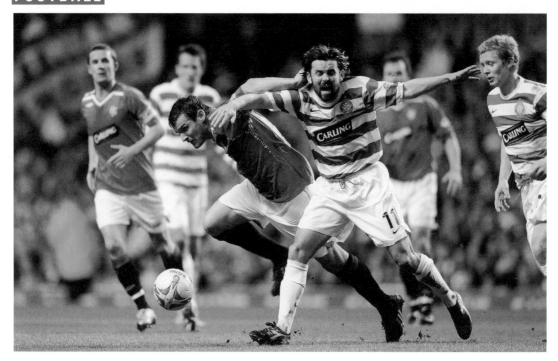

SCOTTISH INDEPENDENCE TO BE DECIDED IN ONE LAST CELTIC V RANGERS GAME

'WE ALWAYS KNEW it was going to boil down to this,' admitted Scottish First Minister Nicola Sturgeon, signing an agreement that will see the future of Scotland decided in what is being described as 'the Old Firm Derby to end them all'.

As per the arrangement, bitter rivals Glasgow Celtic and Glasgow Rangers will once again face off against each other in a 'best-ever-starting-11' format, with a victory for Celtic cementing Scottish independence, while a Rangers win would see the nation stay in the United Kingdom forever.

The match came about after Sturgeon rang the PM following her Scottish Nationalist Party's strong showing in the local elections last week, informing him that a second referendum on independence was a

> **'It's not like you're going to be pro-independence and shout for Rangers, let's face it.'**

matter of 'when, not if'. Faced with a lengthy constitutional battle in the courts followed by an onerous referendum campaign, Johnson suggested instead to just let the Gers and the Bhoys sort it out instead.

'It's really all it comes down to in Scotland, isn't it? Are you Protestant or Catholic? Are you Rangers or Celtic?' said a spokesperson for Johnson today.

'So just let them play and the winner takes all. It's not like you're going to be pro-independence and shout for Rangers, let's face it. Really, we just see this as being a quicker way to the destination. Sturgeon is pretty hard to negotiate with. We promised her zero VAT on Irn-Bru if she just dropped the whole thing, but she insisted on pressing forward.'

Meanwhile, huge numbers of Irish people have got incredibly invested in the clash, as the nation has for many years channelled anti-Protestant sentiment into the exploits of footballers in another country.

CYCLING

BREAKING: 94 PER CENT OF NATION'S MIDDLE-AGED MEN CURRENTLY IN LYCRA AND ON A BIKE

A RED 'LYCRA ALERT' has been issued yet again this weekend as 94 per cent of the nation's middle-aged men insist on pouring themselves into ill-fitting and bulbous cycling gear and taking to the roads.

'We're powerless to stop it, so please stop reporting all budgie smugglers, Lycra lizards and crotch goblins to us,' a Garda spokesperson said of the near 10,000 calls it routinely receives from the public each weekend, begging them to intervene and stop the eyesore.

In some of the worst scenarios shared by Gardaí, members of the public have scratched their own eyes out to avoid having to look at the cyclists for even one second longer, with an increase in unwanted sightings expected as weather improves.

'While I vomit a little in my mouth any time I turn a corner and see a pack of Lycra arses in the wild, I can still handle it. But it's the ones who have dismounted outside shops and insist on stretching their groins and

trying a few squats – why can't they have a normal midlife crisis like men of old and just have an affair,' shared motorist Eileen Dreary.

Querying what advantage is gained by wearing Lycra when you're so unfit that you're trundling along on a bike like a sack of potatoes with pedals made of cement, the motivations behind why middle-aged men

become so enamoured with cycling remain a mystery.

'It gets you out into nature and off the couch. It's definitely my decision anyway, it's not because if I didn't fuck off out of the house and give my wife some peace she'd leave me, I swear,' shared one cyclist admiring a pair of special cycling shades he didn't need to spend €260 on.

THE WORRYING SIGHT of large crowds of celebrating Rangers supporters in Glasgow and on the Shankhill Road in Belfast prompted criticism from authorities and Celtic fans, who can't believe their arch-rivals would so selfishly risk everyone's collective health and jeopardise the progress made in the fight against Covid-19.

'Shameful stuff,' confirmed one Celtic supporter, who confirmed he would have celebrated a historic, never before achieved 10-in-a-row title win all by himself.

'Aye, tanning some tins on the couch, nae putting anyone at risk but that's just the Bhoys through

CELTIC FANS CONFIRM THEY WOULD HAVE CELEBRATED HISTORIC 10-IN-A-ROW AT HOME ALONE

and through, real community club, unlike them bastards,' confirmed the fan, who omitted the fact that he cancelled plans for a Celtic 10-in-a-row-themed carnival once he saw Shane Duffy in defence.

'A woulda done a wee blow of a one o'them wee party flutes but sat meself in the dark alone cus I care fae your families, unlike you lot oot there with your tongues glued to Steven Gerrard's arsehole,' confirmed another Celtic supporter, who was delighted his hatred of Rangers dovetailed nicely with lording it over the moral high ground during a pandemic.

Yet more Celtic 10-in-a-row title-winning celebrations that would have gone ahead instead of mass gathering included fans donating their

own vaccines to developing nations, sewing PPE for nurses, spending money ear marked for bottles of Bucky on food for the needy and voodoo dolls of Alfredo Morelos.

Elsewhere, one or two Celtic fans conceded they can understand the celebrations, as it was the Rangers' first ever league win in their 10 years of existing as a club.

BREAKING NEWS

JOHNSON OFFERS 100K TO ANY FOOTBALLER WHO GOES IN STUDS-UP ON MARCUS RASHFORD

'ONE WOULD THINK, amid all the by-clauses and backdoors and amendments and constitutional rewrites and donkey-and-cart-era bylaws and exemptions sewn into the British legal system, that a prime minister would have found it easier than this to hobble or otherwise kill a mere sportsman,' sighed PM Boris Johnson today, pinning a picture of Marcus Rashford at the top of his 'hit list'.

Rashford, a Manchester United forward and near-constant thorn in the side of the Conservative Party, had drawn the attention of the PM yet again this week, after pointing out that food parcels sent to hungry kids while schools were shut actually turned out to be the contents of a chip shop bin, leading to Johnson's plotting to remove him once and for all.

'If only the bugger played rugby, I know about 50 chaps who I went to Eton with whose sons could absolutely spike him on the pitch,' snarled Boris,

as he watched his ministers fall one by one to embarrassing questioning on TV and in print over the subject.

'But he plays that damned peasant sport. Hancock, quick, find out if we know any footballers willing to give this Rashford bugger a damn good kicking on the pitch. What's a lot of

money to a footballer these days? 100 grand, eh? That's more than they could get paid in a lifetime, I'd imagine. Wait, they earn what?!'

Johnson is to spend the rest of the day completely unable to grasp the concept that this Rashford might just be a 'good person', whatever that is.

LOCAL FATHER CLEARLY TAKING SON'S SPORT ACTIVITY MORE SERIOUSLY THAN DAUGHTER'S

ARTFULLY PULLING the wool over his children's eyes, local father Cathal Curtin believes his children Cian and Ciara are none the wiser to his uneven distribution of attention when it comes to their sporting activities.

Curtin, who threatens the life of his son Cian's referees at least 18 times a game and gives a detailed breakdown of Cian's every touch of the ball, is genuinely of the opinion that half-heartedly repeating 'that's great, love' to Ciara during dinner when she relays her on-field exploits goes unnoticed.

'The dope cried when Cian took his first steps and thought he was going to be the next Messi, but not even a peep when Ciara lined out for the Waterford U14 Camogie team,' Curtin's wife Emer explained.

Rolling his eyes to the heavens whenever Ciara's away matches are more than 3 km from the family home but taking a pay cut and reducing his working week to four days just to make sure he can drive Cian to his hurling training even though his wife is free then, Curtin is blind to the 'burning a hole through his head' stares he is treated to by Ciara.

'Ciara? Ah yeah, she's great at the old netball or whatever one it is she plays,' confirmed Curtin, who uses Ciara's camogie matches as the perfect time to bed down on his phone and catch up on all the lads' WhatsApp banter and videos.

'She might not be able to keep doing it though. The fees and subs, the gear, all that – it's just not worth it. Especially

when Cian will probably be needing new boots and the soccer team have that trip to England planned,' Curtin confirmed, his back to the field of play as Ciara scored a goal.

HORSE RACING

20,000 RACEHORSES DEAD SINCE 2017 KIND OF JEALOUS THEY DIDN'T MAKE THE NEWS TOO

COMMENTING on the fallout from a controversial viral image of an Irish horse trainer sitting on a dead racehorse, some 20,000 deceased animals who failed to make it on the racing track and were slaughtered have admitted to being kind of jealous for not making the news.

The 22,000 figure, which is only from 2017 to 2019, and is probably now double that, continuously goes under the Irish horse-racing outrage radar due to the enormous wealth trainers and stud farms accumulate for the industry, with the dead animals insisting, 'No, go right ahead there

Historical Facts

Less well recorded in history was the 1913 Lock-In, Jim Larkin's pint session with the lads when he came up with the idea for the Lockout.

> **'It's a good thing the horse-racing industry isn't compared to the now struggling greyhound industry, or we would all be out of billions'**

and just be outraged at a single dead horse being sat on. We're used to it at this stage.'

'Sure, over seven thousand of us are slaughtered by the industry and sold for meat every year for not running fast enough, but don't let that stop ye getting outraged over just one of us – at least he made it to the track to be run into the ground,' insisted one dead horse WWN spoke to using a Ouija board and a horse whisperer by the name of Dave. 'Probably best to

continue focusing on the greyhound industry and how they do the same thing on a smaller scale, or better yet, slate and racially abuse an Irish Traveller driving a sulky.'

Figures released by the Department of Agriculture reveal 6,573 horses were slaughtered for human consumption in 2018, with 7,748 in 2017 and 7,618 in 2016, with the highest number occurring during the recession in 2011, when over 24,000 unwanted horses were slaughtered for meat.

'Hey, it's a good thing the horse-racing industry isn't compared to the now struggling greyhound industry, or we would all be out of billions,' shared one horse stud owner who wished to remain anonymous for obvious reasons. 'I couldn't imagine what would happen if people actually found out about the god-awful shit we are at in the back of it all – it's a good thing we're insanely rich and well connected.'

JOGGING

MAN OUT JOGGING WITH FRIENDS NEVER SHUTS THE FUCK UP

FRIENDS AND ACQUAINTANCES of Dublin man Jeremy Hayes have today staged an intervention for the jogging enthusiast over his continued tirade of absolute shite talk while running, calling on him to just take the time to casually chat now and again and enjoy the moment.

Hell-bent on proving how fit he is by continually waffling, Hayes was eventually confronted about his inability to shut up by four of his closest jogging partners, desperate for some peace and quiet and a chance to get their own boring life events across.

'Look, Jeremy, you don't always have to audibly stream whatever thoughts pop into your brain. Sometimes the dead air is nice when we're all

> **'We all know you can keep talking for hours on end, but you don't need to keep doing it.'**

running,' a nervous James Murphy said, opening the intervention, staged on a park bench in a local green. 'We all know you can keep talking for hours on end, but you don't need to keep doing it.'

'Yeah, I'm with James on this one, Jeremy, maybe give your head some time to process the thoughts coming through before just spilling out your entire life story, or whatever happened

> **'Ah, sorry lads, my ear pods were in there, what were ye saying?'**

that day in stunning detail from start to finish. It's kind of ruining our mojo when we're running,' David Walsh chimed in, hoping his point was somehow getting across.

'Ah, sorry, lads, my ear pods were in there, what were ye saying?' Hayes revealed, taking his hood down and his earphones out.

'We were just saying will you ever shut the fuck up when we're all running, give someone else a chance,' a now exhausted Walsh barked. 'You'd give morphine a ball-ache.'

'Okay, okay, lads, Jesus, someone got out of the wrong side of the cage this morning,' he retorted, as they all set off for their run, again dominated by Hayes. 'Ha-ha, that reminds me lads, did ye watch the UFC at the weekend? Jaysis there's some slaps in that … fucking work today then lads you should have smelled the shite Mary from accounts was cooking in the microwave … any of ye try Amazon Prime … some weather all the same …'

> **'We were just saying will you ever shut the fuck up when we're all running, give someone else a chance.'**

SPORTS SCIENCE

WE BUILD THE PERFECT INTER-COUNTY GAA PLAYER

THEY SAID it couldn't be done, but using the latest in sports technology WWN Labs believes it has created the perfect inter-county GAA player.

Football is an unforgiving sport that demands high levels of elite performance. Here is the perfect specimen tailored to all your All-Ireland winning needs:

- Shoulders moulded from the contents of a cement truck, solid enough to withstand a shoulder from any rival player nicknamed 'The Brick'.
- Hydraulic calves fashioned out of parts from a 100C-2 midi JCB excavator.
- Lungs – the equivalent capacity of eight hot air balloons. Enough there for a marathon or two, or one GAA podcast interview, whichever requires more oxygen.

Housing Ladder Tips

If the bank of Mum & Dad turns down your request, consider the bank of Nanny & Grandad.

Predictions for 2022

Several prominent Irish male radio and TV celebrities will suddenly leave their six-figure salaries for no sordid reason whatsoever.

- For free kicks and 45s – a foot fitted with the same GPS accuracy system that US drone military operators use when they want to ensure their missile will land on the right wedding party in the middle of the Afghan desert.

- Studs replaced by miniature trampolines for all those high balls.
- A temperament with a two-switch function marked 'ice cold calculation and focus' and 'Schmozzle rage'.
- No need for the addition of a personality – like trying to reduce the weight on an F1 car, a personality would only take up room.
- Fitted with the forced smile of a four-year-old posing in front of their birthday cake. Comes in handy if they end up on *The Late Late Show* and have to pretend to tolerate Tubridy; also used for 407 county sponsor engagements and photo ops.
- The player comes fitted with a phone containing the numbers of the local priest, businessman, former principal and a dozen others on the off chance he ever needs a character witness.

FITNESS

MAN'S KETTLEBELLS PROVING HUGELY EFFECTIVE AT WIDE RANGE OF NON-EXERCISE USES

ORIGINALLY BOUGHT as a sort of exercise regime or weight-training programme or something or other, the kettlebells sitting in the home of Dublin man Cathal McHogan have proved to be an incredibly useful thing to have about the house, *WWN* can report.

'It's mad, I don't even remember buying them!' laughed the 37-year-old, pushing some of the heavier weights around with his foot.

'But nevertheless, they've come in fierce handy around the house. Not for lifting or anything like that – I gave it a go, it's not for me at all. But I wouldn't be without them, and recommend every house buy a full set!'

Among the uses McHogan has found for his kettlebells are:

- 10 kg and up: ideal for weighing down the kids' trampoline out the back whenever stormy weather is threatened. Also useful for holding when jumping up and down in the green bin if it gets too full. 'It adds enough weight to my own bulk to really smush that rubbish down,' revealed McHogan.
- 6 kg to 8 kg: 'perfect' for weighing down books that contain flowers being pressed, a hobby that is far more in keeping with the amount of energy that McHogan is willing to expend at any given time.
- 5 kg and under: 'Doorstops, paperweights, hey, if you have a bag of evidence that you need to disappear, stick a 2 kg bell into

it and fuck it into a river – gone,' smiled McHogan, before bending over to lift a 0.8 kg kettlebell to show us, at which time he ruptured every disc in his back, blew both his quads and dislocated his shoulder all at once.

RACEHORSE INDUSTRY PUTTING DOWN THOUSANDS OF JOCKEYS EVERY YEAR

A STAGGERING 43,580 horse-racing jockeys were put to sleep last year, a damning CSO report has found on the eve of the Cheltenham festival, highlighting the unforgiving and competitive nature of the industry.

Jockeys as young as 16 were humanely euthanised after they failed to win races, with calls for the breeding of jockeys to be curbed over

the escalating number of deaths.

'A lot of the jockeys who were put down had been injured, and nothing could be done for them, but the large majority were just not pushing the horses fast enough, which is fair enough,' the report read.

Bred for their short size and light weight, jockeys can last up to 30 and even 40 years old before being

sent out to stud; however, younger, less successful riders are usually sent for slaughter and their meat sold to factories abroad.

'Jockey meat is a delicacy in some countries, so they don't totally go to waste,' local jockey breeder Tony Holden explained, before defending the mass killing of tens of thousands of riders every year. 'Once they break a limb, they're rendered useless, as it can take up to eight weeks for them to heal. By that stage, the cost to tend to their injuries and feed them isn't financially feasible, so we have no other option but to put a bolt gun to the back of their ear and pull the trigger.'

Human rights group Amnesty International has called on the horse-racing industry to address the blatant murders, but admitted it did understand the financial side of the industry.

'It just seems like a lot of unnecessary death, and we would suggest some kind of rehabilitation programme for injured jockeys, or for jockey rescue charities to intervene,' Amnesty International concluded.

EXCLUSIVE

The Criminal Courts of Justice

IRISH COURTS STAR EMBROILED IN UFC FIGHT

ONE OF IRELAND'S most promising Irish criminal court stars is facing reputational ruin after he was embroiled in an unseemly UFC fight, *WWN* can reveal.

· 'This was on the eve of what's potentially his biggest court appearance to date, and now it's been ruined with all this UFC business dragging him down,' reported a source close to iconic courts superstar Conor McGregor.

The Year in Numbers

400,879 – the number of times Irish women tried to pass off their own farts as their partners'.

Forced into pre-fight videos, interviews and sparring sessions, many feel McGregor's reputation of being chiefly known for his high-profile appearances in court will be tarnished permanently.

'We told him to keep his head down, stick to what he's good at, but he can't help himself. It's sad, cus some people now know him as just a UFC lad – all his hard work in courts down the drain,' added the source.

McGregor had previously garnered a reputation for inspiring a younger generation of defendants.

'When I grow up, I want to be involved in the sort of thing the Irish media can't report on due to the threat of Ireland's backward libel

laws,' shared one youngster, who still cherishes the autograph he got from McGregor while waiting outside the courts during McGregor's appearance for assaulting a man in a pub.

Others have suggested that this UFC distraction won't in anyway affect the high esteem he is held in within Irish legal circles.

'There's respect out there for him, and even the stuff that doesn't make it to court, people still know him for that – the comparing people to Nazis, calling people f****ts, keeping local snow salesmen in business, no one can take that away from him,' offered one court pundit on the popular court website CourtJunkie.com.

McGregor was last in the news after being the unfortunate victim of a watch scam, when a fraudster sold him a watch you'd find in a claw machine in an arcade for a six-figure sum.

OLYMPICS ▬▬▬▬▬▬▬▬▬▬▬▬▬▬▬▬▬▬▬▬▬▬▬▬▬

PROPOSED OLYMPIC EVENTS IRISH PEOPLE WOULD EXCEL AT

EVERY COUNTRY takes great pride in the Olympics, the pinnacle of sporting spectacle, and although Ireland's success is rare in these quadrennial games, this might change if a number of proposed new events get the go-ahead.

Would Irish people excel at the following disciplines?

Competitive passive-aggression

This is currently a mother-daughter relay event, but it could be expanded to fathers and sons over time. Judges award points for comments that would go undetected by an outsider if they weren't paying attention, but that prove utterly devastating to the person on the receiving end.

Irish mothers are strong gold medal favourites for the next 45 Olympics owing to their talent for oaring in thinly veiled criticism about how their daughters choose to live their lives.

Greco-Roman wrestling with your sexuality

Greased-up rural farmers do battle by wrestling against the unstoppable force of their yearning for the immovable object of their desires: the Cleary's lad back in town with a fierce tan on him after finishing college and doing a summer in the US.

Wait-listing

The gold medal will likely go to the Irish person who can moan the most about being inconvenienced by a queue. Bookies' money remains on strong favourite Orna Healy, who is still in the middle of her 'c'mere and I'll tell ya how long the GP kept me in that waiting room' rant, which started three months ago.

100-second begrudgery sprints

How many insults can you lay at the feet of someone in the public eye enjoying moderate success or praise?

Mental gymnastics

A team event: Irish couples are rewarded for how quickly they can get the hump with each other and get into an entirely avoidable argument about something trivial.

Triathlon (drinking edition)

A multi-discipline event. The competitor who can drink the most cans, take the most safety pisses and cram the most people into a taxi when someone at a house party yells 'taxi's outside' wins.

Conspiracy Corner

The Spire is a silo in which all of Ireland's old Sellafield iodine tablets are stored.

FOOTBALL

'PACK OF GREEDY CUNTS': FOOTBALL FANS FINALLY AGREE ON SOMETHING

FRESH from the announcement that VAR has ruled a move by 12 clubs to form a breakaway 'super league' offside, football fans have put aside their tribal rivalries to finally agree on something and declare the owners of the clubs involved a 'pack of greedy cunts'.

'I'd happily scream abuse at supporters of rival clubs for hours over a disputed throw-in, but today these shameless money-hungry pricks at the top have achieved the unthinkable – getting Man United and Liverpool fans, Barca and Madrid fans, Inter and Milan

fans to wholeheartedly agree with each other that this is the Gareth Bale overhead kick against Liverpool of bad ideas,' confirmed one fan who could piss steam right now they're so angry.

Fan ire at the announcement of the league is the least of the worries for the clubs' owners, as fraud charges have already been brought against those involved for describing anything involving Tottenham Hotspur and Arsenal as an elite 'super league'.

While the make-up of the proposed midweek league hasn't been finalised, rules such as '€2 billion for a goalless draw' and 'the team who pays the biggest dividends to parasitic shareholders and owners at the end of the financial year' being declared the winner of the league have been put forward.

Leaked plans for the league suggest the playing of football will be abandoned entirely and replaced with owners of the clubs, shirtless and oiled up, massaging one another with piles of cash while loading their clubs up with insurmountable levels of debt.

Elsewhere, this brazen contempt shown for football fans everywhere is expected to lead to a 0 per cent increase in Irish people abandoning support for English clubs to take up an interest in the League of Ireland.

TEENAGER WORKING FOR KINAHAN CARTEL DISAPPOINTED TO FIND OUT BOSS INVOLVED IN SPORT

STILL REELING from the BBC *Panorama* documentary into the murky and grubby world of elite boxing, local teenager and Kinahan cartel employee Andrew Profitt has expressed his disappointment in Daniel Kinahan after discovering his links to the controversial sport.

'And to think I looked up to him,' shared Profitt, who was an easy target for the cartel after a life spent being ignored by local representatives and institutions meant to help him from being coerced into a life of crime.

'If I've learned anything from this profession it's that you can't have one foot in drugs and another elsewhere.

He should stick to focusing on poisoning local communities and exploiting young lads like myself,' explained Profitt, in between deliveries.

'Like, take me for example. If I ignored my boss and stayed in school and tried to do something with my life, then he'd probably threaten me, right? And tell me I'm "taking my eye off the ball", and that's how I see it after watching that documentary. It's like do you even take being described in the High Court as the head of a murderous drug gang seriously anymore?'

'How are we supposed to keep our rep as one of the most brutal drug cartels in Europe if he's off pretending

to be Mr promoter man? Donkey King to Muhammad A-Geebag,' continued Profitt, in what are sure to be some of his last words.

Despite the documentary's impact, it's not clear if, finally seeing sense, the drug cartel world will distance themselves from such a controversial boxing figure.

Elsewhere, there was considerable fury at Tyson Fury's lack of fury over fury at Fury's Kinahan links.

GOLF

WOMEN GRANTED PORTMARNOCK GOLF CLUB MEMBERSHIP WILL NEED PERMISSION FROM HUSBANDS FIRST

FOLLOWING the historic news that, after 127 years, women members will finally be permitted to join Dublin's Portmarnock Golf Club, the club's members have sought to clarify some additional information, *WWN* can reveal.

'Of course they're free to join, as long as they have a letter of written permission signed by their husbands and their doctors,' shared one club member *WWN* spoke with.

'They won't be allowed on the grounds if it's that time of the month. We don't want the greens becoming reds if you catch my drift,' he added.

'They won't be allowed on the grounds if it's that time of the month. We don't want the greens becoming reds.'

It's a time of great social change and progress at the club, as a vote on installing women's toilets, tee boxes and tampon dispensers is expected in another 127 years.

'And golf carts are off limits. Have you seen these lot trying to drive their cars?' continued one of the 16.6 per cent of members who voted against the change.

Female players on the course will also be asked to let the nearest man shout 'fore' on their behalf, as male members do not wish to be disturbed by the shrill and grating voices synonymous with women.

'The good-looking ones will have to wear short skirts when retrieving their balls from the hole, and before you say we're sexist, the female captain's prize will be a hoover – it may have been a while coming, this vote, but we're making up for lost time,' concluded the existing members.

County Knowledge

Roscommon

Originally built as a set for the popular comedy show *Moone Boy*, the county of Roscommon was deemed 'too nice' to demolish, and so it still exists there today.

Since voting a majority No in the marriage referendum, Roscommon has been ostracised by the rest of the country, and has been chosen as the fall-guy county when the time comes for Ireland to shed its old ways and fears.

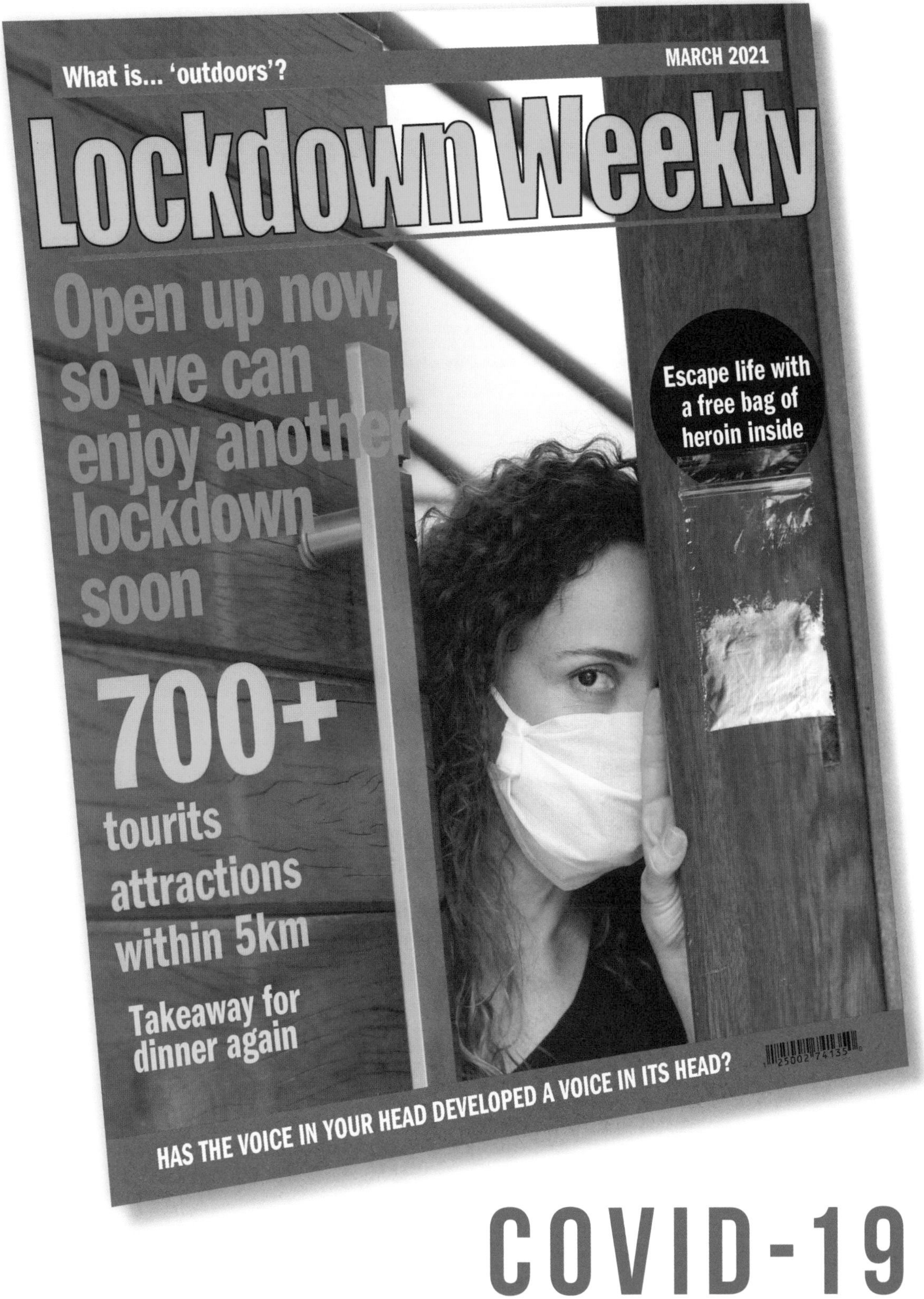

What is... 'outdoors'?

MARCH 2021

Lockdown Weekly

Open up now, so we can enjoy another lockdown soon

Escape life with a free bag of heroin inside

700+

tourits attractions within 5km

Takeaway for dinner again

HAS THE VOICE IN YOUR HEAD DEVELOPED A VOICE IN ITS HEAD?

COVID-19

FOLLOWING ON from a catalogue of public relation disasters, vague leaks and a general incompetence when delivering crucial changes in lockdown restrictions, the government has decided to go back to basics by publishing all future restriction measures on Ogham stones.

Dating back to the fifth and sixth centuries, Ogham inscriptions are the oldest known method of written

LOCKDOWN RESTRICTIONS FOR MARCH TO BE PUBLISHED ON OGHAM STONES

communications in the Irish language, using very basic pictorial-type lines.

'We realise that we may have over-complicated things by releasing dribs and drabs of conflicting information to the press,

so we've decided to make this very easy for people by outlining the next six months of lockdown measures on etched standing stones in a primitive form of our native language,' a letter delivered by a government spokespigeon read today.

A team of illiterate baboon monkeys have been flown in and have already been put to work etching the new measures on the Ogham stones, which will be erected on top of some of the most unreachable hills and mountaintops across the country.

A government source later confirmed that 'we're looking into publishing the findings of all future government inquiries on these stones, and I admit we're kicking ourselves we didn't use them for the Mother and Baby Homes report last month.'

It is understood that hundreds of the stones have already had to be recalled over continual changes being made by the government, but it has been confirmed that the final draft of Ogham stones should be ready by June 2045, or thereabouts.

BREAKING NEWS

GARDAÍ SHUT DOWN HAS-BEENS OPERATING IN SHED

GARDAÍ have uncovered a network of has-beens operating out of a shed in the North County Dublin area. A perfectly serviceable but illegal bar was found, occupied by has-beens and filled with fame-adjacent paraphernalia.

'We found Brian McFadden and Linda Martin chatting away about the time McFadden personally called out ISIS on Twitter,' explained one Garda

on the scene, as Bertie Ahern hovered in the background, refusing to leave.

'The more we explored the premises, the more neglected and spotlight-starved celebrity careers we found,' added one Garda, as he placed 12 long-forgotten Louis-Walsh-related bands in cuffs.

'Five members of Six were here. We think the remaining member scaled the wall to escape, but sure we wouldn't have a fucking clue who he was if we caught him,' added the Garda.

The proprietor, who was also arrested, claimed that the clientele was only permitted in the shed for 15 minutes, but long outstayed their welcome.

'We arrested your man who was in that thing, ah you know him, here hang on, we'll fetch him out of the van,' added another Garda as he frogmarched a man so unfamous he failed to recognise him even after he insisted he had been in an episode of *Love/Hate* or something.

Gardaí also confiscated a number of items, including signed photographs of some of the patrons, which are believed to have a street value of zero euro.

Waterford Whispers News

ISSUE 34,567,432 WATERFORD, MONDAY, JANUARY 26, 1998 £1.99

Crowds Gather to Witness First Panini Arrive In Ireland

DUBLIN airport was awash with thousands of crazed spectators yesterday afternoon to catch a glimpse of the first-ever panini bread to arrive on the island of Ireland, *WWN* can reveal.

As it landed on a chartered jet from Italy, crowds cheered along the perimeter fence, desperate to see the small flat bread emerge on the jet's gangway. Archbishop Desmond Connell held it aloft, before delivering a two-hour mass in the arrival's hall.

'Blessed are the toasted-sandwich makers, for they shall inherit substantially priced ham and cheese paninis,' Archbishop Connell told the crowd, blessing the bread before closing an awaiting grill on top of it. 'Let this bread help Ireland prosper. May its indented grill lines ooze with melted cheddar cheese, forcing an accompaniment of Hunky Dory cheese-and-onion-flavoured crisps and some salad.'

As it made its way from the airport through the city streets, fans of the panini bread swarmed the roads in scenes reminiscent of Italia90, when some first got the taste of foreign bread.

'Aw, 'tis great ta see it here,' explained one weeping man we spoke to, 'it's all we ate over there during the World Cup and now it's finally here.' Debate was strong among the crowds over the proposed recommended retail prices of the new fancy bread, with many café owners calling it a delicacy that should range between £4–£8.

'I can't see this ever taking off,' said another man, 'that kind of fancy shite doesn't fit here. What will they try sell us next, fancy coffees?

Give me a sliced pan ham sandwich and a cup of Gold Blend instant any day over this muck.'

HOME-SCHOOLING

'CONAS ATÁ TÚ ME BOLLIX' CONFIRMS MOTHER WHO REGRETS SENDING KIDS TO GAELSCOIL

A CO. WATERFORD mother with no understanding of the Irish language has admitted to now regretting sending her two children to a local Gaelscoil, with ongoing home-schooling during lockdown rendering her a useless, redundant parent.

'Conas atá tú me bollix!' Darina Kent exclaimed, trying to decipher the latest stream of incomprehensible text delivered via a dated school database.

'This is all Klingon to me. Could they not speak in English for the couple of months while us eejits help them with their homework? It's like Stevie Wonder leading Andrea Bocelli here.'

Previously opting for the well-known Irish-speaking school for its sterling reputation, and not because she wanted to gloat to friends that her children can speak Irish and attend an Irish school, Kent contemplated what

it would be like to speak in a language that didn't put everything backwards in its translation.

'No wonder it's a dying language, it's pure shite talk,' she insisted, before turning to her youngest and not holding back her thoughts. 'How many years have you left in this place, Saoirse, eh? Surely you wouldn't mind if we transferred you to another school, would ya? Make Mammy and Daddy happy?'

Now consoling her traumatised daughter, Kent vowed to try harder during home-schooling, promising herself to at least learn some basic Irish to get her through the next few months.

'Is maith liom cáca milis?' she told her children, before deciding to step out for a well-deserved smoke. 'Tá mommy ag dul go dtí an fags.'

Elsewhere, Darina's husband Paul apologised again for not being able to help out, as he's very busy pretending to work while watching YouTube on his laptop all day.

DAILY COVID BRIEFINGS TO START RELEASING THE NUMBER OF DECEASED BUSINESSES

WITH THE NUMBER of human fatalities thankfully dwindling day by day, Ireland's daily Covid-19 briefings will now count the daily number of deceased businesses across the country, *WWN* has learned.

'Dozens of businesses are dying every single day due to restrictions, so it's best we include them in our Covid daily briefings,' a spokesman for the HSE confirmed.

Despite only a handful of cases nationwide, some 3,500 pubs employing tens of thousands of people across the country will not be allowed to open this coming Monday due to not being able to serve Covid-19's only known vaccine.

'Normal pubs don't have any substantial meals to shield people from the virus. Also, people who frequent pubs always get mad drunk, lose the run of themselves, start shifting each other and end up squirting contaminated sex juice everywhere,' a

government health adviser explained, before addressing the now very irate Vintners association.

'It's quite simple: you bar folk can't be trusted to carry out the same simple guidelines that restaurateurs have successfully kept to over the past few weeks.

'Besides, publicans don't have the IQ level to adhere to such tasks. Pubs and pubs that serve food are two completely different things – one smells of food and the other doesn't,' he added, before being rugby tackled to the ground and torn to pieces by a small group of publicans.

Meanwhile, revellers attending a drive-through bingo game this week have told counterparts hoping to attend a recently cancelled drive-

through music concert that it's not the same thing, and to also stop their whining.

GARDAÍ IN DUBLIN have confirmed they have arrested what is believed to be a drug-dealing Brazilian variant, found cycling a rickshaw along the Cork road and believed to be on its way to work in a local meat-processing plant, *WWN* can confirm.

Using its stringy protein legs to propel the vehicle, the variant brought Gardaí on a 10-mile low-speed rickshaw chase before eventually pulling over on the N25.

'We found a frightening amount of cocaine on the variant, and a follow-up search found dozens of Brazilian variants living in a small room in a city-centre house,' Gardaí stated.

The variants are all believed to be working for a local meat plant

Predictions for 2022

Love Island 2022 gets off to a rough start as the contestants battle with an infestation of genital mites and have to self-isolate throughout the entire series.

DRUG-DEALING BRAZILIAN VARIANT FOUND CYCLING RICKSHAW TO WORK IN MEAT PLANT

owner – who can't be named due to litigious billionaire reasons – and travelled through Dublin airport over the last three months to cut and pack meat for long hours under poor wages.

'Is hiring a highly contagious strain of Covid-19 for our meat plant a bad idea? Probably. But look at it this way: they make us lots of money, so you can't argue with that,' a manager at the plant said.

> **'A follow-up search found dozens of Brazilian variants living in a small room in a city-centre house.'**

Following today's find, the government has vowed to do everything in its power to do nothing to interrupt the country's meat-processing industry.

'Most of the meat plants in Ireland are owned by good men who have far more money than us as a state, so let's not poke the bear,' the Minister for Deflections concluded.

VACCINE LATEST

EU COUNTRIES AGREE TO END PRACTICE OF TRANSPORTING VACCINES VIA TORTOISE

NATIONS BELONGING to the European Union have pledged to rectify the alarmingly slow initial rollout of its Covid-19 vaccination programme, which has been greeted with anger and frustration by citizens.

After a special task force charged with identifying possible errors and inefficiencies within the supply chain reported that delivering the vaccines on the backs of ageing tortoises with arthritic hips and a poor sense of direction was probably not ideal, the practice is to be halted.

'Everyone's an expert after the fact. Yes, the tortoises are bad, but we didn't hear anyone speak up when we said we'd use flightless penguins to fly the vaccines to Ireland,' confirmed one Brussels bureaucrat.

EU officials defended their decision, however, to hedge their bets by placing orders across a dozen vaccine manufacturers only for a few to gain approval, and to enter drawn-out haggling with Pfizer/BioNTech.

'You put a bunch of Europeans into a room and don't expect them to get turned on by the prospect of haggling?' Health commissioner Stella Kyriakides shared, before admitting that maybe the EU took its eye off the ball through increased activity in their 'Shit talk Britain' WhatsApp group.

In the last 48 hours the German and French governments have applied increasing pressure on

Conspiracy Corner

You really think one young boy could kill King Conchobar's prized wolfhound using just a hurley? Wake up, sheeple.

Predictions for 2022

Marking the 100th anniversary of the Irish Civil War, families take up arms against each other over the Anglo-Irish Treaty.

Brussels officials, prompting the EU to pledge to roll out the vaccine with increased haste.

'The vaccine will now be delivered by a select group of intelligent octopuses, each tentacle armed with needle-pointed pneumatic drills. We've increased initial supply by thinning out our current vaccines with water like a teenager would do to their parents' drinks cabinet. We'll pick up the pace in no time,' confirmed Kyriakides.

BREAKING NEWS

MAN SUFFERS PUNISHMENT BEATING AFTER SUGGESTING ZOOM QUIZ

A MAN in his mid-thirties is said to be in a serious but stable condition in Waterford hospital tonight after a group of up to 20 of his co-workers barged into his apartment and kicked the absolute living shit out of him for inviting everyone for 'some Zoom fun' at the weekend.

Arthur Carlon, 35, made the suggestion for a return to 'the good old days' of the early lockdown with a Zoom quiz that he would host during a weekly check-in with his co-workers, prompting flashbacks of dreadful Friday nights spent doing what amassed to unpaid labour with every dose in the office, all from the comfort of your own home.

With bosses leaping on the idea as a good team-building exercise, Carlon's co-workers defied government guidelines to 'keep their contacts to a minimum', by convening at his house in the early hours of the morning and giving him a *Full Metal Jacket*-style towel-beating for being such a lickarse.

'Get it straight. Zoom quizzes were fun for all of 10 seconds back when we were in full lockdown, but that's about it,' said one of the attackers as they fled the scene.

'If you think just because we're probably heading into a second lockdown that we want to go back to spending two hours at our computer screen looking at people we can barely tolerate at the best of times, forget it! And it's not just work; if any of our friends suggests a Zoom games night or a live music gig over Zoom, you're getting beaten to a pulp too!'

Gardaí have confirmed that they are not investigating the incident, as they 'see no crime here'.

TRAFFIC CONE WOULD GIVE ANYTHING TO BE ROBBED BY STUDENTS RIGHT NOW

TRAFFIC CONES and shopping trollies across the country made a joint statement earlier today, saying they would only love to be stolen by students right now, anything to give them a break from the monotony of lockdown, *WWN* can confirm.

A spokesperson for roadside traffic cones, once a go-to item for drunken escapades, made an emotional plea to young people across the country, pointing out that they don't need to be drunk to steal a cone of their choosing, and to just go for it when the urge hits them.

'If you're passing roadworks and see several cones just sitting there, take one and put it on your head,' insisted the spokesman, demonstrating the act and now sounding muffled. 'Even if it's just picking one up and talking through it or just kicking over a cone onto its side – it will all help traffic cones get through this difficult period in time. Plus it's great craic.'

Similarly, the spokesperson for shopping trollies in Ireland made a plea to students to take them for a little spin once in a while, but warned to keep to one student per trolley.

'One student can push another in a trolley as long as they wear masks on their face, elbows and knees,' he said. 'Just think of how boring it is for both trollies and traffic cones right now who have been left abandoned by drunk young students who are all studying from home. It's bad form

really – students need to get their priorities straight.'

VACCINE LATEST

ASTRAZENECA NO LONGER RECOMMENDED FOR DAVIDS UNDER 50 BORN ON A WEDNESDAY

FIRST PLAGUED by issues with the delivery of the AstraZeneca vaccines, now the subsequent decision by the National Immunisation Advisory Committee to no longer recommend its use for any David under 50 born on a Wednesday can be added to its list of teething problems.

'Now this only applies to Davids whose middle names begin with an "S",' confirmed one person with knowledge on the matter.

Davids under 50 born on Wednesdays with a middle name beginning with 'S' who drive VW Golfs won't miss out on vaccinations

completely, however, as there are a number of other vaccines available that make up part of the nationwide vaccination programme.

'Obviously if these Davids had an imminent appointment, it will be a shame and a frustration to have it cancelled, but remember this just affects those cohort of Davids that also went to the Metallica gig in Slane in 2019 – via the N2 or the M1,' confirmed the insider. 'If you're a David over 60, 70, 110, etc., you're laughing.'

Authorities asked everyone to cross their fingers that no other vaccine emerges from further trials with a ban

> **'This only applies to Davids whose middle names begin with an "S".'**

on anyone who had their ear pierced before they were 15 or have operated heavy machinery in the last 100 years from receiving it.

Despite the fact that you are far more likely to die in a car crash than develop blood clots from the AstraZeneca jab, the measure has limited the number of people who can receive it out of an abundance of caution. One sad fallout from this, however, is the exponential increase in your aunt's vaccine-related rants on Facebook.

Elsewhere, the government was seen celebrating wildly at the emergence of fresh nonsense they can blame for failures to deliver a speedy and efficient vaccine rollout.

Historical Facts

At the time, many people were suspicious about why it was being referred to as World War I.

EXCLUSIVE

ALL THE KNOWN SIDE EFFECTS OF TALKING OUT YOUR ARSE ABOUT COVID

WITH THE ROLLOUT of Covid jabs beginning around the world, concerns about the side effects of talking out of your arse about Covid-19 have never been more vocal and prominent.

Are you concerned about a loved one and keen to know what the side effects are? *WWN* has the list you need. Among the most severe side effects from talking out of your arse about Covid-19 include:

- An allergy to wearing face coverings in shops and on private premises.
- Struggling with speech; for example, an inability to form sentences that don't include 'Bill Gates' or '5G'.

Conspiracy Corner

Kerrygold isn't even made from real gold, nor is it made in Kerry.

- A sudden obsession with Sweden that completely disappears when someone points out the country's less than spotless record on Covid-19.
- Blurred vision, which makes it harder to tell the difference between expert immunologists and 'some lad off Facebook'.
- Increase in weight given to George Soros memes; increased appetite for waving a tricolour on Grafton Street for no reason.
- Intense confusion and splitting headache when dealing with news that the coronavirus has directly led to a drop in immigration into the country.
- Insomnia caused directly by staying up until 3 a.m. watching videos that violate YouTube's terms and conditions. Additional side effect related to this can see people

develop compulsion to send links of these videos to everyone.
- Feeling nauseous and dizzy anytime someone says the moon landing wasn't faked.
- Those stating they won't avail of any vaccine often experience an inflated sense of intelligence. This troubling swelling shows no signs of abating. Sadly, this is also true of people who intend on getting the jab.
- The worst possible side effect is being put forward as a general election candidate for Sinn Féin.

LOCAL MAN REGRETTING BASING ENTIRE PERSONALITY ON GOING TO PUBS

THE DECISION to centre every facet of his existence around the culture of drinking is a hen that has certainly come home to roost for Waterford man Ciaran Toher, following the closure of all pubs and parties in the wake of the coronavirus pandemic.

'In hindsight, I should definitely have had at least one pastime that didn't revolve around being among a large group of people in a venue that

sells alcohol,' mused Toher, facing into yet another week of doing nothing except googling 'when are Level 5 restrictions ending'.

'The annoying thing about all this coronavirus stuff is that if the pubs were open, I'd have so much craic talking about it all, the restrictions, the masks, the government, the whole lot. I suppose I could chat with my pals about it anyway, but what's the point if you're not getting locked at the same time?'

Sensing his mounting frustration at not being able to do the one thing in life he loves doing, Toher's friends have encouraged him to take up a new hobby during the long months of lockdown, with the following results:

- Sea swimming: Deemed 'too cold', which would not be so bad if 'you were able to go straight to a pub with a snug for a few whiskies to warm you back up'.
- Playing an instrument: Toher has declared that no music he could play would ever stand up to the sweet sounds of some lad with a keyboard in a pub on a Friday night banging out 'Cracklin' Rosie'.
- Learn a new language: Declared 'pointless', as Toher has no holiday plans this year, and already knows how to order Carlsberg in four languages.
- Meet new people, potentially a partner to spend his life with: 'Ah you'd need a few pints in you for that'.

VACCINE LATEST

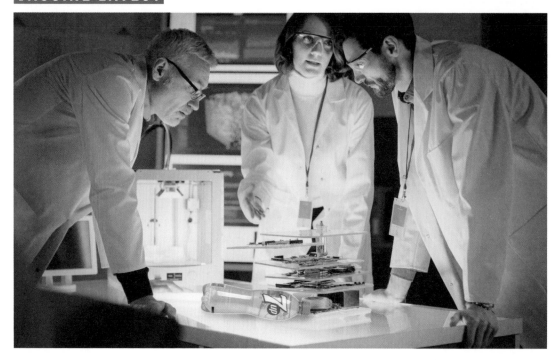

PFIZER VACCINE CREATED AFTER IRISH INTERN ACCIDENTALLY SPILLED FLAT 7UP INTO MIX

HERALDED the world over as the key to ending our pandemic-ravaged lives, Pfizer and BioNTech have confirmed the key part one Irish intern at their Ringaskiddy, Co. Cork plant played in their newly unveiled vaccine.

'The vaccine was about 5 per cent effective until this little idiot intern spilled flat 7UP all over some samples

we were working on, and somehow he has bested the greatest scientific minds in the world,' explained head of Pfizer Dr Albert Bourla. 'We've never seen anything with such a high level of medicinal might.'

Sean Rafflin, 16, a transition-year student on work experience, spoke to *WWN* about the role he played in the defining scientific breakthrough of our times.

'Fuck, Mam's going to kill me,' explained Rafflin, his voice breaking several times as he failed to understand the gift his accident has provided to humanity.

'I can just hear her raging at me now – "Do you know Uncle Larry had to beg his boss in Pfizer to get you that work experience? And look what you've gone and done, ye big eejit", "Did ye not see the 'No eating or

drinking in the labs' signs, ye clown?",' Rafflin continued, getting teary-eyed and failing to see scientists popping champagne in the background.

Rafflin explained that he slipped on a loose sausage that had fallen onto the floor from his jumbo breakfast roll, and in the process accidentally spilled the contents of a bottle of 7UP in his hand at the time, dousing vaccine samples.

Asked if he was unhappy that the founders of BioNTech, Ugur Sahin and Özlem Türeci, both the children of Turkish immigrants in Germany, were getting all the credit, Rafflin remained humble.

'Jesus Christ, please, you won't say anything to my Mam, will you? She's picking me up in a minute. She'll have a conniption.'

EMPLOYMENT

LOCAL BARMAN WILL MISS THE COVID-19 UNEMPLOYMENT PAYMENT WAGE RISE

DUSTING OFF his old black shirt, black trousers combo, local barman Jason Ryan reminisced about his last six months of living the high life, lounging around and enjoying his work-free day, secretly wishing for yet another lockdown.

'Back to this old shite again,' Ryan grumbled, his sphincter spasming from the thought of having to work shite hours for shite money in a job that has now become even shittier with the introduction of compulsory facemasks, visors and general customer chaos.

'Great, just 30 hours this week at a tenner an hour,' the 32-year-old said, checking his roster and rolling his eyes at a split shift on Saturday and Sunday next, varicose veins already pulsing in his calves. 'I can't wait to see all the old regulars again … oh, no, wait, most of them are probably either dead

now or too scared to come out near the place – this should be a barrel of fucking laughs.'

Used to the Covid-19 pay rise of €350 per week for the past 25 weeks, Ryan welcomed the news that the payment was recently cut, making it just about even now with his current weekly wage, not making him feel all that bad.

'Bus, lunch, few pints after work – I'm only working to be able to go to work at this stage,' he added, contemplating slipping on a wet floor or something, anything to get him out of working in Ireland's new bastard normal. 'I can't wait for customers to not be able to understand me, forcing me to pull down my mask at

every order, cleaning everyone's mess up again and hearing my favourite phrase, 'When yer ready, pal', again. Hopefully, I'll catch the fucking thing and we'll have to close.'

Desperate for an out, Ryan applied online for a local meat factory job, processing meat.

'It can't be much worse than this. At least the Gardaí won't be in every two seconds checking if we're doing our job right,' he concluded, before sending his CV.

Historical Facts

Oliver Cromwell ordered the destruction of Drogheda after receiving a bad pint there while on a stag do.

The Year in Numbers

103,644,789 – the number of potholes in Cavan.

BREAKING NEWS

GARDAÍ BREAK UP STREET PARTY OF NEWLY VACCINATED OVER-85S

UNEDIFYING SCENES were captured by news cameras last night as Gardaí broke up a large gathering of newly vaccinated over-85s in the Limerick City area of the country.

'I've been cooped up long enough, ya gowls, you can cocoon this,' one pensioner was heard to say moments before headbutting a Garda and fleeing the scene.

The street party, which was attended by anywhere between 100 and 140,000 people, depending on which tabloid is trying to get you to rage-click their headline, has been heavily criticised by people who say it sends the wrong message to younger people not yet vaccinated.

'You'll have 70- to 80-year-olds now influenced by this behaviour – mark my words, we'll be breaking up some septuagenarian sex parties before the week is out,' confirmed a Garda spokesperson.

Among items confiscated at the party included bags of MDMA tablets, 600 bottles of Buckfast, several sets of decks and a lighting rig that was used by octogenarian DJs supplying tunes to the party, as well as other party paraphernalia, including gimp masks, fireworks, neon face paint and half-eaten kebabs.

> **'We'll be breaking up some septuagenarian sex parties before the week is out.'**

County Knowledge

Wicklow

The Wicklow Mountains have been consecutively voted as one of the best places to dump a body in Ireland from 1965 to 2021.

Wicklow is home to Bray, and that must be a tough pill to swallow, in fairness.

The government has formally thanked all those holding parties and large gatherings, confirming that they will use these events as an incomprehensible excuse for a slower-than-expected rollout of vaccines if and when that occurs.

Elsewhere, a spokesperson for the University of Limerick has apologised for holding a practical in-person, on-street exam for students of its Events Management course, which also resulted in a street party in the city.

The Year in Numbers

0 – the number of babies buried in unmarked graves on the grounds of Mother and Baby Homes, according to PR specialists.

only €100mn

Vulture Fund
Aficionado

5 warm and fuzzy alternative names to 'vulture'

Leaving properties vacant for the craic

"YOU'RE GRAND LADS, I HAVE YA COVERED"

- exclusive Paschal Donohoe interview

Setting up a shell company for your shell company

Shaking down renters like the piggy banks they are – we show you how

12345 678 900 0

PROPERTY

ESTATE AGENTS

ESTATE AGENT HAS 'SOMEONE'S COME IN WITH AN OFFER ABOVE YOUR ONE' BULLSHIT DOWN TO AN ART FORM

'NOW I KNOW I said you went "sale agreed" but …' began estate agent William Traynor down the phone to a stressed-out pair of first-time buyers for what must be the 15th time this week.

Mistakenly believing he was coming across as relatable, empathetic and 'on your side', Traynor's latest attempt to gouge would-be homeowners and set them up in a bidding war against a dozen couples in a similar situation was seen through in record time.

'Woah, woah, I'm not the bad guy here. I'm afraid this is just a case of the seller getting an offer out of the blue,' counselled Traynor unconvincingly in response to a torrent of swear words.

'Alright, I'll give you two a chance to mull it over, but as I said you just need to match this bid, which is €40k above your offer, which was already €25k above the sale price, which was already €90k above what the house is actually worth,' said Traynor, closing out the conversation shortly

before repeating the same routine on another call.

Speaking to *WWN* about the tough market out there for buyers, Traynor admitted some estate agents earn their poor reputation with some of the underhanded tactics they pull.

'You can fuck right off with that. It's not me you're mad at, it's the market. Go find another fucking agent and they'll tell you the same fucking thing pal,' offered Traynor in an apology screamed in this reporter's face.

AN INTRO TO IRISH RENTING AD LINGO

NEW TO THE IRISH rental market and unsure of the terminology you come across when browsing the dozens of property rental sites in Ireland? Look no further than this indispensable primer for common phrases and what they mean:

- 'Hartigan Estate Agents is proud to present …' – the balls on this crowd.
- 'Spacious' – small, cramped.
- 'By appointment only' – easier to reject your request when you've formerly identified yourself as having a foreign-sounding name in an email or text.
- '5 minutes from the Luas' – a long journey akin to Jesus's 40 days and nights in the desert.
- 'New build' – the repeatedly flagged fire safety issues could help you make the front page of newspapers after a fire.
- 'Bespoke furnishings' – same cheap shit everyone buys in IKEA.
- 'Bright interiors' – you have to light a flare after 4 p.m. to see anything.
- 'Newly refurbished' – last saw a lick of paint when Pope John II visited Ireland.

- 'Studio apartment' – the mattress is placed over the top of a bathtub, the plug-in electric heater doubles as your grill. The front door is a window that never shuts.
- 'Reference required' – from you of course, what, you didn't think a landlord should give you a reference from a previous tenant?

Jesus, then how would they ever find some gullible fool to rent this shithole?

- 'One month's deposit up front' – you're not getting that back.
- 'Is sure to go quick' – that's right loser, we hold all the cards in this godforsaken nightmare they call 'renting in Ireland'.

IGNITING A DRUGS FEUD TO LOWER HOUSE PRICES IN AN AREA YOU WANT TO BUY A HOME, A GUIDE

SKYROCKETING house prices across all our cities have left would-be homeowners with only one option: to provoke a bitter gangland turf war in a bid to deter investors and pick up a three-bedroom at an affordable price.

Here's how:

1) Learn your local dealers
Despite what you may be led to believe, there are dealers in every area in Ireland. Chances are you've dealt with them yourself if you wanted a bit of smoke for the weekend or a bag for a stag do. Find out as much about them as you can. Be on the listen for any boss-style names. Fat Jack, Baldy Finnegan, The Exhaust, things like that.

2) Loose lips sink ships
Once you know a few of the local characters, get real sloppy with your discretion. Loudly mention how you got really great coke at an unbeatable price from The Lizard while you walk past one of Catface Sean's young lads on the corner. Keep fomenting dissent. Maybe even throw in a few tall tales. 'Arsefeet Malone told me the other day that he doesn't think there's a slap in Gutters McKenna or any of his lads,' you might say.

3) Things will get worse before they get better
All-out drug war won't kick off overnight, so expect house prices to continue to rise for a few months until the inevitable happens. Just as the government are powerless to stop the vulture funds scooping up housing supply, the guards are powerless to stop drug gangs from killing each other. Or maybe they just don't want to. The government, that is. And the cops, now that we think of it.

4) The keys are all yours
After a few years of the deaths of people who were 'known to Gardaí', as well as the ensuing media furore about how the streets of [insert your target location here] are no longer safe to be on, house prices should plummet back down to what you can afford to pay, and you're set! You now live in the area of your choice, and all you have to do to live peacefully for the rest of your days is kick back and watch an even bigger Eastern European gang waltz in and chase off the dealers in the area, bringing some degree of stability to the area.

5) Your kids can fend for themselves
No plan is foolproof – you and your kids now live in what's considered 'a bad area', so they may find it difficult later in life when it comes to attaining a good education, career, all the rest. But hey, life wouldn't be fun without a challenge, right?

Predictions for 2022
They said he'd never do it, but 2022 will be the year Dad finally uses that electric chainsaw he bought in Aldi 14 years ago.

RENTING

LANDLORD UNDER THE IMPRESSION HE'S YOUR BOSS OR SOMETHING

USING THEIR SECURITY deposit as collateral, local landlord Kieran Tobin has kindly asked tenants David and Ciara O'Doherty if they wouldn't mind giving the garden a once over, and if they could also give the windows a good wipe down too, thanks, that would be great, he revealed.

Calling by unannounced for the second time this month for a visit that is legally required to come with a week's written notice, Tobin was putting his key in the door to make his way inside the rented accommodation, about to break another rule.

'Oh, Kieran, I didn't hear you knock. Is everything okay?' David O'Doherty asked, now completely

subservient to his landlord of two years, knowing his 'traits'.

'Yeah, I just need to cut that hedge out back there, it's annoying me,' Tobin said, unaware it was 9 a.m. on a Saturday morning and really not a good time to illegally enter a tenant's home.

'Ah, okay, just let me get dressed there. Do you mind going around the side … ah, yeah just come in sure,' the tenant said, realising his landlord was already making a beeline for the back door, through their rented home.

'Jesus, that grass is long, David, is the lawnmower broken?' Tobin pointed out, before grimacing at three empty bottles of beer on the

kitchen table like it was any of his business. 'Ah, late one I see?'

'Ah, no, Kieran, you fucking cunt, we've been working all week, you know, trying to make the money to pay for the €1,800 rent you charge us for a small one-bedroom townhouse every month that you keep fucking calling into unannounced,' fellow

tenant Ciara O'Doherty wished she could shout from the comfort of her bed, as she listened to the prick come in and give orders to her partner once again.

Finished with his errand, Tobin made it his business to point out several fixes around the house before heading off again to terrorise another tenant down the road.

'Well, that's me done. Don't forget those gutters too, David, they'll clog up now in a good blast of rain and you don't want the front yard to be flooded, thanks,' he barked, before taking off in his 2021 Mercedes.

EMIGRATION

HIGH RENTS, HIGH UNEMPLOYMENT: WHY WON'T YOUNG PEOPLE GET THE MESSAGE AND EMIGRATE?

DUE TO BEING held in higher esteem by young people than TikTok, *WWN* has been asked by the Department of No Jobs to use its influence to engage with younger generations and ask why they can't take a hint.

'I would emigrate only there's a pandemic you fucking clowns' is an understandable response to such inquiries from the government, but its special Seriously Though, Fuck Off Unit (STFOU) couldn't have made its feelings any clearer. It's almost like you want to be stuck in Ireland, priced out of a life.

'We just don't get it, we're trying our best here to make it a foregone conclusion, but we're worried you don't feel robbed of a decent chance

at a nice life enough to head off to Australia, the UK or Canada,' confirmed a STFOU spokesperson.

'We made Simon Harris join TikTok, for Christ's sake, we can't make our condescending contempt any clearer. We've no homes or jobs for you lot, so time to head off.

'Terrible pay and working conditions for nurses and doctors, zero respect for teachers, making Dublin hard to afford even if you're Elon Musk ... if we can do much, much less to help you, please let us know, whatever gets you looking up Skyscanner flights,' added the spokesperson.

'We clearly need feedback and getting back to the drawing board, because all the gaslighting doesn't seem to work either. We banned co-living while also letting it just carry on, for example. We love boasting about social progress, upping the minimum wage, paternity leave and

all that bollocks, but we probably need to work harder at crushing your resolve, so any tips are welcome,' they continued.

'Do you need to see more tents? Cus we can do more tent villages if ye like. Just say the word and we'll have a treasured cultural institution flattened and replaced by a sparkling hotel within the hour,' the spokesperson enthused.

Conspiracy Corner

Countess Markievicz was the sixth Spice Girl.

PRODUCT RECALL ISSUED IN IRELAND FOR FAULTY PROPERTY LADDERS

AN EMERGENCY RECALL of Irish-built property ladders has been issued by manufacturers citing a number of serious faults that render the product virtually unusable.

Certified as 'grand' by the Department of Housing, the property ladders, sold exclusively in local free markets, have now been deemed not fit for purpose after routine health and safety checks.

'See this one? Well for a start it's covered in grease. You try getting on that you'll slip right off,' explained product testing expert Brian Carmody.

Carmody also found that 100 per cent of ladders tested had a defect

whereby the bottom rung breaks off completely once a person has themselves climbed to the second step, while a number of previous ladder owners reported losing their shirts.

'It's shocking that anyone thought these property ladders were a good idea,' added Carmody after discovering the ladders are also completely user-unfriendly for renters.

'When the first rung breaks away it causes panic in the person trying to get on, and out of a desire to preserve one's place further up the ladder, those on a higher rung tend to kick down.'

Despite the urgent recall, a number of estate agents, second homeowners and developers have been seen clutching onto their ladders for dear life and claiming that they would resort to violence if anyone tried to take them away.

In response to the news of the product recall, the government rubbished the move, stating that only experienced ladder climbers they knew personally or investment funds should ever be allowed to purchase a ladder.

TIMELINE
THE HOUSING CRISIS: A TIMELINE

1566 AD – English Crown forces begin confiscating land from Irish people. Early forms of US vulture funds begin furiously taking notes. The act of kicking out native populations in favour of 'civilising' areas with foreign workers is also said to be the inspiration for modern-day Grand Canal Dock, Dublin.

1641 Rebellion – Phelim O'Neill leads a bloody uprising against the confiscation of land from native Irish people. It results in the deaths of an estimated 4,000 Protestants, often through indiscriminate attacks. People will be familiar with the modern equivalent to O'Neill's fight today, which involves a tweet with a picture of a daft.ie bedsit going viral.

1695–1778 Penal Laws – A series of discriminatory laws, which included a number of property laws discriminating against Irish Catholics and Protestant Dissenters. Successive Fine Gael governments have been accused of largely plagiarising aspects of the laws.

1879 The Land Wars – Irish National Land League set up by Michael Davitt, who leads agitation for 'the land for the people'. The Land Commission, which allowed farmers to buy farms from landowners, is set up. Famously, according to current Sinn Féin historians, his final words were 'carry on my legacy, Mary Lou McDonald'.

1913 Lockout – The working poor refused to accept the squalid living and working conditions as well as the stagnant wages that existed as a machine of profit for absentee landlords. More on this later.

1930s–1950s – Some 55 per cent of all housing built was social housing. Poor people were offered dignity, and believed they had a right to a decent life and contentment. Foolish Irish politicians vow to never make this mistake again.

1950s–1980s – With the encouragement of successive governments, property developers tear down characterless Georgian buildings across Dublin and replace them with the iconic grey office blocks we know and love today.

1930s–1980s – The government saves on social housing for single mothers by locking them up in Laundries and Mother and Baby Homes. This is regrettably not an option now, thanks to something called 'feminism'.

1990 Celtic Tiger – What sort of loser doesn't own 12 apartments in Bulgaria?!

2008 Banking Crisis – Helpless bankers left with no choice but to accept taxpayers' money from the government. Subsequently, helpless property developers accept money from NAMA for worthless assets.

2011 – Ghost estates haunt the dreams of landlord TDs. NAMA sells apartment blocks to cuckoo funds for the price of a Freddo bar.

2018 – Helpless property developers accept public land from the

Historical Facts

Archaeologists have surmised that the Salmon of Knowledge was actually the Eel of Cute Hoorology.

The Year in Numbers

678 – the number of 'Live Laugh Love' signs in your aunt's house.

government to build houses on as part of the Land Development Agency.

2019 – Government economists and PR spin teams explain why your brain is too small to understand why giving €700 million in Housing Assistance Payments every year to landlords is better than building homes.

2020 – The working poor and working-actually-doing-alright-for-myself refuse to accept the squalid living and working conditions as well as the stagnant wages that existed as a machine of profit for absentee landlords.

Present day – The government discovers a housing crisis. Opposition parties confirm they have the secret solution to the crisis, but you have to vote for them first.

HOME OF THE YEAR

'BE A NIGHTMARE TO HEAT THOUGH', CONFIRMS MAN OF EVERY HOUSE ON 'HOME OF THE YEAR'

ONE LOCAL MAN has revealed a talent for scoffing at every single entrant into RTÉ's popular *Home of the Year* TV show, *WWN* can confirm.

Whether it's a restoration, modern build or one-off ambitious architectural feat powered by 100 per cent carbon-neutral notions, Eoin Neyland can't stop himself from disparaging every home on the grounds of how they would be a nightmare to heat.

'You wouldn't just be burning peat with that one, you'd be burning your money. Good luck, I'd take our home

over that monstrosity,' shared Eoin with his wife Mairead, as *HOTY* judge Hugh Wallace made his way round an open-plan home with energy-efficient underfloor heating and a kitchen made out of solar panels.

'Sure, it's nice, but ESB would be riding ya with the bills,' tutted Eoin, narrowing his eyes in search for obvious draught points in the home.

Working in perfect tandem, Mairead has exclusive rights to disparage all interior decor in the homes, while sitting on the couple's pinky-brown couch with matching Batman curtains

they've had for the last 15 years.

'Yuck, who decorated that, Stevie Wonder?' Mairead offered, as Eoin correctly identified an open window in the background.

'An open window? And this was probably filmed in winter? Jesus, they'll be personally funding pay rises at Electric Ireland,' observed Eoin.

The couple then rounded off their watching of the show by complaining about how the winning home was less deserving of a place in the final than a slowly collapsing shed.

County Knowledge

Limerick

The affluent county of Limerick maintains a lavish lifestyle thanks to a fortune made from the sale of short, five-line humorous poems.

Home to actor Richard Harris, the first person to drink a table under him.

Residents of Newcastle West speak with an impenetrable Geordie accent.

FOR SALE

HERE'S SOME IRISH HOUSES FOR SALE FOR UNDER €100K, YOU POOR SAD PATHETIC PRICKS

HERE'S AN ARTICLE on cheap Irish property to satisfy those of you who can't afford a respectably priced home, provided as an act of kindness in the hopes of balancing out all the unaffordable homes we've been paid to write about over the past decade.

We promise not to scoff at the following dwellings, despite the fact that you can still barely afford any of them, you poor sad pathetic pricks.

2 Bedroom Terraced ▶ House Somewhere Inaccessible to Anywhere for €87k
Would you look at the fucking state ... okay, I know we said we wouldn't belittle these properties, but wow, what a shithole, right? Surely we can come up with something better and for less money than this ball of shite. Moving on.

2/3 Bedroom Detached ▶ Home in Driving Distance to Anywhere in Ireland for Just €99k
Well, at least it's detached, we suppose. It comes

with detached windows too. Detached chimney, detached electrical wiring from the grid, detached feelings of resentment when you're looking at how much it will cost to refurbish this mess. Sure, once you've

those windows in, you can recycle the timber boards and make some rustic kitchen units. Imagine the fun you'll have, creating. Just think of it as a blank canvas you found in a skip.

▲ 1 Bed Detached Cottage Overlooking Some Ditches for €50k

We've had to do the old black-and-white desaturation trick here to hide the shit-stained walls, but if you close your eyes hard enough you can imagine this property teeming with life. Microbiological life, but life none the less. It even has its own tree growing through the cracks. Cool.

▼ 4 Bedroom End of Terrace Redbricked Family Home

Ideal for people who don't mind homes with violent histories, this fantastic period property will set you back €150k and will make … ah shite, sorry. We've just realised this is way over your budget. Far too big for your lot, anyway. Ye'd only get notions.

5 Bedroom Country ▶ Manor Complete with Its Own Garage for €70k

Technically in Ireland, this Aran Island home is ideal for people who want to recreate the time and effort it took to build the Pyramids in Giza. Imagine all the fun in working out how in the name of fuck you're going to bring all the materials needed to this barren landscape. Yes, it will probably take a lifetime and cost an arm and a leg to do up, but at least you'll have something to give to your kids to sell off the moment you're dead.

▲ 1/2/3/4/5/6 Bedroom Doer-Upper for €98k

We're pretty sure the beautiful red bricks alone would cost €98k, but seriously, don't take our word on that. Yeah, it might seem like a lot of work, but just look at how sunny it is there. Like, do you even need a roof, really? This would make a great project for someone who loves camping and living in the great outdoors. You know the types. We're sure this will be snapped up.

▲ 2 Bedroom Mountaintop Cottage with Own Windows for €76k

Now you're talking. This is right up your street. However, the nearest street is about 90 kilometres away. But it comes with its own installed windows and original door. Imagine the history attached to this place, and the solitude of being on top of one of Ireland's highest mountains. This is truly an amazing find. No need to thank us.

▼ 3 Bedroom Fully Elevated Prefab Home for €25k

This flood-proof property in Athlone is ideal for the family on the go. It was originally based upstream, so why not enjoy the ride, as seasonal flooding brings your family to a new field annually. This fully fitted mobile is highly recommended, and we expect to see it go quite fast, depending on the current.

EDITOR'S NOTE:
Unfortunately, the estate agent you were dealing with has confirmed that someone else has come in with a bid that is €150k above the asking price. Can't match that? Have you considered just starving yourself and putting money you normally spend on food into your savings?

WWN GUIDE

LOOPHOLES FOR CUCKOO FUNDS, A GOVERNMENT GUIDE

ARE YOU an investment fund planning on hoovering up the Irish housing market but worried that new rules introduced by the government might harm your chances?

Well then, this is the guide for you. Worry not, the Irish government is on hand to personally guide you through all the loopholes you can easily exploit:

- First off, for the few of you investment funds we didn't already give a heads up to about all this, or who didn't give us some of our best ideas, don't worry, this is very much a case of doing the bare minimum to the point of doing fuck all.
- All that rent you're collecting, don't worry, the old 'you don't have to pay any tax on that' arrangement is here to stay.
- We've added a rate of 10 per cent stamp duty on any individual or fund buying 10 homes or more over a 12-month period. But there's nothing stopping you setting up a bunch of shell companies to buy multiple sets of nine homes, thus avoiding the 10 per cent charge.
- But hey, with billions to invest it's not like you'll even hesitate to carry on buying 10 units that once cost you €350k each that will now cost €385k each. It's almost like this doesn't act like a deterrent at all.
- It'll be a few years before any of this takes effect, and existing planning permissions will be exempt, so for the time being make like a young one in pyjamas sprinting through a reopened Penneys and buy fucking everything! Don't say we don't look after you guys!
- Now, some of you have reported sightings of Eoin Ó Broin and Cian O'Callaghan staring a hole through your souls from behind the bushes outside your offices. Sadly, we can't do anything about that at the minute. Maybe we can pay for the therapy if you require it.
- As everyone, including ourselves in government, knows, only idiot losers would think an apartment qualifies as a 'home', which is why we didn't extend the rule, which means 50 per cent of new housing estates must be sold to owner-occupiers.

- Oh, and you see that 50 per cent figure? That's actually at the discretion of local councils. So a council can reduce that 50 per cent to 0 per cent if they like.
- Basically lads, the country's cities are yours to do what you want with. And don't worry, we'll keep paying you hundreds of millions in HAP as a thank you for buying apartments that could have fallen into the wrong hands, aka working families.
- We increased councillors' pay to €25k there the other day, so that eliminates any risk that a councillor could be induced to side with investment funds in exchange for a future roll with a property company or the like.
- Irish Residential Properties PLC's share price rose by nearly 4 per cent off the back of our announcements to 'crack down' on funds, and we in government can only apologise that we couldn't facilitate a bigger increase. We'll endeavour to do so next 'crack down' time.
- If you need any customer service assistance and further hand holding when it comes to making the most of the loopholes, we are reachable at the usual number!

Predictions for 2022

Pavee Point intervenes after Wanderly Wagon makes the news for parking on a public lay-by in a standoff with the local council.

COUPLE GET THAT DUBLIN IS OVERPRICED KIP BUT THEY'RE STILL NOT MOVING TO CARLOW

DESPITE NEWS that Dublin rental prices decreased to levels that mean a rancid bedsit the size of a shrivelled grape is only €1,400 a month, one local couple have maintained their stance that the capital is not enough of an overpriced kip to consider moving to Carlow.

'Stabbings becoming an Olympic sport, soul-crushing rent, traffic looking like a sequel to *The Human Centipede* – it's not all that bad when you consider the alternative,' explained tired, exhausted, sick of everything couple Tracy Lownes and David Fillon.

The Year in Numbers

1.5mn – the number of houses Sinn Féin said it would have built this year if it was in power, all for a fiver too.

'Sure we're halfway to becoming Travis Bickle in this good-for-nothing city, but c'mon, Carlow or wherever isn't the answer,' the couple offered, batting back the prospect of cleaner air, lower rent, better quality of life, all the good things.

While they wouldn't go so far as to say they're 'happy' living in an epidemic of hotel-building, the couple are suffering from pronounced 'Dublin Syndrome', which leaves them unable to see that living in the capital is draining them of their life force.

'It actually kind of helps pass the time, going for a stroll and pointing at

> **'It actually kind of helps pass the time, going for a stroll and pointing at hotels and saying things like "that used to be a pub, music venue or people",'**

hotels and saying things like "that used to be a pub, music venue or people",' offered David.

'And there's our jobs – sure the jobs market in Dublin, that's where it's at,' Tracy added, of the jobs the couple can easily do via working from home these days.

Unwilling to put a figure on a high level of rent that would force them out of the city, the couple remained optimistic that Dublin would turn things around.

'We've the white-water rafting facility on the way, don't forget, and we'll have great fun watching people who can actually afford to pay to use it,' said the couple.

PLANNING

OBJECTION ERECTION: MEET THE FREAKS WHO GET OFF ON LODGING PLANNING OBJECTIONS

WHILE THE WORLD remains in a state of near-constant chaos, thankfully some things remain reassuringly normal.

The hardcore and seedy behaviour of serial planning-permission objectors is a central part of Irish life. To get a

better understanding of those who pursue objection erections, *WWN* met the freaks who climax at the thought of striking down someone's hopes and dreams of building a south-facing front porch.

'I sometimes take pictures of planning permission signs for wank material later,' shared one freak, who admitted he and his fellow objection fetishists sometimes delayed gratification by waiting until the very last possible minute to lodge an objection.

'Even just imagining the sound of some poor soul hammering a planning application notice into the ground outside their home can get me hard. All that hope, consulting with an architect, the fees involved, and

> **'Even just imagining the sound of some poor soul hammering a planning application notice into the ground outside their home can get me hard.'**

they've no idea I'm going to steamroll in with "not in keeping with the tenor of the area" or "blocks out the sunlight". Fuck it, I've just done a mess in my pants,' confirmed one excited freak.

The objection community frequently send each other lewd images of families standing outside homes with measuring tapes saying, 'imagine a seomra here', getting off on the prospect of halting their dreams.

'I can sniff out a planning application notice from 500 metres away,' shared a veteran PPRS (Planning Permission Rejection Sadist).

Others in the objection community also get off on having their own applications rejected.

'It's no good having it rejected by some other PPRS deviant, it needs to be done by your average member of the public. Last year I applied for permission to build a 14-storey apartment block where my garden shed is. I picked something really ridiculous, cus I knew the objections would come flooding in,' explained a Planning Permission Rejection Masochist.

However, sometimes their pursuit of the next objection-based titillation can go wrong.

'I went a bit far one time; for a laugh I lodged an application for a white-water rafting place in Dublin city centre. Fuck me, even though it was initially accepted – the amount of objections – I was ejaculating dust after a while. They'd sucked me dry, I nearly died from it,' confirmed one sick puppy.

MINISTER FOR HOUSING DREADING JOB WHEN THERE'S NO COVID EXCUSE

WAKING from yet another lucid dream where he's now a Minister for Housing in a post-pandemic world free of lockdown restrictions and excuses, Fianna Fáil TD Darragh O'Brien desperately reached for

a glass of water beside his bed to wash down that coarse, horrible feeling of pressure in his throat.

'Urgh, how much longer can I get away with this coasting? Hopefully someone will call an election or reshuffle before I actually have to do some work,' he croaked to himself, beads of salted sweat gathering on his pale, throbbing chest.

With future newspaper headlines now spiralling around his frantic mind, O'Brien began attempting to excuse his future inevitable failures, many of them too predictable and all too real for his liking.

'"Housing Minister with Shares in Cuckoo Fund Is What's Wrong with

Irish Politics", "O'Brien Responsible for Lowest Social Builds in Ministerial History", "Mica Homes to Cost State Billions" – oh boy, I wish there was a pause button for this role right now,' he yelped, now humming and rocking in his bed to bring calm.

When he rang the Taoiseach in a panic, O'Brien's number was screened by the country's leader, sending him straight to voicemail.

'If this is Darragh again, relax, breathe,' began the pre-recorded answering machine of the Taoiseach. 'We've talked about this before. Remember, we don't have to do anything about this. We just have to *say* we are. Repeat after me – "we can't solve the housing crisis overnight". Now, that bought Fine Gael 10 years, so it should do the same for us. Back to bed now like a good lad.'

Waterford Whispers News

VOL 1.20156136   WATERFORD, SATURDAY, NOVEMBER 11, 1989   20p

Calls For Veil Ban on Oppressed Irish Women

RENEWED calls were made this week to ban head and facial coverings for Irish women who have remained oppressed under the Catholic church regime for the past several hundred years, *WWN* reports.

Currently, women of all ages have been pressured by the church to cover their heads and face while also being expected to wear long ankle-length skirts to hide their bodies from vulnerable men.

'The fact that every single woman in Ireland walks around covered from head to toe is indicative of the power the Catholic church has over its followers here,' said a campaigner to allow women wear what they want. 'Ireland seems to be living in some kind of religious bubble based on fear with male

priests and bishops at the helm – dictating what society does and even wears.' The proposed ban on shawls and headscarves is expected to be discussed in the Dáil later this week; however, local bishop Dermot Lacey has slammed the calls as the work of Satan himself.

'I knew this would happen; didn't I say that when we gave them the vote? Next, they'll be asserting their opinions on things. That's Ireland ruined for centuries. I actually talked to plenty of women who say their minds are too small and fragile to be given the responsibility to dress themselves, and that they're happy for men to decide for them.'

'No, you can't talk to them, but that's word for word what they said.'

FINANCE

VULTURE FUNDS SEEN CIRCLING OVER ULSTER BANK BRANCHES

DESPITE ROBUST LAWS in place to protect mortgage holders and a pledge for a gradual closing down to take place over several years, Ulster Bank branch security guards have spent the day trying to fend off ravenous packs of vultures, *WWN* can confirm.

With the departing bank's mortgage book presenting a tempting investment opportunity for anyone with enough money and absolutely no concern for mortgage holders, the skies outside branches have been dominated by the sight of birds of prey.

'Jesus, it's like someone sewed a few seagulls together and injected them with pure evil,' shouted one employee as he waved a broom in the air trying to disperse the growing presence of vultures, who love nothing more than to claw away at carcasses.

'We thought we could just shoot them for being a nuisance and intimidating customers, but it turns out they're a protected species with special treatment from the government,' added the guard, who sadly will be one of 2,800 people to lose their jobs as a result of Ulster Bank leaving the Irish market.

A spokesperson for the vultures said that there is nothing to worry about, and that, if anything, Ireland doesn't know how lucky it is to have these vultures circling them constantly, and no, you're mistaken, the vulture didn't just shit on you.

'Look, I understand. I'd be a bit scared by the sight of vultures trying to swoop down on my mortgage too, but protections are in place, which means your mortgage could end up being

County Knowledge

Tyrone

Every Toblerone in the world was made in Tyrone until the mid-1980s, when production shifted to Europe due to a shortage of triangles.

Tyrone: not bad for a county named after a lad off of *Coronation Street*.

Tyrone is one of the most likely Irish counties to sleep with yer ma.

switched to a number of banks such as this one here that shafted thousands, this one that was bailed out by the taxpayer or this other one that was always bailed out too,' confirmed a Central Bank official.

WW news
Waterford Whispers News

It Was A Different

TIME

JANUARY 2021

Nun The Wiser: Our Guide
To Losing The Records Of
What Child Went Where

"She's only lying,
don't listen to her"

€8bn In Funds:
The Church Hasn't The
Money For Compensation

Not Sure Adoption Is Right
For Your Baby? Let Us Decide

NOTHING TO SEE HERE | NO SUCH FILES EXIST, SORRY | ENOUGH TIME HAS PASSED

WWN GUIDES

CRYPTO

'CLASSIC PUMP AND DUMP', AND OTHER ANNOYING PHRASES YOUR CRYPTO MATES HAVE PICKED UP

CONDUCTING the proper research on cryptocurrencies such as Bitcoin may require a would-be investor to explore many complicated areas. One such area is simply learning the basic crypto jargon to impress your fellow peers. *WWN* has compiled the best and most used phrases for your perusal.

'Classic pump and dump'
You will hear this go-to phrase a lot from 'crypto bros' who want to denounce any currency that's not of their liking, mostly high-risk 'fad' cryptocurrencies such as Dogecoin. Thrown around a lot, 'classic pump and dump' refers to the orchestrated investment in a new coin, causing it to temporarily surge, and then selling it off before it crashes. However, this is never to be confused with investing in Bitcoin, as Bitcoin isn't like that, and probably safer than houses if houses were virtual and stored on servers and online cloud-based systems in the most secure place to keep your money in the world – the internet.

'Fuck Elon Musk, the fucking prick'
Usually said after one of the weekly Elon Musk tweets that send all crypto crashing, 'fuck Elon Musk, the fucking prick' is probably one of the most common phrases your crypto mates use to express their dismay at their Bitcoin value plunging below their initial investment. This phrase is usually followed by an uncertain facial expression and an unconvincing quip of 'ah no, it's okay though, I'm in it for the long game anyway – Bitcoin is the future'.

'I really wish Musk would shut his hole'
You will find that a lot of common crypto phrases include the South African billionaire, as 'the world's most revolutionary new currencies' seemingly depend on his every word, but don't let this put you off, as Bitcoin is the future and 'will become one of the most important ways to pay for things and transfer assets', its whole price depending of course on what Elon Musk tweets that week. But don't let that stop you investing all your money in it. Bitcoin is the future of humanity and will kill all the corrupt banks.

'Why have you not got onto crypto yet?'
Usually said in between Elon Musk tweets during a steady, uninterrupted surge in price, proud crypto bros will utter this phrase in the hopes of getting you on board and making themselves feel like some kind of super clued-in cryptocurrency guru destined for billionaire stardom. This is usually followed by lengthy jargon-ridden waffle that they're just regurgitating from Reddit with promises of 'I'll show you how'.

'Ah for fuck's sake, Musk, shut up, you absolute bollocks'
Yes, there is a bit of a pattern here, but investing in crypto is the future, despite the whole thing seemingly being influenced by an unhinged billionaire.

SOCIAL MEDIA

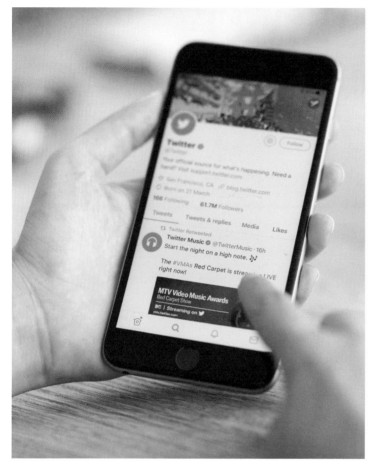

2) Double down

When called to task over something you tweeted by a fellow Twitter user, a hate crime victim or indeed the family of a grieving celebrity that ended their life after an online pile-on that you contributed to, don't back down. In fact, go harder again. What's the worst that can happen? If the first tweet has ruined your life, what's a few more? If anything, your follow-ups should be even more outrageous. You're a loose cannon, baby! You're just telling it like it is!

3) Enjoy your new job

So okay, you've been booted out of your job for comments made on Twitter that, in a certain light, could be construed as being 'sexist' or 'anti-Semitic'. Don't fret – if you've done it right and you've got enough Twitter followers to begin with, you can easily parlay this negative energy into a successful career in the media. RTÉ, Newstalk, VM1, Today FM, they'd all love to have you on as 'balance' during arguments that you've no experience in. You might even get a weekly newspaper column out of it! You've made it! It's all gravy from here!

PS: What you're saying on Twitter doesn't have to be offensive, ill-timed or hurtful to ruin your life. It can also just be really, genuinely stupid.

RUINING YOUR LIFE WITH A TWEET, A GUIDE

Ah, Twitter. Since its inception, millions of people have managed to totally wreck their entire lives with the swipe of a finger – but if you're still not sure how to get cancelled in 280 characters or less, then follow these steps.

1) Don't fact check

Yes, you could do a little research into each tweet you send, but that would fly in the face of the rollercoaster ride that is social media. Just tweet it! If you're wrong, who cares? Sure, a lot of people will be angry with you, maybe your boss might want a word or two, but there's every chance that as many as six people will give you a 'like' on your post. That's free dopamine right there!

GLAD-HANDING

THE LOST ART OF BROWN ENVELOPING

'Some younger politicians today, if you gave them an envelope it'd be like handing a child a slinky. Only us old timers are keeping the skill alive'

THE ADVENT of online banking and offshore accounts has ruined the noble art of glad-handing and bribery, according to a new report that reminisces fondly on the days that when you wanted something done, you first had to make a trip to the stationery store.

'If I wanted to get a politician to grant me planning permission today, I'd have to get one of my grandkids to do that whole cryptocurrency, dark web transaction craic. Back in the day, it was much more personal,' said one ageing property developer we spoke to, enjoying his retirement in luxury despite being officially declared bankrupt.

'People always say "brown envelope", but any colour would do, and you'd stuff it full of cash. You kids have probably never smelled five grand in twenties, have you? Amazing smell. Then you'd ring the guy. Not text, ring, and arrange to meet him someplace, and then the switch was made. He wouldn't even count it, because he knew you and knew he was dealing with an honest guy.'

Although the art of physical brown enveloping may have died off during the economic disaster, when the birth of the smartphone meant it was too risky and traceable to actually meet with the person you were bribing, many purists still to this day forgo the

much easier, much more untraceable world of offshore banking for that thrill of a wad of money in your overcoat pocket.

'It's a muscle memory – you never lose it,' said one former politician we spoke to, who can still get things done for the right price.

'You never put your hand out for it; you just take it when it's offered. Never discuss the business there and then, just talk about golf or the weather. Then walk away with it. It's an art form. You can't teach it.

'Some younger politicians today, if you gave them an envelope it'd be like handing a child a slinky. Only us old timers are keeping the skill alive, and soon we'll be gone. Then all bribery is going to be online, which I think is a shame.'

Further investigation into the decline of brown enveloping has shown that it's been years since a politician has asked their tailor to make extra-large overcoat pockets – just another economic casualty of regulation gone mad.

Predictions for 2022

If the US can spend two decades and trillions of dollars in Afghanistan to replace the Taliban with the Taliban, then you can convince your ex to take you back.

DRINKING

ALCOHOL-FREE GUINNESS NOT BAD WITH A SHOT OF GIN IN IT: READ OUR REVIEW

MADE FROM A SECRET recipe that Arthur Guinness demanded he be buried with, Guinness 0.0 promises drinkers the same Guinness taste that everyone loves and agrees is the best part of Guinness, but without any of that cumbersome drunkenness that has had people on the fence about the stout from day one.

So how is Guinness 0.0? Well, the can opens with a familiar widgetty hiss that suggests you're about to have an experience just as amazing as any other can of half-warm Guinness you ever poured into a Budweiser glass you stole from a pub, and the pour is sure to draw as many 'you're not doing it right' heckles from onlooking amateur barmen as ever before.

The quintessential Guinness taste of rusty nails hits the palette with the same 'I'll just have one but really sixteen' rush as before, but the zero-alcohol nature of the drink really begins to sink in after the fourth can, when all your worries, woes and problems remain as front and centre as they ever were, in no way washed away as they normally are at this stage.

In fact, this reviewer felt no urge to text his ex after even six cans, prompting a gearshift in order to salvage what was turning out to be a pretty ho-hum wake.

It seems the key ingredient of Guinness, the alcohol, is missing in this new Guinness zero product, and they really weren't messing – you can drink

this stuff all day and not even get a bit of a buzz; trust us, we tried it. As our cans floated one by one down the water of the canal we sat beside, we didn't feel the warm embrace of a beer coat. In fact, we felt cold and emotionless. Something had to be done.

We added clear spirits such as vodka and gin to the pour, which maintained the classic black Guinness pour but added the joy of booze back into the mix. And in a stroke of good fortune, our six pack of gin-powered Guinness 0.0 worked out cheaper than just buying normal cans of Guinness, given that the zero variety of Guinness has already ended up in the '8 for a fiver' bargain bin. Result!

Historical Facts

World War II was single-handedly won by the Russians, the Americans and the British.

GETTING YOUR PARENTS BANNED FROM SOCIAL MEDIA FOR GOOD, A GUIDE

THEY'RE AT IT again. No matter how hard you try to avoid their public social media rantings and trolling comments with questionable racial undertones, your parents continue to live and breathe online in some kind of warped punishment that you never earned.

Surprisingly, or not, Facebook has never banned your folks for their online behaviour. Sure, Dad was banned for 24 hours for that Hitler joke about the gas bill that time, but contrary to all morality, relying on a social media platform to make sure people are compliantly social isn't down to the social media platform, apparently, so let's get creative.

Hiring a team of Singapore-based hackers to infiltrate your mother and father's social media accounts to plant horrific posts denying the Holocaust might seem like a very expensive and extreme move, but have you seen Mam's latest Journal.ie comment regarding her stance on Meghan Markle? Seriously, you are either in this or not.

Ask the hackers to throw in some texts orchestrating a terrorist cell. Call the FBI and report them. Interpol too. The last thing you want is Facebook giving them a lame 30-day ban and your parent returning to haunt your life once again with more vile opinions.

Now, we're not saying planting thousands of euros worth of drugs in your parents' home is the way forward here, but it's certainly a goer. Let's face it: it's only a matter of time before they join TikTok, so framing your folks in a bid to have them locked away for 5 to 10 may be a fantastic option for you. By the time they leave prison they'll be so old and tired they'll have lost all will to live and never log on again. Let's see Dad giving out about Direct Provision in 2031 then! Lol.

Sometimes you've got to get your hands dirty. Anything to stop your mam's comments about the Travelling community on news articles showing up on your feed, so accusing her of having an affair will not only get Dad angry, but it may also cause them to split up and finally highlight the dangers of social media to both of them. Play both parents off of each other. Telling your dad that Mam has been cheating on him with several people online since before you can remember will leave him devastated, but at least you will never again have to see his confusing pro-Sinn Féin anti-Republicanism posts.

Some easier ways to get them banned:

- Tell them to post a picture of a nipple on their feed as part of a cancer awareness campaign.
- Report them for slightly criticising Israel's settlements in the West Bank.
- Report any songs or music they shared in the past for copyright infringement.
- Or simply claim they called Mark Zuckerberg a thin-skinned little prick.

Predictions for 2022

With workers now opting to work remotely, Dublin quickly becomes a barren wasteland ruled by Mad Maxesque working-class pirates terrorising the streets on e-scooters.

IN-DEPTH GUIDE

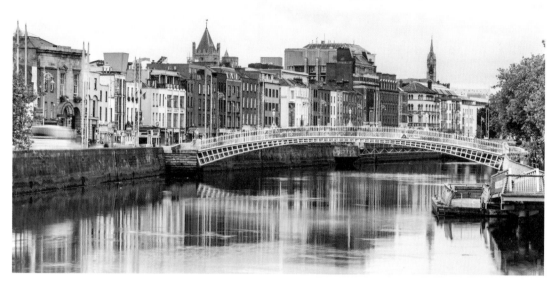

TAKING PEOPLE FROM DUBLIN DOWN A PEG OR TWO, WE SHOW YOU HOW

WITH ALL THE ARROGANCE of Cork, but marginally more insufferable accents, people from Dublin think too highly of themselves, it's often said.

WWN is here to help you take them down a peg or two lest they drown in their notion-riddled smugness:

- Always accompany the phrase 'The Big Shmoke' with condescending air quotes. Otherwise, only ever call it 'The Pale'.
- Point out that Dublin's only any craic at all because of the townies and culchies that moved there.
- Ask them how much rent they're paying. Warning: this one isn't for the faint-hearted; expect tears.
- Continuously edit the Dublin Wikipedia page to state that the city was founded by Vikings as somewhere to stop off for a slash on the way to a good city.
- Talk about O'Connell Street the way you would an intriguing trip to the zoo.
- Throw in a 'Sure, we have a rampant drug problem as well, but at least we have the decency to hide it.'
- Denigrate Trinity College at every turn. (This may prove hurtful to your non-Dublin friends who went there. This is an added bonus.)

'Sure, we have a rampant drug problem as well, but at least we have the decency to hide it.'

Housing Ladder Tips

Secure your home by bidding €400k over the asking price.

- Sometimes it is best to just sit back and let Dubliners eviscerate their own county, which is basically just one giant hotel at this point.
- Start giving the city a derogatory nickname so awful, for example 'Stablin' or 'Druglin', that it will irritate Dubliners to such an extent that they'd sooner rip their ears off than hear it one more time.
- Slowly steal everything in the city. There's thousands of non-Dubs living in town, so next time you head home to see the folks, take something with you. A hanging basket. A park bench. Clean the place out, it'll only take a few months.
- Remind them repeatedly about all the miniature Union Jacks they waved at the visiting queen or king or whoever it was that time, just remind them, the pricks. And never let it go.
- Laugh at the fact that they have no idea what a Zetor is, or how to drive one. Losers.

EDUCATION

GUIDE TO BEING A MATURE STUDENT

ARE YOU ONE of the thousands of Irish adults who has realised that holding down a mediocre job in a post-pandemic world doesn't have the same security it once held, and are now actively seeking to up-skill and re-educate yourself out of fear of being yet another discarded citizen stuck on the fringes of a spiralling rich/poor divide?

Great! WWN has put together this handy go-to guide for budding mature students returning to college this year.

Before you begin, please don't be intimidated by the fact that you are an older student attending a college full of young, energised teenagers. By the time they get their heads out of their phones you will already be halfway through your first year. Plus, they will blatantly ignore you anyway, once they find out how old you are.

They will either think you're a bit slow or a narc planted there to lift the lid on the college drug scene. Either scenario leads to the same treatment.

While attending lectures, always make sure to keep all of your obvious questions until the very end of the class to hold everyone else up from leaving the room/Zoom. Ignore all the deep sighs from your younger college peers while the lecturer stares vacantly at your ridiculously stupid question.

Relish in the fact that you're the only one listening to the obvious answer that you should have already known but didn't due to working at the same monotonous job for the past 20 years that has left your brain redundant.

Never speak to younger members of the opposite sex unless spoken too. Even the bare mention of a little johnny joke can have you put on the sex offenders register these days, so just be mindful that what was funny in the 1980s is now a full-blown crime, carrying with it severe consequences.

Don't tell anyone your real age, as people under the age of 25 are unable to comprehend why an 'old person is back in college'. Such thoughts in young people can lead them to understand that life isn't as predictable and rosy as those people in the TikTok videos.

Never reveal the reasons why your partner left you and why your own kids don't talk to you anymore, and that this is your last chance at making something of yourself – these kids need hope and optimism, not the exact opposite, e.g. your life.

If forced to attend a 'night out', always just stick around for the one before sneaking off right before the shots stage. If you stay post-shots, you're destined to end up creeping on someone half your age before ending up crying on the steps outside a nightclub, stuffing bits of kebab into your mouth that you drunkenly dropped on the wet road.

Finally, just have fun with it. This will be the best six months of your life before you finally drop out due to stress from the academic workload and end up taking a range of benzos for the remainder of your life. And never forget: at least you tried.

EMPLOYMENT

UNEMPLOYED? HERE'S HOW TO GET A JOB ACCORDING TO A LAD WHO WORKS FOR HIS DAD

WITH CSO FIGURES revealing that Ireland's unemployment rate remains stubbornly high, it's never been more important to take advice on the job market, and today *WWN* hears from employment expert Joshua Daly, currently employed by his father.

'Unemployment is a state of mind at the end of the day.

'If I've said it once I've said it a thousand times, you don't have to be poor – it's a choice. Look at me, I could have been poor, but I made the choice to accept my dad's offer of a high five-figure salary.

'And before you have a go and spout off your unfiltered raging jealousy, I got my job on merit when I dropped out of college in first year without any relevant experience, and Dad's mate in the guards tidied up all that "unpleasantness" from that college party.

> **'I could have just gone on the dole like a pathetic person, but instead I let my dad give me a job after weeks of my mother crying and begging him to do it.'**

'Dress for the job you want, not the one you don't have. Take me for example. I could have just gone on the dole like a pathetic person, but instead I let my dad give me a job after weeks of my mother crying and begging him to do it.

'It's really that easy, and if you haven't done what I've done, chances are you're lazy and you're wrongly blaming others for your predicament and not taking responsibility.

'Taking responsibility is huge. I should know: if I hadn't paid the cleaner's son for a clean piss sample, I would've had to serve out the suspended sentence for that other thing my dad's mate in the guards couldn't tidy up.

'Get out your phone and just get in touch with whatever family member is independently wealthy and can afford to take on some dead weight that adds absolutely nothing to the company.

'Or do like my mate Roggo and just get a friend who is already in the company to hire you over much more qualified candidates.

'And fucking quit it with the "my whole industry has been shut down by the pandemic" sob story. Jesus, you lot want something for nothing, don't you? You should have thought about your career choice properly years ago and accounted for a pandemic occurring at some point.'

PARENTING

PHRASES TO USE IN PUBLIC TO CONVINCE PEOPLE YOU'RE A GREAT PARENT

PORTRAYING YOURSELF as the perfect mother or father in a public setting is one of the hardest things you can do when dealing with contrary, anxiety-inducing kids who are too dumb to even get the concept of reputation. Choosing the right phrases to say loudly so everyone can hear is key to saving face in public. Below you will find some quick and easy phrases to use to show everyone how great a parent you are.

'And what begins with the letter "A", Lorcan? That's right, an apple! Good boy'

You're out walking with your moaning toddler. A stranger is about to walk past and judge you. You need to think fast before your little shit breaks into a cry. Smile and look like you're being really attentive to the child and say, 'And what begins with the letter "A", Lorcan?' The stranger won't know or hopefully hear if the child replied, so simply add, 'That's right, an apple! Good boy.' Job done: you're not only a caring parent, but an educational one too. Lorcan may be confused at your sudden politeness, but just go back to normal when the stranger has gone.

'Say hello to the nice man/ woman, Lorcan'

Sometimes you've got to distract both child and passing stranger, especially if the stranger is being uber nosy and staring.

Simply turn the attention back at the stranger by forcing your child to engage, and this should hurry them the fuck on past you.

This is called deflection, and works a treat when you need to think on your feet. Also don't forget to remind your child to never talk to strangers, and ground them for a day to make sure they get the message.

'Don't worry, we'll get you some fruit when you go home'

Sometimes a crying child is inevitable, and nothing can be done to stop their whingeing, so why not make it sound like they're crying for healthy food products like fruit and/or veg?

People in audible range will be impressed at your parenting skills and child's propensity for healthy food. When they're gone, lob a biscuit into their gob to shut them up until you get home and lash on the chicken nuggets. Perfect.

'Oh Lorcan, why are you upset? This isn't like you at all. Please, someone, for the love of God help me. My child's eyes are leaking!'

There is nothing more embarrassing than a full-on tantrum when there are dozens of people around. For extreme cases, extreme measures are needed.

When your child kicks off, act like you've never seen this before. Pretend you don't even know what tears are and freak the fuck out.

Someone will hopefully rush to console you and reassure you that the liquid pouring out of your child's eyes are called 'tears', and quickly defuse your overreaction. Ask them, 'Are you sure this is natural? He's never done this before.' Witnesses to this will be left in absolute awe of your parenting and how nice a family you must be.

'Lorcan, shut up or Mammy will throw your iPad in the fucking bin when she gets home'

Look, sometimes you've just got to be yourself and let it all out. Who cares what people think anyway – Lorcan can be a little bollocks at times.

> **Historical Facts**
>
> Ancient Egyptians worshipped cats, despite the cats not really giving a bollocks about them.